"Esteemed Bookes of Lawe"
and the Legal Culture of Early Virginia

EARLY AMERICAN HISTORIES

Douglas Bradburn, John C. Coombs, and S. Max Edelson, Editors

"Esteemed Bookes of Lawe"

AND THE
LEGAL CULTURE
OF EARLY VIRGINIA

☙❧

Edited by
Warren M. Billings
and Brent Tarter

University of Virginia Press
CHARLOTTESVILLE AND LONDON

University of Virginia Press
© 2017 by the Rector and Visitors of the University of Virginia
All rights reserved
Printed in the United States of America on acid-free paper

First published 2017

1 3 5 7 9 8 6 4 2

Library of Congress Cataloging-in-Publication Data
Names: Billings, Warren M., 1940– editor. | Tarter, Brent, 1948– editor.
Title: "Esteemed bookes of lawe" and the legal culture of early Virginia / edited by
  Warren M. Billings and Brent Tarter.
Description: Charlottesville : University of Virginia Press, 2017. | Series: Early
  American histories | Includes bibliographical references and index.
Identifiers: LCCN 2016030554 | ISBN 9780813939391 (cloth : alk. paper) |
  ISBN 9780813939407 (e-book)
Subjects: LCSH: Law—Virginia—History. | Law—Virginia—Bibliography—History.
Classification: LCC KFV2478 .E84 2017 | DDC 349.75509/033—dc23
LC record available at https://lccn.loc.gov/2016030554

CONTENTS

Acknowledgments vii

Introduction 1

English Legal Literature as a Source of Law and
Practice in Seventeenth-Century Virginia 11
WARREN M. BILLINGS

Law Books in the Libraries of Colonial Virginians 27
W. HAMILTON BRYSON

The Library of the Council of Colonial Virginia 37
BRENT TARTER

English Statutes in Virginia, 1660–1714 57
JOHN RUSTON PAGAN

John Mercer:
Merchant, Lawyer, Author, Book Collector 95
BENNIE BROWN

The Library Reveals the Man:
George Wythe, Legal and Classical Scholar 113
LINDA K. TESAR

The Law Library of a Working Attorney:
The Example of Patrick Henry 137
KEVIN J. HAYES

A Virginia Original:
George Webb's *Office and Authority of a Justice of Peace* 157
WARREN M. BILLINGS

A Handbook for All:
William Waller Hening's *The New Virginia Justice* 179
R. NEIL HENING

St. George Tucker: Judge, Legal Scholar, and
Reformer of Virginia Law   195
CHARLES F. HOBSON

Notes on Contributors   221

Index   223

ACKNOWLEDGMENTS

Mark K. Greenough and E. Lee Shepard, two of our tablemates at the Richmond legal-history dinners, were early enthusiasts for this book; they also helped identify likely contributors. We thank the contributors for their outstanding essays. From beginning to end their willing cooperation eased our task as editors. Thanks to Richard Holway, history and social sciences editor at the University of Virginia Press, for his keen support of the book. Carol D. Billings, Mary Sarah Bilder, Stephen Blaiklock, Sally Hadden, and James S. Heller read the manuscript in all or in part, and we are most grateful for their thoughtful suggestions. We acknowledge the Manuscript Division of the Library of Congress; the Earl Gregg Swem and Wolf Law Libraries, College of William and Mary; the Library of Virginia; and the *Virginia Magazine of History and Biography* for permission to reproduce items in their possession.

Warren M. Billings
Brent Tarter

"Esteemed Bookes of Lawe"
and the Legal Culture of Early Virginia

INTRODUCTION

In 1666 the General Assembly required county courts and the General Court to purchase acts of Parliament and other "esteemed Bookes of Lawe." "An act for the supplie of each Countie with Lawe bookes," Virginia 1662–1702, Laws (Charles City Manuscript), 189, Thomas Jefferson Papers, ser. 8, vol. 9. (Courtesy Library of Congress)

Before the establishment of modern law schools in the nineteenth century, people prepared for a career at the bar not by studying law as we describe the process now but, in their revealing phrase, by "reading law." Law books and the legal profession were and are inseparable, and in those days both were equally inseparable from statecraft. Excepting perhaps clergymen, no group of Virginians or early Americans was as dependent on books as lawyers and judges. A minister might say he needed only one special book, but every lawyer admitted that he needed many more. Law books, and how lawyers and judges used them to serve their clients and fellow subjects and citizens, were among the most important elements of the print culture in the colonies and the new nation.

Virginia men of law constituted one of the first learned professions in colonial America. Their work engaged them in a centuries-long tradition of legal scholarship and adjudication, whose essence their books transmitted to them. Those books were vital to them. Learning how they acquired and used books becomes of utmost importance to an understanding of colonial legal culture. Analyzing their collections illuminates the history of the book, providing clues about who purchased books, how they acquired books, how they used books, and what the books contained of England's history and legal traditions. Virginians owned treatises, practical manuals, and compilations of case reports that informed them about the details and principles of English statute and common law. The loss of most colonial appellate-court records has obscured the importance of printed English reports in the courts, even though surviving private case notes indicate that lawyers often turned to those reports in arguments before the General Court. Practical manuals taught how to manage professional work. Theoretical or historical treatises contained the essentials of English law. And case reports contained precedents and arguments for applying those essentials in Virginia.

Insights derived from studying the ownership and use of law books in turn provide valuable tips on how men of law in the colonial and Revolutionary periods learned their craft, did their work, and shared their learning with young men who read law under their tutelage. That these individuals shared law books with their colleagues and also had access to an excellent law library in Williamsburg demonstrates the professionalization of the law in Virginia long before the American Revolution.

The reach of law books extended far beyond a small community of practitioners. From the very beginning, members of the General Assembly relied on books when they legislated for their new colony. Besides legislators and lawyers, at any one time hundreds of justices of the peace sat on the county courts, which constituted the tribunal of first resort for men and women of all classes, who turned to those courts to collect a debt, prosecute a villain, probate an estate, or settle a property dispute. Those justices seldom had any significant education in the law. When presented with novel or complex cases, they relied on their own personal working collections of law books. But their courts also maintained law libraries, a fact that students of the colony's legal history have almost entirely disregarded. County-court law libraries originated in a 1666 act of assembly requiring local magistrates to purchase Michael Dalton's manuals for justices of the peace and sheriffs, Henry Swinburne's treatise on wills, editions of parliamentary statutes, and "Some other esteemed Bookes of lawe."[1] Statutes of the realm in force before 1607 were good law in Virginia, as were later acts that specifically applied to the colonies or were incorporated by the General Assembly and the courts. Beginning in the 1660s, county courts also shared concurrent jurisdiction with the General Court for enforcing the English acts of trade and navigation. Those and other legal responsibilities meant that justices of the peace needed access to reference works on the common law as well.

These aspects of the legal culture of early Virginia have been little studied. Indeed, beyond some institutional analyses of the legislative and judicial processes, scholarship on the legal history of colonial Virginia still contains more holes than solid studies. An understanding of how lawyers, judges, and ordinary people relied on law books illuminates several critical elements of the colony's legal culture. It also brightens the beginnings of a highly professional bench and bar that emerged during the nineteenth century. Moreover, these insights shed new light on the colony's intellectual history. Men who owned law books often added volumes of history, theology, and the classics of Greek or Roman antiquity—either in the original language or in English translation—to their libraries. In turn, these findings suggest corresponding developments in the legal cultures of other colonies and early states where circumstances may not have departed radically from conditions in Virginia.

These ten essays explore aspects of the law and intellectual culture of Virginia from the seventeenth century to the early years of the nineteenth century by looking at legal bibliography very broadly defined. They offer new answers to several important questions about the professional lives of lawyers and justices of the peace. Who acquired law books, and how? What books did they have? Who used them, and how? What do the contents of law libraries disclose about their owners? How did young men read for a career in the law? And why and how during the eighteenth century did Virginians begin creating a distinctively Virginian legal literature to meet the needs of the people in the English king's oldest colony and the new nation's largest, most populous, and arguably most influential state?

This book had its origins in conversations among people with similar interests in legal history and bibliography, and six of its ten essays made their debuts at sessions of the annual Virginia Forum. In 2011, Linda K. Tesar and Warren M. Billings presented papers on law books. Tesar, of the Wolf Law Library at the Marshall-Wythe School of Law at the College of William and Mary, reported on her initial re-creation of the holdings in the personal library of George Wythe, the distinguished colonial attorney, signer of the Declaration of Independence, law professor, judge, and mentor to numerous accomplished attorneys, statesmen, and jurists. Billings, Distinguished Professor Emeritus at the University of New Orleans, was teaching legal history at the William and Mary law school then. He extended up to the Civil War his earlier findings about the influence of English law books on seventeenth-century Virginia legal institutions and later published an expanded version of his conference paper as "'Send us ... what other Lawe books you shall thinke fitt': Books That Shaped the Law in Virginia, 1600–1860."[2]

Within weeks of that conference, at the informal semiannual dinner of Richmond-area legal historians and others who have an interest in legal history, Brent Tarter, of the Library of Virginia, suggested that some of the participants organize a panel discussion on colonial Virginia legal history for the 2012 Virginia Forum. At that conference, E. Lee Shepard, of the Virginia Historical Society, offered an overview of the primary sources for studying colonial legal history. Billings also participated, using the needs-and-opportunities essay in his *Magistrates and Pioneers: Essays in the History of Early American Law*[3] to issue a plea for in-depth studies of some vital but neglected topics. W. Hamilton Bryson, of the T. C. Williams School of Law at the University of Richmond, working from his earlier research, discussed the value of studying legal bibliography. John Ruston Pagan, also of the University of Richmond law school, commented on how aspects of colonial Virginia law evolved as local and provincial judges made choice of law decisions that determined which colonial or parliamentary statutes applied to specific cases in the colony. And R. Neil Hening, an independent scholar in Richmond who first assembled the Richmond legal-history group in imitation of John Marshall's famous law dinners, reported on the biographical research he had done on his ancestor William Waller Hening, whose legal and historical reference works, published between 1795 and his death in 1828, were the most numerous and important Virginia law books of the time.

The two Virginia Forum sessions and the evening discussions in Richmond persuaded Billings and Tarter that more than enough good, original work on early Virginia legal history and bibliography was in the offing to make up a collection of essays that would not only make a useful contribution to the field of legal history in Virginia but also appeal to anyone with an interest in early Virginia history in general or curious about Virginia's legal and intellectual past. In that sense, then, such a book would reach across the boundaries of legal bibliography, history of the book, print culture, state history, and legal studies. Hence this volume.

From the beginning, it was obvious that because Billings's previously published "English Legal Literature as a Source of Law and Legal Practice for Seventeenth-Century Virginia" was a pioneer study in the field,[4] it merited inclusion in this collection. And because Bryson had done additional research to supplement his pathbreaking *Census of Law Books in Colonial Virginia*,[5] a report from him on his updated findings was entitled to a prominent place in the collection. His contribution on private ownership of law books in the eighteenth century picks up where Billings's work ends. Both essays make abundantly plain that most available law books came off the presses of London printeries in all shapes and sizes and in an ever-widening array of subject matter. Thus they set the stage, as it were, for the remaining eight essays, which focus on discrete topics in greater detail.

Brent Tarter presents a history of the library of the colonial Council of State. Sometimes referred to as the General Court library, it was the nearest thing to a "public" library in the colony. Founded in 1620, by the eve of the Revolution it had become the largest law library in Virginia, and it was not only used by councillors but open to anyone with legal business in the capital. Tarter blends multiple manuscript sources into a discussion of holdings, their acquisition, and, sadly, their dispersal and subsequent loss.

John Ruston Pagan's search of Virginia court records from the period 1660–1714 revealed abundant references to English statute books. His essay asks why Virginians acquired those volumes; it explores the influence of acts of Parliament on the colonial legal system; and it illustrates ways Virginians used English statutes to regulate commerce, shape local laws, and adjudicate cases as they fashioned their hybrid legal order.

Given their subject matter, the essays by Bennie Brown, Linda K. Tesar, and Kevin J. Hayes group together logically. Brown, an independent scholar in Williamsburg, Virginia, brings to the fore an all but forgotten lawyer, John Mercer, a born bibliophile who was by turns merchant, lawyer, judge, legal writer, book dealer, collector, and creator of one of the largest private law libraries in the colony. That library sustained his vast law practice; coincidentally, it also educated his nephew George Mason, author of the Virginia Declaration of Rights. Linda Tesar has turned her Virginia Forum paper into a comprehensive analysis of George Wythe's library. No less passionate a booklover than John Mercer, Wythe amassed his collection to enhance his study and teaching of law and to indulge his lifelong fondness for the Greek and Roman classics. Kevin J. Hayes, Professor of English Emeritus at the University of Central Oklahoma, investigates the law books that Patrick Henry owned, how he read law, how he used his library, and what that usage says about the renowned lawyer-statesman. Hayes's essay extends the detail and scope of a portion of his *Mind of a Patriot: Patrick Henry and the World of Ideas.*[6] Together these essays reveal much about the collecting habits, the literary tastes, and the intellectual influences of their books on three prominent eighteenth-century Virginia men of law.

The final three essays fall into another logical group and were jointly presented at a session of the 2015 Virginia Forum. Their spotlight is on three legal scholars who founded a distinctly Virginia brand of legal literature. Warren M. Billings looks into why and how George Webb compiled and published his *Office and Authority of a Justice of Peace* in the 1730s.[7] Not only was Webb's volume the earliest legal reference manual composed by a Virginian and printed in Virginia but it was also first in a line of Virginia-specific law books that began in Webb's time and stretches to the present. R. Neil Hening's essay resurrects a little-remembered late eighteenth- and early nineteenth-century Virginia legal scholar. Between 1795 and his death in 1828, William Waller Hening published numerous legal reference books that were among the most read of his time. Of these, none was more significant than his *New Virginia Justice,*[8] which superseded Webb's *Justice.* Neil Hening has painstakingly pulled together bits and pieces to form an account of how the *New Virginia Justice* came to be, and along the way he also comments on the vagaries of printing and bookselling in post-Revolutionary Virginia. Charles F. Hobson considers the example of poet, legislator, revolutionary, soldier, statesman, jurist, and teacher of law St. George Tucker. He explains Tucker's tailoring of Blackstone's *Commentaries on the Laws of England* to Virginia and American settings, his difficulties with publishers, and how Tucker's *Blackstone* was a favored reference and textbook well into the nineteenth century.[9] Hobson also draws notice to his edition of St. George Tucker's manuscript law notes and reports, which the University of North Carolina Press published for the Omohundro Institute of Early American History and Culture in 2013.[10] That part of his essay contains a compelling discussion of Tucker's importance to the shaping of the republican legal order of Virginia and the new nation.

Each essay, in its own fashion, is anchored in the particulars of its subject, but together they speak of broader matters. Although historians of the book have remarked widely and often about early American print culture, their tendency has been to ignore law books as worthy of close study. This collection argues otherwise, demonstrating the importance of law books to a deeper appreciation of studies of the book in early America. Read as state history, the essays constitute a sharp reminder that law, always a pervasive dimension of life in the Old Dominion, has never garnered its proper due. These essays offer a much-desired corrective. Perhaps they will inspire others to take up the cause.

Taken as an errand into legal studies, the authors' venture into that realm highlights how little attention legal scholars have given to the relationship between law books and the rise of colonial legal cultures. Anyone looking for answers to such basic questions as who wrote law books, who printed them, who marketed them, who collected them, and who used them quickly confronts two frustrating realities. Few books about law books exist. An accumulation of articles and book chapters are strewn about as entries in the odd state historical magazine, law review, library journal, or other serial publication. This collection scarcely fills that void, to be sure, but it is a step in the right direction.

Law books and the men who read, used, and made them exercised a powerful influence in colonial Virginia. Many of the Virginia statesmen who helped found the United States were practicing attorneys, and some of them were profound students of the law. Without their knowledge of law books, we could not have had the full corps of remarkably talented Virginians who took part in the American Revolution, wrote a constitution for the new state, helped write one for the new nation, and served in their legislatures and courts. The essays in this volume, based on original research and full of new revelations, help us see more clearly how the law operated and changed in colonial and Revolutionary society. This is an important part of the large story of how English law traveled to North America, how it worked, and how it was transformed into Virginia law and American law.

NOTES

1. "An act for the supplie of each Countie with Lawe bookes," Virginia 1662–1702, Laws (Charles City Manuscript), 189, Thomas Jefferson Papers, ser. 8, vol. 9, Library of Congress.
2. Warren M. Billings, "'Send us . . . what other Lawe books you shall thinke fitt': Books That Shaped the Law in Virginia, 1600–1860," *Virginia Magazine of History and Biography* 120 (2012): 314–39.
3. Warren M. Billings, *Magistrates and Pioneers: Essays in the History of American Law* (Clark, NJ, 2011), 417–55.
4. Warren M. Billings, "English Legal Literature as a Source of Law and Practice for Seventeenth-Century Virginia," *Virginia Magazine of History and Biography* 87 (1979): 403–17.
5. W. Hamilton Bryson, *Census of Law Books in Colonial Virginia* (Charlottesville, 1978).
6. Kevin J. Hayes, *Mind of a Patriot: Patrick Henry and the World of Ideas* (Charlottesville, 2008), 33–47.
7. George Webb, *The Office and Authority of a Justice of Peace and also the Duty of Sheriffs . . . Adapted to the Constitution and Practice of Virginia* (Williamsburg, 1736).
8. William Waller Hening, *The New Virginia Justice, Comprising the Office and Authority of a Justice of the Peace in the Commonwealth of Virginia* (Richmond, 1795).

9. *Blackstone's Commentaries: With Notes of Reference, to the Constitution and Laws, of the Federal Government of the United States; and of the Commonwealth of Virginia,* ed. St. George Tucker, 5 vols. (Philadelphia, 1803).
10. *St. George Tucker's Law Reports and Selected Papers, 1782–1825,* ed. Charles F. Hobson, 3 vols. (Chapel Hill, 2013).

ENGLISH LEGAL LITERATURE AS A SOURCE OF LAW AND PRACTICE IN SEVENTEENTH-CENTURY VIRGINIA

Warren M. Billings

THE COUNTREY JUSTICE:

Containing the Practice of the

Justices of the Peace

Out of their

SESSIONS.

Gathered for the better help of such Justices of Peace, as have not been much conversant in the Study of the LAWS of this REALM.

By MICHAEL DALTON of Lincolns-Inn, Esq; and One of the Masters in Chancery.

To which is now added,

The Duty and Power of Justices of Peace in their Sessions;

An Abridgment (under proper Titles) of all *Statutes*, relating thereunto.

A large TABLE of the Principal Matters herein contained.

With two other TABLES, One of the CHAPTERS in this BOOK; and the other of such ACTS of Parliament, as concern the Office of a Justice of Peace.

Justice is the Staff of Peace, and the Maintenance of Honor. Cic.

LONDON:

Printed by G. Sawbridge, T. Roycroft, and W. Rawlins, Assigns of Richard Atkyns, and Edward Atkyns, Esquires. And are to be sold by H. Twyford, F. Tyton, J. Bellinger, W. Place, T. Basset, R. Pawlet, S. Heyrick, C. Wilkinson, T. Dring, W. Jacob, C. Harper, J. Leigh, J. Amery, J. Place, and J. Poole. 1677.

Michael Dalton's Countrey Justice, first published in 1618, was an essential reference work for magistrates in seventeenth-century Virginia. Michael Dalton, *The Countrey Justice: Containing the Practice of the Justices of the Peace Out of their Sessions*, 12th ed. (London, 1677). (Courtesy Wolf Law Library, College of William and Mary)

THE BROAD DIMENSIONS OF VIRginia's legal history in the seventeenth century are well known. For colonial Virginians the interval between 1607 and 1700 was a period of experimentation during which they ransacked their heritage to discover laws and legal institutions suitable for a novel environment. Gradually, they devised acceptable legal practices grounded alike in an ancient tradition and a new environment, thereby setting the stage for the maturing of Virginia society in the next century. Although there is a familiar ring to this summary, the details of how the colonists proceeded to mold their legal inheritance to their use remain obscure. For as David H. Flaherty has aptly observed, the Old Dominion's legal history has languished from serious neglect.[1] Consequently, inadequate answers have been provided to some fundamental questions: Who was responsible for adapting English law to colonial needs? What was the extent of the colonists' legal training? And how did they acquire their knowledge of English law and its practice?

Throughout the nearly two decades that the London Company managed the colony, company officials recruited the colony's leaders from England's ruling classes. Therefore, the men whom the company selected as its governors and councillors had more than a passing acquaintance with the realm's customs. They had, after all, enjoyed the educational and professional advantages of their privileged station. At all times before 1624 offices in the colony were filled by experienced men who had attended the universities or the Inns of Court and who possessed close ties with the king's court or Parliament.[2]

Despite the qualifications that they brought to their places, these men left a negligible impression upon Virginia's legal system. More than a few succumbed to the rigors of settlement. Others found Virginia too great a hell to endure and fled home at the first opportunity. Still others had no intention of remaining in Virginia any longer than it took to slake their thirst for adventure. The inability of early leaders to adapt to Virginia plus the uncertainty about the direction in which the colony should proceed postponed necessary decisions and reserved to those colonists who assumed positions of leadership after 1624 the greatest influence in shaping English law to fit the colonial setting.

Those men who assumed leadership upon the demise of the London Company fall into two groups. The smaller but more conspicuous of the two consists of the royal governors whom the crown selected throughout the remainder of the seventeenth century. In background and in training these individuals were similar to their company counterparts, and in virtue of their position they were situated so as to be able to shape colonial law. In London's view theirs was the most powerful and prestigious office in Virginia, and their royal masters often counseled them to rule "as near as may be to the laws of England."[3] Moreover, as the king's surrogates and the colony's chief magistrates they could propose laws to implement their instructions and to facilitate their government of colonial affairs. One might therefore conclude that Virginia's royal governors played a preeminent role in transferring English law to the colony, but such a conclusion is unwarranted.

From 1619 onward, governors shared with the General Assembly the responsibility for making laws for Virginia, and as the century wore on the assembly came to enjoy a greater measure of legislative authority. Furthermore, the accretions of local custom lessened the governors' influence, particularly in cases of their acquiescence, which were often made necessary by a lack of royal guidance and support. In the end, default as much as design guaranteed that other hands than those of the governor would assume the task of reforming English law to suit Virginia's needs.

The other hands belonged to men who were part of that migration of "vexed and troubled Englishmen,"[4] who following the company's downfall left a disturbed homeland committed to finding a stable and prosperous life in America. By the mid-1630s what had begun as a trickle of settlers became a flood that did not run its course for more than forty years.[5] Arriving in such numbers, these new immigrants soon burdened Virginia's existing legal and institutional structures beyond their capacity to meet the requirements of an expanding frontier community. Responding to the need for a fundamental change in the colony's government, the General Assembly as early as the 1630s established the county court system, thereby creating a need to adapt more English law to new conditions.[6] Beyond that, the new system proliferated the number of offices in the colony, and the prospect of acquiring one of these posts lured ambitious colonists. Thus it was the post-1630s immigrants who became clerks of court, justices of the peace, sheriffs, burgesses, and councillors, who were most responsible for effecting the transfer of England's legal patrimony to Virginia.

Unlike their predecessors, the post-1630s colonial leaders did not spring from the traditional ruling stock. They arose instead out of that variegated social class of seventeenth-century England called "the middling sort." Their background was quite different from that of the men they succeeded. To be sure, some were gentlefolk, but for the most part they were merchants, bakers, salters, vintners, or practitioners of some other skilled calling. As such, they were not, however, part of the mercantile establishment that had promoted colonial undertakings at the beginning of the century. Rather, they belonged to that group of commercial men who assumed a controlling interest in the colonial trade after 1624.[7] While a majority of these men resided in London or Bristol at the time they left England for Virginia, they were often of country origin and had gone to the metropolis in search of opportunities. Frequently in their formative years they had benefited from the improved educational opportunities that were an English hallmark in the years between 1560 and 1640. But no more than a handful were university graduates or matriculants at the Inns of Court.[8] Such formal training as the majority of them received likely went no further than grammar school or an apprenticeship. The remainder of their education came in the school of hard knocks.[9] These men differed from their earlier company counterparts in one other important respect. They lacked close connections with the home government, and until they settled in Virginia[10] they had little experience in drafting laws or administering justice.

Given these circumstances, how did men with seemingly so little expertise in so complex an institution as the law succeed in transporting it to Virginia? There are several possible answers to the question. In the first place, the men who effected the transfer were not completely ignorant of the law and its customs. No Englishman was, nor could be, because the law was very much a part of his culture. A belief that a set of rules governed society and its members had long been a guiding cultural assumption in England, and for centuries successive generations of Englishmen learned to respect the law as the sinew that bound society together. Almost from birth the colonists slowly absorbed this conception of law. By mere observation, they discovered the rules that governed their families' households. As they grew older, they came upon the more formal regulations that touched the relationships between their own and other families, and individuals, the church, the guilds, and the state. Little by little, they came to understand that a well-ordered society was a regulated community that kept its members at peace with one another and out of harm's way. Hence, by the time they became adults, they had learned to appreciate a fundamental maxim of English law: *"salus populi suprema lex est,"* that is, "the safety of the people is the chief law."[11]

This view of the law's purpose was an important item in the post-1634 immigrant's intellectual baggage. In order to transform his perceptions into usable laws for Virginia, a colonist did not need to be a lawyer. He needed only an awareness of this general function of law, a concern for the well-being of his fellow settlers, and a willingness to act.

Then too, colonial lawmakers had received more than a cultural exposure to English law. Their backgrounds in commerce and the skilled trades frequently led to participation in legal proceedings. In the normal course of doing business they gained practical experience in drafting documents such as powers of attorney, charter parties, deeds, bills of exchange, indentures, and even wills. Settling debts or other business disputes brought them into contact with the judicial process. These contacts were valuable lessons in how to bring suit, how to take and give evidence, and how to discharge the duties of attorneyship. Together, these and similar encounters gave the lawmakers a layman's working understanding of how the English system of justice operated.

These acquired talents explain why some of the men had gone to Virginia in the first place. Their skills qualified them to promote new outlets for business as well as to protect the established interests of family and close friends. Once in the colony, they soon discovered that a proficiency in legal matters facilitated their entrance into the local political life. And it required little effort for them to employ their practical knowledge in helping to create Virginia's legal system.

Besides cultural inspiration and practical acquaintance, the colonists drew their legal knowledge from the large corpus of printed works about English law which had come into use in the one hundred fifty years before Jamestown's settlement. Since the invention of printing made books far cheaper to produce, the middle of the fifteenth century witnessed a revolution in learning. By the 1480s the first printed law books were available in England.[12] Throughout the next century the number of legal titles multiplied as their popularity increased and as more learned lawyers sought to pass their knowledge on to others through the medium of print. By 1600 more than fifty volumes of a variety of legal works were already in circulation.[13] The great constitutional struggles of the seventeenth century insured that the law would remain a lively topic, and authors and printers struggled to keep pace with demand. Numerous editions of Sir Edward Coke's monumental *Reports* and the *Institutes,*[14] for example, were printed between 1606 and 1697. Sir Francis Bacon's *Elements of the Common Lawes of England*[15] went through three editions, while John Kitchin's *Jurisdictions*[16] and Sir William Noye's *Compleat Lawyer*[17] went through five and eight printings, respectively. Here, then, was a vast treasure-trove of legal information to which Virginia lawmakers could turn for guidance.

Documenting the colonists' use of the literature that was available is easy enough. In addition to estate inventories in manuscript and in print, there are numerous studies written about the colonial Virginian's reading habits.[18] These sources provide a reasonably accurate indication of the titles that circulated in Virginia. They show a wide variety of subjects—abridgments of statute and case law, legal dictionaries, case reports, and books that dealt with the law's philosophical and procedural underpinnings.[19] Another group consisted of books of a more practical nature, which might be termed "how-to-do-it" books. Examining the contents of some of these books reveals the wide range of legal information which a Virginia lawmaker could command.

Abridgments of statutes and case law were among the first legal books printed in England.[20] The compilers arranged their summaries in roughly alphabetical order, according to subject matter.[21] A reason for their existence seems to have been a desire to furnish law students with convenient finding aids to the statutes and the yearbooks, the predecessors of the law reports.[22] Since the abridgments facilitated access to both statute and case law, they became popular with lawyers, and their popularity caused them to be reprinted in many editions prior to 1700.

Of the many abridgments compiled down to the end of the seventeenth century, those of Sir Anthony Fitzherbert,[23] Sir Robert Brooke,[24] William Rastell,[25] and Edmund Wingate[26] enjoyed wide use in England, and copies of all four authors' works found their way to Virginia. Their influence, as well as that of lesser-known abridgments, upon Virginians is questionable, however. Abridgments of case law were printed in Latin or law French, which most colonial legislators probably could not read. The appearance of Fitzherbert and Brooke in some inventories does, of course, suggest that certain individuals had the facility to read those works and draw inspiration from them. But no direct evidence which links either Brooke or Fitzherbert to colonial statutes or court decisions has been forthcoming. Because they abridged statute law, Rastell's and Wingate's compilations may have been helpful to the colonists; they could be used both as guides to English statutes and as models for colonial laws.

Although their contribution is difficult to document precisely, the utility of law dictionaries for colonists without formal legal training is readily apparent. At least six compilers of legal dictionaries flourished between the 1520s and 1700, but John Rastell's *Termes de la ley* and John Cowell's *Interpreter* probably had the most extensive circulation in Virginia.[27] Composed by the printer John Rastell, the first edition of *Termes de la ley* appeared in 1527.[28] The first dictionary of any sort ever printed in England, its popularity was such that it went through twenty-eight editions before going out of print in 1819. Early editions of *Termes de la ley* were more limited in scope than later dictionaries; they contained only the most commonly used legal terms and a bit of antiquarian lore about the origin of words and phrases. Later editions included an expanded number of definitions as well as a parallel English translation of the entire dictionary.

Cowell's *Interpreter*[29] is of a wholly different character. Its coverage is more extensive, its author was more erudite than Rastell, and its publication entirely in English was an improvement over Rastell's dictionary. Published by a professor of civil law at Cambridge, the *Interpreter* initially appeared in 1607. Unlike Rastell, from whom he borrowed heavily upon occasion, Cowell cited precedents, statutes, and authorities for his definitions. That the prose is lucid and direct in its explanation of sometimes complicated terminology is the *Interpreter*'s great strength. Despite its value, the *Interpreter* was suppressed in 1610 because of a parliamentary controversy over certain passages which Cowell had written about the monarch's absolute sovereignty.[30] It reappeared in 1637 and was republished with additions six times in the next ninety years.

To read through *Termes de la ley* and the *Interpreter* is to gain some feeling for their probable effect upon the colonists. Certainly both dictionaries are quite helpful in rendering seventeenth-century English law and practice more intelligible to modern scholars.

Case reports came into vogue shortly after the compilation of the last of the yearbooks was completed around the year 1535.[31] At first the reports resembled the yearbooks in that they were little more than notes or rough summaries of selected cases. In time their reportage became more formal and complete, thereby making them a more valuable reference tool than their predecessors. By the seventeenth century, a number of compilations of reports were already in print, and those attributed to James Dyer[32] and Edmund Plowden[33] were especially esteemed until they were superseded by the reports of Sir Edward Coke. Coke, of course, soon dominated this branch of legal literature just as he did every other matter of law that attracted his interest. Such was his reportorial prowess that the work of other compilers, like Edward Bulstrode[34] and Sir George Croke,[35] seems pale by comparison.

Dyer, Plowden, Coke, Bulstrode, Croke, and other reporters all appear in colonial inventories, but the degree of their influence in Virginia is difficult to determine. The fact that the early reports were in law French probably precluded their widespread use in the colony. Coke's *Reports* were not published in English until 1658, about the same time that Bulstrode's and Croke's English reports appeared. It may be, then, that reports of any kind did not have much of an effect until after mid-century. That they were used in Virginia after that time is substantiated by the presence of the reports among the law books belonging to men who migrated to Virginia or who came to intellectual maturity after 1650. William Fitzhugh, Ralph Wormeley (d. 1703), Richard Lee (d. 1714), and Arthur Spicer, for instance, all owned some parts of Coke's *Reports,* and Fitzhugh's surviving correspondence shows that he at least consulted Coke frequently.[36] Moreover, in a case heard before the Westmoreland County Court in 1685, Coke's authority was invoked by the defendant in a dispute arising from an alleged violation of the Navigation Acts.[37] Other examples of the reporters' influence must await further study of the relationship between the reports and an evolving Virginia legal system.

There were many books that dealt with the philosophical and procedural aspects of law published in England before 1700. Such titles as Coke's *Institutes of the Laws of England,*[38] Henry Finch's *Law, Or a Discourse Thereof,*[39] Sir John Fortescue's *A Learned Commendation on the Politique Lawes of England,*[40] William Fulbeck's *A Direction or Preparative to the Study of the Lawe* and his *A Parallele or Conference of the Civill Law, the Canon Law and the Common Law of this Realme of England,*[41] and Sir Thomas Littleton's *Tenures*[42] enjoyed a wide circulation throughout the English-speaking world.

Coke's *Institutes* are too renowned to require any comment here, other than to lament the lack of a modern edition and to suggest the need for someone to undertake a careful assessment of their use by seventeenth-century Virginians. By the seventeenth century, Fortescue's and Littleton's works had already been recognized as classic commentaries on English law. A charming little book, *A Learned Commendation of the Politique Lawes of England* was written around 1471 to instruct the young Prince Edward in the mysteries of England's legal customs. Fortescue constructed the book in the form of a dialogue between himself and the prince. In it he stressed two main themes, the rule of law and the limited character of the English monarchy—two ideas whose time had come by the 1600s. Whereas Fortescue was concerned with general legal principles, Littleton's *Tenures* is a technical treatment of English property law. In the book Littleton discussed estates, types of tenures, joint ownerships, and the special doctrines of real property that were known when it was published in the 1480s. Littleton's intelligent style, his reduction of complex law to a logical system, and his abstraction of sound legal principles made the book a required text for all who would become proficient in the laws of real property. The more obscure writings of Finch and Fulbeck are noteworthy not so much for their authors' erudition as for what their use reveals about the readers. Neither author is now remembered for having any lasting effect upon the course of English legal history; their works are rather pedestrian. But use of both books by the colonists suggests a certain eclecticism on the Virginia lawmakers' part. It was as though the Virginians turned to any and every theoretical study that might aid them in finding serviceable legal traditions. Furthermore, their use of these books should alert scholars to the necessity of going beyond the obviously seminal treatises, like Littleton and Coke, to examine the work of numerous lesser lights.

To this point, the discussion of colonial tastes in legal literature has centered on those books whose influence was more general than specific. For that reason, it is particularly difficult to measure a book's effect. The impact of the "how-to-do-it" books can be calculated with much greater certainty.

How-to-do-it books were an important element in the legal literature to which any sixteenth- and seventeenth-century Englishmen could turn for instruction. A source of practical knowledge, they covered a broad range of subjects, and they were usually authored by men who were highly competent in their fields. A case in point is William Lambarde. The author of a very popular guide for justices of the peace,[43] Lambarde was himself a member of the bench in Kent.[44] As he noted in his preface, he was moved to write the book because upon coming to his office he had known so little about it. Accordingly, he hoped his work would be an inspiration to others. Lambarde's was but one of a large number of similar manuals for justices of the peace.[45] There were, in addition to the manuals for justices, directories for clerks, sheriffs, constables, and lawyers, as well as guidebooks on how to plead cases, write wills, convey property, or draft a variety of legal documents.[46]

In form, all how-to-do-it books were pretty much alike. If the author discussed the duties of a justice or a sheriff, he began with an examination of the office and traced its development down to his own time. Then he described the duties of the officeholder and what powers were vested in him. Generally these descriptions were arranged alphabetically in a fashion similar to the abridgments of statute and case law. In those situations where the officeholder was likely to confront breaches of law, the manuals gave instruction in what constituted criminal offenses, and told how to make arrests, collect evidence, and hold trials. Books that dealt with the preparation and keeping of legal records were basically alike. They explained the importance of records, the derivations of particular documents, their functions, and the conditions under which they should be employed. Most important of all, such guidebooks furnished the reader with sample copies in English and Latin of each instrument.

Of all the how-to-do-it books which the colonists owned, Michael Dalton's *Countrey Justice* and Henry Swinburne's *Briefe Treatise of Testaments and Last Wills* deserve special attention. Apart from their being superior examples of the genre, each made a demonstrable impression upon Virginia law. In a word, they provided many of the models for both law and procedure in the colony.

"For the better conformity of the proceedings of the courts of this country to the lawes of England," an act of the General Assembly in 1666 required both volumes to be purchased by the county courts, the General Assembly, and the General Court.[47] Even before the legislature ordered their use in the colonial courts, however, there are indications that some magistrates had long depended upon Dalton and Swinburne for advice on legal matters.[48] Copies of both volumes are recorded in some inventories that date from the 1640s and 1650s. In Lower Norfolk County the justices bought the *Countrey Justice* as early as the 1650s. And Swinburne's comments on the heritability of status seem to have been influential in persuading the Assembly in 1662 to entail slavery upon mulatto children whose mothers were held in life service.[49]

The appeal of such books to Virginians is clear. For men with no formal training, a scrivener's guide like William West's *Symboleographia* was an invaluable pattern upon which to model a county's records. Dalton's or Swinburne's opinions on the magistrate's duties or on the making of wills gave the necessary advice on how these responsibilities should be discharged. The statutes, precedents, and other authorities that these writers cited could be invoked to provide a foundation of tradition upon which to rest law and procedure in the Old Dominion. One had merely to lift appropriate sections out of these volumes and apply them to a given problem. That Dalton, Swinburne,

West, and other authors of how-to-do-it books were more popular with colonial lawmakers than Coke, Bacon, or Littleton is evidence of their collective work's considerable effect in Virginia.

Their writing had another significant consequence for Virginia's early legal history. Since it drew attention to how local officials discharged their public obligations, it tended to magnify the eminence of these officeholders. It also emphasized the importance of local law and custom. That emphasis served mainly to reinforce the colonists' previous exposure to English law by calling to mind their past experience and by sanctioning the idea that local traditions were the most suitable to their own needs in the New World. Colonial dependence upon the how-to-do-it books is therefore one proof of the preeminent role English local law played in seventeenth-century Virginia.

In the end, the combination of culture, experience, and book learning produced surprising results. Some, like the emergence of a body of law governing slavery and Indian relations, were tragic and had the most unhappy consequences in the long run. The amalgamation of various civil, criminal, admiralty, equity, and administrative jurisdictions into a single system of local courts, which was under one appellate court,[50] simplified the judicial process. That change probably made the dispensation of justice somewhat more efficient in Virginia than it was at home. Using the vernacular in all laws, court proceedings, and documents was an improvement over the situation in England, as was the employment of the county courts for the safekeeping of all kinds of legal records.[51] The county courts' gradual assumption of the powers of ecclesiastical courts and control over church-related affairs led to a secularization of colonial society and the eventual decline of the church's hold over the worldly activities of colonial Virginians.

These and other breaks with the past may be explained as the offspring of necessity or as the inevitable consequence of crude attempts to imitate things badly remembered. The compulsion of necessity cannot, of course, be overlooked. In the absence of firm direction from home, the demands of a harsh environment often forced the colonists to depart from tradition. No one can deny the fact that the men who brought English law and institutions to Virginia were often woefully ignorant of the system's basic customs. Over time, ignorance produced differences between how things were done in England and in Virginia.

The variances may also be explained another way. That explanation is revealed in a paradoxical attribute peculiar to so many of the Englishmen who transformed their legal heritage in its Virginia setting after the 1630s. Being English, they strove mightily to render a faithful replication of that birthright. But being laymen in the law as well, they did not have the same sort of dedication and reverence for the law and its forms as did judges and lawyers. Theory and general principles often gave way to practical considerations; substance was more important than form. What worked, in short, was frequently more significant than either precedent or the wisdom of the ancients.

Nowhere perhaps are the implications of this behavior more clearly illustrated than in a 1662 statute that defined the status of bastard mulatto children born to black bondswomen. An increase in the number of such children had heightened concern about the children's condition. In part, the worry was due to an inflation in the incidence of court actions brought by mulattos claiming that their English paternity prevented their enslavement.[52] English hostility to blacks, mulattos, and bastards also played a part in the legislators' quest for a statutory means to prevent the increase of such children. Searching the past for help provided few guidelines. English local law, the statutes, and case law were of little help because none of these had contemplated the mulatto's existence or the situation that brought him into the world. Lacking the sanction of common law, the Assembly borrowed the civilian doctrine *partus sequitur ventrum*, which some burgess probably had found while rummaging through his copy of Swinburne: It made a mulatto's freedom or bondage dependent upon his mother's condition of servitude. In English common law such a manoeuvre would have been most irregular, but because it worked, it satisfied the Virginians. Moreover, because their solution had come from an authoritative source, it satisfied their urge to remain faithful to the past while solving the immediate legal problem of what to do with a peculiar species of person.

At the end of the seventeenth century Virginia boasted a legal system that was already verging on maturity. The handiwork of men lacking in formal legal education, it resembled its English parent, but was different enough in certain aspects to claim a nearly unique distinctiveness. Still in a fluid state, it was receptive to infusions from English legal traditions other than the local ones that had dominated developments since 1618. Such changes would be brought about in the next century by more professional men of law who had a much better acquaintance with English procedure and case and statute law than did their predecessors. Their task would be made easier because they had inherited a common characteristic from their colonial forebears—a temperamental willingness to accept change and variance with the past as the price for doing business in the New World.

NOTES

This essay was originally published in *Virginia Magazine of History and Biography* 87 (1979): 403–16. The notes have been updated to bring them abreast of scholarship since 1979 and to conform to the style of this book.

1. David H. Flaherty, ed., *Essays in the History of Early American Law* (Chapel Hill, NC, 1969), 12.

2. Bernard Bailyn, "Politics and Social Structure in Colonial Virginia," in *Seventeenth-Century America: Essays in Colonial History*, ed. James Morton Smith (Chapel Hill, NC, 1957), 92–94; William Strachey, comp., *For the Colony in Virginea Britannia, Lawes Divine, Morall and Martial, etc.*, ed. David H. Flaherty (Charlottesville, 1969), xv.
3. Instructions to Sir William Berkeley, 10 Aug. 1641, in *The Papers of Sir William Berkeley, 1605–1677*, ed. Warren M. Billings (Richmond, 2007), 29.
4. The phrase is that of the historian Carl Bridenbaugh, *Vexed and Troubled Englishmen, 1590–1642* (New York, 1967).
5. Wesley Frank Craven, *White, Red, and Black: The Seventeenth-Century Virginian* (Charlottesville, 1971), 1–39.
6. William Waller Hening, ed., *The Statutes at Large; Being a Collection of all the Laws of Virginia from the First Session of the Legislature in the Year 1619*, 13 vols. (Richmond, 1809–23), 1:224. The rise of Virginia's legal institutions is too well known to be rehearsed here. See, for example, Philip Alexander Bruce's monumental *Institutional History of Virginia in the Seventeenth Century, An Inquiry into the Religious, Moral, Educational, Legal, Military, and Political Condition of the People Based on Original and Contemporaneous Records*, 2 vols. (New York, 1910); Wesley Frank Craven, *The Southern Colonies in the Seventeenth Century, 1607–1689* (Baton Rouge, 1949); Edmund S. Morgan, *American Slavery, American Freedom: The Ordeal of Colonial Virginia* (New York, 1975); Warren M. Billings, *A Little Parliament: The Virginia General Assembly in the Seventeenth Century* (Richmond, 2004).
7. Robert Paul Brenner, "Commercial Change and Political Conflict: The Merchant Community in Civil War London" (PhD diss., Princeton University, 1970), 1–145.
8. Louis B. Wright, *Middle Class Culture in Elizabethan England* (Chapel Hill, NC, 1935), chap. 2; Martin H. Quitt, "From Elite to Aristocracy: The Transformation of the Virginia Ruling Class," paper read at the annual meeting of the Southern Historical Association, Houston, 1971, 6–8.
9. The experience of Obedience Robins is typical of these immigrants. Born in Northamptonshire in 1600, at age twenty Robins was bound as an apothecary's apprentice in London. He moved to Virginia in 1621, settling on the Eastern Shore, where he became involved in the area's political life, serving as a monthly court judge, justice of the peace, burgess, and councillor. At his death in 1662 he had amassed large landholdings and was a power in colonial politics at both the provincial and county levels. These data were complied from the court minute books of the Worshipful Company of Apothecaries at the Guildhall in London and the records of Northampton County, Virginia.
10. The conclusions drawn in this paragraph rest largely upon information compiled for Virginia's local and provincial officeholders in the period from 1619 to 1700. That information was taken from the Virginia county court records, guild records at the Guildhall Library, London, the archives at the Bristol Archives Office, Bristol, microfilms of English records that comprise part of the Virginia Colonial Records Project, the family papers that are housed at the Virginia Historical Society, and such gene-

alogical sources as the *Virginia Magazine of History and Biography* and the first and second series of the *William and Mary Quarterly.*

11. The seventeenth-century legal writer William Fulbeck expounded these views at length in his *A Direction or Preparative to the Study of the Lawe* (London, 1600), chap. 1.
12. Except where otherwise noted, the bibliographic data mentioned in this paragraph were compiled from A. W. Pollard and G. R. Redgrave, eds., *Short-Title Catalogue of Books Printed in England, Scotland and Ireland, and of English Books Printed Abroad, 1475–1640* (London, 1926), and D. G. Wing, ed., *Short-Title Catalogue of Books Printed in England, Scotland, Ireland, Wales, and British North America and of English Books Printed in Other Countries, 1640–1700,* 5 vols. (New York, 1945–51).
13. Bertram Osborne, *Justice of the Peace, 1361–1848: A History of the Justices of the Peace for the Counties of England* (Shaftsbury, Dorset, 1960), 12.
14. Pollard and Redgrave, *STC,* 121–22; Wing, *STC,* 350–51.
15. Pollard and Redgrave, *STC,* 27.
16. Wing, *STC,* 301.
17. Ibid., 496.
18. A useful guide to printed inventories of estates that included their owners' libraries, as well as studies of reader habits, is David Gillespie and Michael H. Harris, comps., "A Bibliography of Virginia Library History," *Journal of Library History* 6 (1970): 72–90. I derived my list of law titles read by seventeenth-century Virginians from these sources and others that are mentioned below. Mr. Harris kindly provided me with a copy of the bibliography. See also W. Hamilton Bryson, *Census of Law Books in Colonial Virginia* (Charlottesville, 1978).
19. For an example of what a seventeenth-century colonist's law library might contain see "An Inventory of the Goods Chattels Wares and Merchandizes belonging to the Estate of Arthur Spicer 8 Feb. 1701/02," Richmond County Wills and Inventories (1699–1701), fols. 36–41.
20. A useful bibliographic guide to the abridgments is John D. Cowley, comp., *A Bibliography of Abridgments, Digests, Dictionaries and Indexes of English Law to the Year 1800* (London, 1932). Cowley's introduction acquaints the reader with some of the mechanics of publishing legal literature from the fifteenth to the nineteenth centuries.
21. For example, see the entry "accon sur le case" in Sir Robert Brooke, *La Graunde Abridgement, Collecte a escrie per le judge tres reverend Syr Robert Brooke Chivalier, nagdairs chief Justice del Common banke* (London, 1576), fols. 4–8.
22. Theodore F. T. Pluncknett, *Concise History of the Common Law,* 5th ed. (London, 1956).
23. Sir Anthony Fitzherbert, *La Graunde Abridgement, Collecte par le Judge tres-reverend monsieur Anthony Fitzherbert . . . ,* 2d ed. (London, 1565). The first edition, published in 1516, had no attribution of Fitzherbert's authorship (Cowley, *Bibliography of Abridgments,* xliii–xlvi).
24. Brooke's abridgment was first published in January 1573/74 (Cowley, *Bibliography of Abridgments,* 30).
25. William Rastell, *A Collection of all Statutes (from the beginning of Magna Carta unto*

the yere of our Lords, 1557) which were before that yere imprinted (London, 1557). Between 1557 and 1625 Rastell was reprinted, with additions, twenty times.

26. Edmund Wingate, *An Exact Abridgment of All Statutes in Force and Use* (London, 1641).
27. Among the other dictionaries available to the colonists were Henry Spelman's *Archaeologus* (1626), Edward Leigh's *Philogicall Commentary, or, an Illustration of the Most Obvious and Useful Words in the Law* (1652), and Thomas Blount's *NOMO-ΛΕΞΙΚΟΝ: A Law Dictionary* (London, 1670). See also Cowley, *Bibliography of Abridgments*, lxxxi–xc.
28. The original title was *Expositones terminorum in legum anglorum*. Because the dictionary was first printed in law French, it soon became popularly known as *Termes de la ley*.
29. John Cowell, *The Interpreter: or Book Containing the Signification of Words . . .* (Cambridge, 1607).
30. The story of this controversy, plus a brief biography of Cowell, may be found in the 1727 edition of the *Interpreter*.
31. For a listing of the various reports published before 1776 see John William Wallace, *The Reporters, Arranged with Incidental Remarks . . .*, 4th ed. (Boston, 1882).
32. Sir James Dyer, *Cy ensuont ascuns nouel cases* (London, 1585). Dyer's reports went through nine printings in law French down to the year 1622. Five abridgments in English appeared after 1648.
33. Edmund Plowden, *Les Commentaries, ou les reports de deyvers Cases . . .* (London, 1571). The *Commentaries* went through a succession of printings before an English abridgment was done in 1650.
34. Edward Bulstrode, *The Reports* (London, 1657–59).
35. Sir George Croke, *The Reports, Collected and Written in French by Himself; Revised and Published in English by Sir Harbottle Grimston* (London, 1661).
36. Richard Beale Davis, ed., *William Fitzhugh and his Chesapeake World, 1676–1701: The Fitzhugh Letters and Other Documents* (Chapel Hill, NC, 1963), 49–50, 65–66, 66n, 68–69n; Louis B. Wright, *The First Gentlemen of Virginia: Intellectual Qualities of the Early Colonial Ruling Class* (San Marino, CA, 1940), 202–3, 225; "An Inventory . . . of the Estate of Arthur Spicer."
37. Westmoreland Co. Order Book (1675–1689), 374–77.
38. The *Institutes* were first published in London in four parts between 1628 and 1644 and went through numerous editions thereafter.
39. Finch's work first appeared in 1627.
40. Fortescue's book was first printed in Latin. The parallel Latin and English edition cited here was published in London in 1567. A modern translation is S. B. Chrimes, *Sir John Fortescue De Laudibus Legum Anglie* (Cambridge, 1942).
41. Fulbeck's books appeared in 1600 and 1601, respectively.
42. First printed in 1481, Littleton's *Tenures* went through many editions. An English translation appeared in 1604.
43. William Lambarde, *Eirenarcha: Or the Office of Justices of Peace . . .* (London, 1581). Between 1581 and 1620 the *Eirenarcha* went through thirteen editions.

44. On Lambarde's judicial career see Wilbur Dunkel, *William Lambarde, Elizabethan Jurist* (London, 1965).
45. Among these were Sir Anthony Fitzherbert, *The New Boke of Justices of Peace* (London, 1554); Michael Dalton, *The Countrey Justice: Contayning the Practice of the Justices of the Peace Out of their Sessions* (London, 1618); *The Compleat Justice, Being an Exact and Compendious Collection Out of Such as Have Treated of the Office of Justices of the Peace . . .*, 7th ed. (London, 1661); Wa. Young, *A Vade Mecum, or Table Containing the Substance of Such Statutes; Wherein Any One or More Justices of the Peace are Inabled to Act . . .*, 7th ed. (London, 1663); William Sheppard, *The Whole Office of the Countrey Justice of the Peace* (London, 1650); Joseph Keble, *An Assistance to the Justices of the Peace, for the Easier Performance of their Duty* (London, 1683). There was a marked tendency for the writers of such manuals to borrow most liberally from each other's work.
46. See, for example, George Billinghurst, *Arcana clericala: or The Mysteries of Clerkship* (London, 1673); Michael Dalton, *Officium Vicecomitum, The Office and Authoritie of Sherifs* (London, 1623); William Lambarde, *The Duties of Constables, Borsholders, Tithingrnen, etc.* (London, 1583); Sir William Noye, *The Compleat Lawyer* (London, 1651); Henry Swinburne, *A briefe Treatise of Testaments and Last Wills* (London, 1590); John Godolphin, *The Orphans Legacy: Or a Testamentary Abridgment* (London, 1674); William West, *Symboleographia, Which May Be Termed the Art, Description, or Image of Instruments, Covenants, Contracts, etc. . . .* (London, 1590).
47. Hening, *Statutes at Large,* 2:246; Lancaster Co. Order Book (1661–80), fol. 132; York Co. Order Book (1665–72), 361.
48. Compare the oath administered to Virginia magistrates in Hening, *Statutes at Large,* 1:169, with the justice's oath in Dalton, *Countrey Justice,* 12th ed. (London, 1677), 13; Accomack Co. Order Book (1666–70), fols. 150ff., 179ff.
49. Compare Swinburne, *A Briefe Treatise of Testaments and Last Wills,* 75–76, with the act defining the status of mulatto bastards in Hening, *Statutes at Large,* 2:170. The citation to Swinburne used here is taken from the third edition, which was published in London in 1635.
50. Until the 1680s the General Assembly could hear appeals from the General Court. See Billings, *A Little Parliament,* 149–73.
51. Land records and wills, for instance, were not recorded in English county archives.
52. For an example of such a suit see Northumberland Co. Record Books (1652–58), fols. 66–67, 85; (1658–60), fol. 28; and Northumberland Co. Order Book (1652–65), fols. 40, 46, 49.

LAW BOOKS IN THE LIBRARIES OF COLONIAL VIRGINIANS

W. Hamilton Bryson

A TREATISE OF TESTAMENTS AND LAST WILLS,

Fit to be understood by all men, that they may know, Whether, Whereof, and How, to make them.

Compiled out of the Laws Ecclesiasticall, Civill and Canon, as also out of the Common Laws, Customes and Statutes of this Realm.

By HENRY SWINBURNE, sometimes Judge of the Prerogative Court of YORK.

The Fourth Edition, very much enlarged with many choice Cases, and all such Statutes relating to this Subject as have been published unto this time. With an exact Table to the whole.

2 KINGS 20. 1.
Put thine house in order, for thou shalt die, and not live.

LONDON,
Printed by *George Sawbridge*, *Thomas Roycroft*, and *William Rawlins*, Assigns of *Richard Atkins* and *Edward Atkins* Esquires, 1677.
Cum gratia & privilegio Regiæ Majestatis.

Henry Swinburne's Treatise of Testaments and Last Wills, first published in 1590–91, was the standard reference work for lawyers and magistrates charged with overseeing the probate of estates. Henry Swinburne, Treatise of Testaments and Last Wills (London, 1677). (Courtesy the Library of Virginia)

OF ALL PROFESSIONALS, LAWYERS are the most dependent on books. All of their resource material is in written form. To know the quality of the practicing bar, the bench, legal studies, and legal scholarship in general, one must know the books on which they are founded. A census of law books present in the libraries of colonial Virginians can shed some light on the law and the lawyers who shaped the colony and the nation.[1]

Virginia was the largest and most populous British colony in North America. From the Stamp Act crisis through the American Revolution and for the next half century Virginians had a disproportionate influence in founding the United States. Virginians trained in the law late in the colonial period exercised that influence, which makes understanding the quality and abundance of the legal literature available to them both interesting and important.

To say that this essay covers the colonial period calls for a warning. It includes the entire span from 1607 to 1776 as far as the presence of law books in private libraries can be identified, but because the relevant records from seventeenth-century Virginia were not always as carefully made and have not been as well preserved as those from the eighteenth century, almost all of the information comes from the period from about 1700 to 1776. Moreover, Virginia before 1700 was neither so populous nor so prosperous as it was later, and fewer books of any kind would have been present in most households in the early years.

The types of libraries that included law books varied. Some professional lawyers, such as Richard Hickman (d. 1731) and John Mercer (1704–1768), had large, comprehensive law collections. The libraries of the great landowners William Byrd (1674–1744) and Robert "King" Carter (ca. 1663–1732), who sat on the General Court in Williamsburg, show that they had much more than a superficial understanding of the law.[2] The lesser gentry, an extensive class in Virginia, were justices of the peace and composed the county courts, the quarter sessions of colonial Virginia. In addition, they usually handled their own legal affairs, and legal manuals and guides appeared commonly in their more modest libraries.

This description of private libraries is based on printed sources, some manuscripts that have come to hand, and inventories of decedents' estates. The printed sources are for the most part transcriptions of inventories filed among the probate records of the county courts. One of the major limitations of this compilation is that not all of the county records have survived the fires, wars, and other vicissitudes of time. One particularly serious loss was that of the probate records of Williamsburg, the colonial capital during the eighteenth century, the seat of the General Court, and the residence of many prominent lawyers, including the attorneys general. With the loss of those records went references to a large number of law books in the colonial capital. Moreover, some of the manuscript county records have not been systematically surveyed to identify every surviving estate inventory, and eighteenth-century Virginia law allowed people to specify that their executors not file inventories, so that some collections never got catalogued in that way. Many of the surviving inventories contain incomplete lists, and some tantalize with vague entries such as "law books" or "old legal books."[3] Books also perished during the lifetimes of their owners and were thus never listed on estate inventories. Fires were frequent in private homes. The library of Thomas Jefferson (1743–1826) at Shadwell, which was composed mostly of law books, was accidentally burned in 1770.[4] People also lent books that were never returned, and other books were lost to overuse, dampness, and vermin.

On the other hand, it is possible that a single book has been counted more than once, because it is impossible to trace migrations of most individual volumes from owner to owner. That executors or administrators listed the titles demonstrates that those men understood that the books were of importance and had been important to the owners. They were not going to discard the volumes, but heirs with no pressing need or desire for law books may have sold them or given them away. No pattern is discernible in the acquisition or ownership of the various copies of the same title; therefore, with the exception of the rare surviving volumes that contain evidence of a chain of ownership, one cannot make any conjecture that a person got his copy from a particular individual, though he may have.

Furthermore, the number of titles is certainly not the minimum number present in the inventoried libraries of colonial Virginians, because many entries in the inventories are too terse to permit identification of the title. Some of them may duplicate, and probably do, some of the fully identified entries. Even when titles are given, the number of volumes is not always known, because law books were occasionally published in different numbers of volumes when issued in new editions, and some of the entries probably represent incomplete sets. Nevertheless, the errors of omission and commission may cancel each other. While the statistics that follow are cautious and conservative, they are probably representative with respect to the relative abundance in those libraries of the different classes of law books and to which titles in each class were most numerous. The published estate inventories refer to 1,571 copies of 482 identified titles and 360 copies of 179 unidentified titles. Many of the unidentified titles are probably additional copies of identified books, but some certainly are not. We must keep this caveat in mind when noting that the census gives a total of 1,931 copies and 661 entries.

The primary sources of the law represented in the identifiable titles are the reports of judicial decisions and editions of the statutes of Parliament and of the Virginia General Assembly. The secondary sources of the law are abridgments, digests, and treatises prepared by practicing lawyers, law publishers, and, beginning late in the eighteenth century, legal academics, the first and foremost of whom was Sir William Blackstone (1723–1780). Those were works of legal theory, legal history, legal philosophy, and jurisprudence.[5]

The inventories identify 345 copies of 91 reports and accounts of trials, 6 copies of 3 or 4 indexes to reports, and 12 copies of 6 unidentified collections. These reports would have been of little practical value to most laymen, and thus the presence of several in one library suggests that the owner was a practicing lawyer or a person with aspirations in that direction. Of course, a volume of reports could have strayed into a gentleman's library by gift, bequest, or ill-advised purchase. Thus, the list of reports shows the professional and intellectual level of the bar of colonial Virginia.

As one would expect, the most popular of the reporters was Sir Edward Coke, with 20 copies of his reports, including incomplete sets and abridgments. The next highest number is 14 copies of the reports of Sir George Croke. Thirteen copies each of reports by Sir Henry Hobart and William Salkeld appear in the estate inventories, as well as 9 copies of the reports of Sir Henry Pollexfen and of Sir Peyton Ventris. At least one copy of almost all the then-printed reports was present in the private libraries of Virginia before 1776. Of the 98 reports then in print, 91 are known to have been available to one or more members of the colonial Virginia bar, and some of the others may have been. The exceptions were reports of Sir Robert Brooke, William Bunbury, Timothy Cunningham, William Mosely, Joseph Sayer, Francis Vesey Sr., and George Wilson, most of them published after 1755. The Virginians who owned the largest numbers of reports were John Mercer, who owned 97; William Byrd, with 33; Robert Carter, 26; George Johnston (1700–1766), 25; Peyton Randolph (ca. 1722–1775), 24; and Richard Hickman (d. 1732), 21. Five other men each owned between 10 and 20.

A second class of legal reference works consists of collections of state trials and published accounts of individual cases, most of which were criminal trials. The estate inventories identify 43 copies of 24 titles. Virginians probably acquired these books for their historical-interest value rather than for their limited use in legal research or in the routine practice of the law.

Editions of statutes constituted a third class. Most of the English collections of parliamentary statutes were entitled *Statutes at Large,* making it difficult in some instances and impossible in others to ascertain how many titles, editions, and volumes Virginians owned. The inventories record at least 104 copies and sets in their libraries. Collections of statutes that the General Assembly of Virginia adopted, either in full text or in abstract, are easier to identify because editions were fewer in number. The colony's laws are represented by 16 titles and a total of 133 copies.

The secondary English legal literature comprises the great bulk of the books present in eighteenth-century Virginia libraries, 1,007 copies of 346 identifiable titles and 305 copies of 162 unidentified ones. This class of law books includes everything from scholarly treatises to form books and manuals for laymen. English manuals for justices of the peace, 63 copies of 21 titles, were the most abundant. The most popular were the works of Michael Dalton (as might have been expected),[6] whose treatise was represented by 17 copies; of Joseph Keble, 5 copies; and of Richard Burn, 5 copies. Michael Dalton's *Country Justice: Or the Office of a Justice of Peace Out of their Sessions* was first published in 1618 and superseded in popularity William Lambarde's *Eirenarcha: Or the Office of Justices of Peace, in Foure Bookes*. Dalton's work was enormously popular in England as well as in Virginia and went through many editions before Robert Burn's *Justice of the Peace, and Parish Officer* replaced it. The presence of only five copies of Burn's book is not really surprising. His manual was highly successful in England, but because the first edition was not issued until 1755, it had serious local competition from George Webb's *Office and Authority of a Justice of Peace,* published specifically for Virginia justices of the peace in 1736.

Justices of the peace in Virginia presided over the county courts, which had civil as well as petty criminal jurisdiction, but in England justices were invested only with criminal jurisdiction and some quasi-criminal administrative duties. The English manuals for justices dealt largely with matters of criminal law. Webb's manual was much more useful to Virginia magistrates because it offered them guidance on a much wider variety of subjects that came before them. It appears in forty-three estate inventories and was one of only three works by a colonial American. The other two were also manuals for justices of the peace. The inventories identify one copy of William Simpson's *Practical Justice of the Peace and Parish-Officer,* published in Charleston, South Carolina, and six copies of James Parker's *Conductor Generalis: Or the Office, Duty and Authority of Justices of the Peace,* which went through three editions in the middle Atlantic colonies before 1776.

In addition to the manuals for justices of the peace, other types of books dealt with the criminal law and its administration, such as three guides for sheriffs. The inventories record at least 7 copies of Michael Dalton's *Officium Vicecomitum: The Office and Authority of Sheriffs* and a single copy of John Wilkinson's *Practical Treatise on the Office of High Sheriff and of the Complete Sheriff,* published without an author's name. The lists also include two books for constables, one by George Meriton and the other by Edmund Wingate, and two for clerks of assize. Forty copies of twelve titles deal with the criminal law in general. The most popular of them were Sir Edward Coke's *Third Institute of the Laws of England* (10 copies), Sir Matthew Hale's *Historia Placitorum Coronae: The History of the Pleas of the Crown* (8), and William Hawkins's *Pleas of the Crown* (7).

By far the most commonly owned law books in colonial Virginia were practical guides, handbooks, and collections of forms for pleading in court and for the conveying of land. These books were the foundation of the practicing attorney's professional library, and they were also very popular with laymen who handled their own legal affairs. The most common of the 117 titles in 359 volumes were Giles Duncombe's *Trials per Pais; or, The Law Concerning Juries by Nisi-Prius* (15 copies); Sir Anthony Fitzherbert's *New Natura Brevium* (13); Thomas Manley's *Clerk's Guide* (11); and William West's *Symboleography* (11). Eleven other titles appeared in inventories of between five and ten private libraries.

Books on the subject of real property (21 titles and 68 copies) far outnumbered books on other branches of the substantive common law, such as contracts, slander, and fraud. This large preponderance of books on property law reflects the fundamental importance of real estate, the major form of wealth in England as well as in Virginia. Property law was also the most well developed and sophisticated branch of English law. Certainly the most important of the titles was *Coke upon Littleton,* which constituted the first part of Sir Edward Coke's *Institutes.* It was an elaborate and deeply learned commentary on Sir Thomas Littleton's *Tenures,* first published in 1481. *Coke upon Littleton* was the standard text until the appearance of the first volume of Sir William Blackstone's *Commentaries on the Laws of England* in 1765. At least 27 copies of *Coke upon Littleton* were in Virginia libraries. The second most popular such work was John Perkins's *A Profitable Book . . . Treating the Laws of England,* which was in at least eight libraries.

Twenty-six copies of 13 titles dealt with procedure and practice in equity, the other major branch of English law, and there were 10 copies of 6 works on the substantive principles. General reference works such as law dictionaries,[7] abridgments, and encyclopedias, accounted for 28 titles and 132 copies. Giles Jacob's *Law Dictionary* was the most popular title in the general reference category, with 23 copies. The other titles that appeared most often in inventories were John Rastell's *Termes de la Ley* (17 copies); Thomas Wood's *An Institute of the Laws of England* (14); William Sheppard's *Abridgment* (7); Sir Francis Bacon's *Elements of the Common Laws of England* (6); and John Cowell's *Interpreter* (6).

Five other works are entitled to special notice because of their antiquity and scholarship: *Tractatus de Legibus et Consuetudinibus Regni Anglie,* putatively authored by Ranulf de Glanville (d. 1190, commonly called Glanvill), with subsequent revisions or editions attributed to Henry de Bracton (d. 1268) and John le Breton, commonly called Britton (d. 1275); John Selden's *Ad Fletam Dissertatio;* and Christopher Saint Germain's *Doctor and Student,* the last included in eight inventories. All five of these works were on the shelves of William Byrd's library at Westover, Robert Carter owned copies of Bracton and Britton, and John Mercer had a copy of Britton. Indeed, the presence of these books and others of equal scarcity and erudition in other fields contributes to the high reputations of Byrd and Carter and of their libraries.

Virginians also owned books treating those branches of the civil law of the Continent that were grafted onto the trunk of English jurisprudence: ecclesiastical law, including the law of wills; and the law of merchants, including maritime law and the levy of customs duties. Inventories contain references to 24 copies of 20 titles dealing with the various aspects of church law concerning tithes, canons, convocations, and parishes. That only 2 titles appear more than once suggests the relative unimportance of this general group of books. On the other hand, the works dealing with wills and executors were very useful and were present in relative profusion, 72 copies of 11 titles. The most numerous were Henry Swinburne's *Treatise of Testaments and Last Wills* (23), Thomas Wentworth's *Office of Executors* (13), John Godolphin's *Orphan's Legacy* (11), and George Gilbert's *Law of Devises* (8).

The number of Continental legal works is not great, but it is larger than one might have expected, 65 copies of 34 titles. The library of William Byrd of Westover accounted for 28, and they were among the more esoteric. The remainder were standard texts, often English translations, scattered thinly among the colony's libraries. The inventories list 20 copies of Samuel von Pufendorf's two popular treatises, 10 of Hugo Grotius's *De Jure Belli ac Pacis,* 6 of Justinian's *Institutes* (a textbook of Roman law), and 2 of Jean Domat's *Lois Civiles,* or in its English translation, *Civil Law in its Natural Order.*

Almost all free Virginians derived their income from farming, and they were dependent on British merchants and shippers to provide them with manufactured goods and to market their agricultural products. Fifty-five copies of 20 reference books on commerce appear in the inventories. The single most popular book was Charles Molloy's *De Jure Maritimo* (18 copies), followed by Gerard de Malynes's *Lex Mercatoria* (6) and what was usually referred to as "the book of rates," the schedule of the statutory customs duties established by the English Act of Tonnage and Poundage (Stat. 12 Car. 2, c. 4) (12).

As one would expect, the standard legal manuals and guidebooks for laymen were the most numerous law books in colonial libraries. People needed to know what their powers and duties were as justices of the peace, collectors of customs, sheriffs, constables, vestrymen, and administrators of estates. They needed to know how to make wills, how to convey land, how to draft bills of exchange, and how to collect a debt or prosecute a thief. In addition, many of the practicing attorneys, justices of the peace, and judges of the General Court owned copies of the various reports of cases and collections of statutes. The wealthier and more highly educated also had erudite volumes of jurisprudence, legal history, and international law. The most fabulous library of all, that of William Byrd in the rooms at Westover, also included books of the Roman and canon laws of the Continent.

The law books that residents of colonial Virginia owned ranged from a single manual, form book, or statute book in many houses to more than a hundred volumes in a small number of well-stocked libraries. The ownership of law books was widespread throughout the colony, making it obvious that Virginians were concerned with their legal rights and that they looked to the English common law for their definition. Virginians frequently lent books to their neighbors, and the doors of their libraries were evidently always open to friends. With both large and small collections available throughout the settled areas of the colony, people could often borrow books that they did not own.

The scope of the legal literature available to eighteenth-century Virginians was remarkably deep and broad. The availability in eighteenth-century Virginia of the relevant law books, especially the reports of cases, the foundational books, shows that the common law of England was more than just a theoretical concept. It actually governed the community and was applied in the courts. This was true not only of the General Court in Williamsburg but also of the county courts throughout the colony.

NOTES

An earlier version of this essay appeared in W. Hamilton Bryson, "Private Law Libraries before 1776," in *Virginia Law Books,* ed. W. Hamilton Bryson, Memoirs of the American Philosophical Society, vol. 239 (Philadelphia, 2000), 479–87.

1. The statistics in this essay are based on the information found in W. Hamilton Bryson, *Census of Law Books in Colonial Virginia* (Charlottesville, 1978), and upon further, subsequent research done primarily in the Virginia county-court records of wills and inventories of decedents' estates.
2. Kevin J. Hayes, *The Library of William Byrd of Westover* (Madison, WI, 1997); Lyon G. Tyler, "Libraries in Colonial Virginia." *William and Mary Quarterly,* 1st ser., 3 (1895): 248–51; Louis B. Wright, "The 'Gentleman's Library' in Early Virginia: The Literary Interests of the First Carters," *Huntington Library Quarterly* 1 (1937): 3–61.
3. For example, "1 law book" (Benjamin Brown, 1762), "15 law books" (Joseph Heenning, 1718), "13 law books" (Robert Tucker, 1723), "20 law books" (John Eustace, 1702). "Books in Colonial Virginia," *Virginia Magazine of History and Biography* 10 (1903): 389–405.
4. Dumas Malone, *Jefferson, the Virginian* (Boston, 1948), 126; Thomas Jefferson to

John Page, 21 Feb. 1770, and Jefferson to James Oglivie, 20 Feb. 1771, in *The Papers of Thomas Jefferson,* ed. Julian P. Boyd et al. (Princeton, NJ, 1950–), 1: 34–35, 63.

5. David J. Ibbetson, "Charles Viner and His Chair: Legal Education in Eighteenth Century Oxford," in *Learning the Law: Teaching and the Transmission of Law in England, 1150–1900,* ed. Jonathan A. Bush and Alain A. Wijffels (London, 1999), 315–28.

6. L. R. McInnis, "Michael Dalton: The Training of the Early Modern Justice of the Peace and the Cromwellian Reforms," in Bush and Wijffels, *Learning the Law,* 255–72.

7. Gary L. McDowell, "Politics of Meaning: Law Dictionaries and the Liberal Tradition of Interpretation," *American Journal of Legal History* 44 (2000): 257–83.

THE LIBRARY OF THE COUNCIL OF COLONIAL VIRGINIA

Brent Tarter

The library of the Council of State in the capitol in Williamsburg was the most nearly comprehensive law library in eighteenth-century Virginia. Bookplate of the Council of Virginia. (Courtesy the Library of Virginia)

A VISITOR TO WILLIAMSBURG, VIRginia, early in April 1773 walked through the rooms of the colony's capitol and recorded his observations. In the stately chamber where the Council of State met, the Bostonian Josiah Quincy Jr. looked over "a large, well-chosen, valuable collection of books, chiefly of law."[1] That library contained one of the best collections of law, history, and general reference works in Virginia, and the law books probably had a greater influence on the people of the colony than any other one set of books. Those books were important and influential artifacts of English civilization. They transmitted to Virginia—Great Britain's oldest, largest, and most populous North American colony—and preserved for Virginians the essence of centuries of evolving English legal principles and practices.

By the eighteenth century numerous affluent Virginians, as well as practicing lawyers, had law books in their personal libraries. Their books provided practical and theoretical guidance for the settlement of complex or unusual legal problems that arose from time to time, and those men often shared copies of scarce reference volumes with one another.[2] The books in the library in the capitol in Williamsburg probably were more numerous and represented a more nearly comprehensive collection than any of the private libraries by the time Quincy visited Williamsburg, and they were available to a large number of unusually influential Virginians. Most of the leading men in Virginia visited the capital from time to time, either when the General Assembly was in session, to apply to the secretary of the colony or to the governor and Council of State for land grants and other important documents, or to look after their personal affairs during the regularly scheduled meetings of the General Court. That was especially true for lawyers during the eighteenth century because virtually all the colony's most important civil and criminal cases were tried in the General Court, which met in the capitol, where the books were useful to attorneys and judges alike. Members of the House of Burgesses and gentlemen of learning also consulted the books as they worked on legislation or legal issues of more than routine interest; and many of the talented men who guided Virginia during the 1770s and 1780s from royal colony to American state and who guided the thirteen colonies into nationhood also knew and used those books.

The little city of Williamsburg, which was the capital from 1699 to 1780, was a very bookish place. Beginning in the 1730s the printer of the *Virginia Gazette* stocked books for sale at the printing office. Several residents, including clergymen and some of the attorneys general, had noted book collections, as did several clerks of the Council of State and the General Court, some of the governors, and other officers and practicing attorneys who had been called to the bar from the Inns of Court in London. The College of William and Mary also had a library, about which only a little is now known.[3] The library Quincy viewed in the capitol was undoubtedly the largest in Williamsburg, no doubt had the best collection of law books in the colony (with the possible exception of William Byrd's great library at Westover), and was open to every gentleman in Virginia. Because lawyers often borrowed books from one another or from the Council of State library, the capital city's libraries in effect offered them an informal version of the Social Law Library, founded by men in Boston during the American Revolution to pool their collections of legal reference works. Considering the great variety of questions on which a large proportion of the colony's attorneys and political leaders could have gone to the council library to seek information for themselves, for the benefit of their clients, or on behalf of others, the library must have exercised a considerable influence over the political and intellectual life of the entire colony. Anyone from county-court lawyer to General Court judge should have been able to find just about any reference book on English law in Williamsburg. The first place to look was the council's library.

Unfortunately, most of the volumes present in the library when the American Revolution began disappeared during or after the war, as have many of the records documenting the compilation of the library and the fate of the books it contained.[4] Only about seventy-five surviving volumes have been positively identified, but a list of law books the president of the Virginia Court of Appeals compiled in 1791 and the contents of an 1828 printed catalog indicate what kinds of books were in the library at the end of the colonial period.[5] That and other scattered bits of information about the library allow some educated deductions about the library's holdings and its overall quality.

The library's origins stretch back almost to the beginning of the English settlement of Virginia in 1607. In the early years books pertinent to the business of governing were in short supply. George Thorpe, an officer of the Virginia Company, wrote to London on 15 May 1621, "In the matter of our Government here wee are many times perplexed sometimes for lacke of Legal officers & some times for wante of books I woulde therefore intreate you to send us the newe booke of thabridgment of Statutes and Stamfords pleas of the Crowne and mr wests presidents and what other Lawe books you shall thinke fitt and if you please likewise t[o] send us Gerards Herball thereby to make comparison of the simples of the Countrey."[6] The titles he requested indicate that the company's governor and his advisory council most needed practical guides and a good, up-to-date set of statutes. Sir William Staunford's *Les Plees del Coron* (1560), although in the antique language known as law

French, contained valuable guides for court proceedings in various kinds of cases; and William West's *Symboleographia* (1592) contained forms for writs, deeds, and various legal processes by which the men in charge of the government in Jamestown could secure people's property rights and administer justice. John Gerard's *The Herball, Or Generall Historie of Plantes* (1597) would have assisted them in identifying native Virginia plants—"the simples of the Countrey"—with medicinal or commercial value.

The need for English law books undoubtedly increased after Virginia became a royal colony in 1625. At the center of the royal government were the governor and the Council of State, made up of about a dozen of the most eminent, wealthy, and well-connected men in Virginia. Most of them were well educated by the standards of the day, and some of the eighteenth-century council members had attended the Inns of Court in London and studied the law. The councillors were executive advisers to the governor and helped make governmental decisions that ranged across the entire scope of colonial affairs. They also participated directly in the adoption of the colony's laws, first as members of a unicameral General Assembly and after 1643 as the upper house of the colonial legislature. The councillors were also the only members of the General Court, which met quarterly during part of the seventeenth century and semiannually thereafter; and during the eighteenth century they were also the only members of the Court of Oyer and Terminer, which met midway between the sessions of the General Court to hear criminal cases that arose in the interims. These were the colony's highest courts and the only ones with jurisdiction over felonies and the most important civil actions. The councillors sat as judges in both trials and appeals, which covered an extremely broad legal terrain. Their numerous important responsibilities required them to have a reference library in the statehouse in Jamestown in the seventeenth century and in the capitol in Williamsburg in the eighteenth that could inform them accurately about British statute and common law, Virginia civil and criminal law, land law, equity pleading, and practical politics. The members of the council and other political leaders during the seventeenth century were well aware of the importance of legal records and precedents and of the need to have reliable authorities and texts of British laws and judicial decisions to guide their work. In short, books on English law were essential to them and to the Virginians they governed.[7]

During the early years when the English population of Virginia was small and none of the settlements was far from Jamestown, the governor and council attended to virtually all the settlers' legal needs. In the absence of ecclesiastical courts to prove the authenticity of wills and to oversee the executors or administrators of estates, the governor and council did that work, or it would not have been done. From the 1620s to the 1650s the governor and council or the General Assembly gradually delegated specific legal tasks to local courts, such as recording land transactions, keeping the peace, and the increasingly onerous duty of proving wills and probating estates. Those courts developed into county courts of record, which freed the governor and council of much of the time-consuming work.[8]

The creation of county courts required local justices of the peace and county clerks to perform important and occasionally complicated legal business and therefore increased the number of Virginia men who from time to time needed to consult a law book or guide. "Whereas for the better conformitie of the proceedings of the Courts of this Country to the Lawes of England," the General Assembly's 1666 "Act for the supplie of each Countie with Lawe bookes" began, the legislators required the General Court and all county courts to purchase a set of parliamentary statutes and "some other esteemed Bookes of Lawe," including "Dalton's Justice of the peace and office of a Sherriff, and Swinburnes book of Wills & testaments."[9]

The books were the standard reference works on their subjects. Michael Dalton's *Countrey Justice, Conteyning the Practise of Justices of Peace out of their Sessions*, first published in 1618, specified the duties of county justices of the peace in England and their individual responsibilities when the court was not in session. It also included forms for standard writs and other documents a country judge would need. Dalton's manual could easily serve the same needs for Virginia's seventeenth-century justices of the peace, as could his *Officium Vicecomitum, or the Office and Authoritie of Sheriffs* (1623) for Virginia's county sheriffs. Henry Swinburne's *Briefe Treatise of Testaments and Last Willes*, first published in 1590–91, contained what a justice of the peace would ordinarily need to guarantee that an estate was properly probated.

A few subsequent purchases of books for the council's use are recorded, but in very imprecise language. The council reimbursed the auditor, William Byrd (ca. 1652–1704), on 19 July 1694 in the amount of £16 9s. paid to a "Stationer for Law Bookes, paper &c for the use of the Councill Chamber," and on 31 May 1695 the sum of £5 7s. "for bookes and paper for the use of the Councill."[10] Byrd's son and successor, William Byrd (1674–1744), owner of the great library at Westover, continued the purchases and received reimbursement of £59 19s. 3d. on 2 November 1705 "for Law Bookes & other things for the use of his Excellcy and the Council."[11] Crown officers, either the receivers general or the auditors general of the colony, purchased the books throughout most or all of the colonial period. A former member of the council recalled in 1792 that the "Library was bought out of the Fund comonly called the King's Fund," revenue arising from port duties, quitrents, or fees royal commissions authorized, which is why almost no references to the library appear in the ordinary records of the General Assembly or in the statute books.[12]

Several statehouse fires in Jamestown may have destroyed some of the original law books. A disastrous fire in October 1698 occurred just at the time a special joint committee of the General Assembly was beginning a comprehensive revisal of the colony's laws. In July 1699 the joint committee ordered several law books from London, either to replace lost volumes or to augment the stock of reference works. The committee members ordered several up-to-date editions of practical guides, some of them in new editions, among them Sir Edward Coke's *Book of Entries of Declarations* (1614; 2d ed., 1671); the fourth edition of William Rastell's *Collection of Entries* (1687); the revised edition of Richard Garnet's *Book of Oaths* (1689); and the fourth edition of Ralph de Hengham and Simon Theolall's *Registrum Brevium Tam Originalium* (1687). The committee also ordered a recently published volume of New York laws.[13] After the committee of revisers completed its work, those books, if the committee obtained what it had ordered, probably became part of the council library.

Information about the library is only a little more abundant and detailed for the eighteenth century, when the council met in the capitol in Williamsburg. Fortunately, few or none of the books were destroyed when the first Williamsburg capitol burned during the night of 29–30 January 1747. The fire broke out in the attic, and the wind providentially changed direction, giving men time to save all the books and records "of any Consequence." When they threw them out the windows of the council chamber, the volumes became "intermixed with many of the Books and Papers" belonging to the House of Burgesses and the secretary of the colony. That occasioned "very great Labour and Pains in sorting and separating the same." John Collett, the council's doorkeeper, rented storage space for the books until the second Williamsburg capitol was completed.[14]

Members of the council and the clerks of the council and of the General Court probably all participated in deciding which books to add to the library. They doubtless received helpful advice from other men, such as the brothers Peyton and John Randolph, both of whom were barristers educated at the Inns of Court in London, served as attorney general of Virginia, and acquired valuable private libraries. A book-collecting attorney, Benjamin Waller, was clerk of the General Court from about 1740 to 1776 and undoubtedly played an important role in the selection of books. Nathaniel Walthoe, clerk of the council from 1743 to 1770, was also a barrister and book collector, as well as a relative of the London printer and bookseller John Walthoe Jr., one of eighteenth-century London's most important purveyors of law books. The Walthoes were no doubt responsible for the addition of volumes to the council library. The last clerk of the council and custodian of its library during the colonial period, John Blair, had also been educated at one of the Inns of Court. He later served in the conventions that drafted the first constitution of Virginia and the Constitution of the United States and was the first Virginian to serve on the Supreme Court of the United States.

The year before Walthoe became clerk of the council, some of the books in the library acquired a permanent mark of identification. A Williamsburg artisan affixed a stamping that read "Virginia Council Office 1742" on the front covers. While Walthoe was clerk, the council obtained a bookplate for the library. The plate bears the arms of the colony and the identifying legend "Virginia Council Chamber."[15] Those marks of identification suggest that the clerk was proud of the collection or perhaps intended the marks to remind men who borrowed books to return them. A century and a half later the antiquarian Robert A. Brock wrote that he had seen some volumes with the colonial arms "in gilded impression on the backs of books appertaining to the chamber." What he had probably seen were copies of the two-volume 1752 edition of *Statutes of Virginia Now in Force,* which the assembly had specified be bound "with the Arms of *Virginia* stamped on each Book." The General Assembly ordered a thousand copies for the use of the assembly and for distribution to the county courts.[16]

Changes in the nature of legal practice also accounted for the expansion of the council library's holdings. Acts of assembly passed in 1732 and 1748 regulating the licensing of lawyers recognized a bifurcation of the legal profession that had taken place by then. Barristers and a select number of unusually well trained lawyers practiced before the General Court, but men of lesser skill had to confine their practices to the county courts.[17] The General Court lawyers were a distinguished company, and on the eve of the Revolution that bar was as impressive as any in British North America. The trials and appeals at which General Court lawyers appeared required an equally impressive law library.[18]

Documents dated 1763 and 1770 contain lists of titles that help establish what books were and what books were not in the council library during the decade before Josiah Quincy described it on the eve of the American Revolution. A note dated 20 May 1763 in the minute book of the council reads, "The Receiver General was requested to write for the following Books, viz. Hayne's State Papers; Robertson's History of Scotland; Anchitel Grey's Parliamentary Proceedings; Hume's History of England; Guthrie's New British Peerage; Continuation of Acts of Parliament."[19] The surviving letterbook of Deputy Receiver General Richard Corbin at the Colonial Williamsburg Foundation Library contains no record of book orders. However, Corbin may have done as instructed; William Adair, the absentee receiver general, resident in Britain, may have executed the purchases; or an agent acting for one of them may have obtained some of the volumes.

"Continuation of Acts of Parliament" was not a title but an order to purchase the volumes of statutes published after the most recent ones then in the library. Samuel Haynes's *Collection of State Papers Relating to Affairs in the Reigns of Henry VIII, Edward VI, Mary, and Elizabeth, from 1542 to 1570* (1740), probably purchased as a result of the 1763 directive, still belongs to Virginia and is in the collections of the Library of Virginia. William Robertson's *History of Scotland during the Reigns of Queen Mary and of King James VI*, in two volumes (1759; 2d ed., 1763), and David Hume's six-volume *The History of England, from the Invasion of Julius Caesar to the Revolution in 1688* (1762) appear on a 1770 list of titles to be purchased and were therefore not procured under the 1763 directive. It is not known for certain whether the library ever acquired the ten-volume *Debates of the House of Commons, from the Year 1667 to 1694,* edited by Anchitel Grey (1763), or William Guthrie's *A Complete History of the English Peerage,* in two volumes (1763).

A "List of Books necessary for the Council Chamber made out by Phil: L: Lee June '18, 1770" is much longer. The council member Philip Ludwell Lee began it, but three other men added titles or additional details to the list, suggesting that Lee circulated it to other people or that council members discussed the list at a formal meeting or over drinks in the evening and added to it in the process.[20] In fact, it is a list of books that were not in the library as of that date. Standard legal reference works absent from the list were almost certainly already in the library. The list also suggests that Lee and perhaps other members of the council wanted to add more works on English history to the collection.

The list begins with "Journals of the house 'Lords all that can be had in Print," journals of the House of Commons, "Votes of Both Rules & orders of both," as well as "Statutes at large from 6th. George '3d."—that is, since 1766—to bring up to date the library's holdings of parliamentary records and statutes. The list also includes references to *A Collection of the Parliamentary Debates in England from the Year 1668 to the Present Time,* which the printer John Torbuc issued in 1744, and Richard Chandler's *History and Proceedings of the House of Commons from the Restoration to the Present Time* (1742). The notation "Petits Law of Parliament" could have referred to either of two late seventeenth- or early eighteenth-century treatises, George Petyt's *Lex Parliamentaria; or, a Treatise of the Law and Custom of the Parliaments of England* (1690; 2d ed., rev., 1734) or William Petyt's *Jus Parliamentarium: or, The Ancient Power, Jurisdiction, Rights and Liberties of the Most High Court of Parliament Revived and Asserted* (1739). The last three titles could reflect an increased or increasingly sophisticated appreciation of the subtleties and complexities of parliamentary procedure as it had evolved by then in the Virginia General Assembly or—and this would have been of prime importance in the years immediately after the Stamp Act crisis—the scope of and limitations on parliamentary authority.

Lee's amended list also includes "Laws of all the English Colonys in North & South America compleat to this time," beside which in a different handwriting is an unanswered question: "Q. What English Laws in So. America." As with many other entries on the list, that line provides two insights: one is that at that time the library probably did not include a comprehensive set of laws of other English colonies; and the other is that at least some council members believed it would be wise to add to or complete the collections of other colonies' laws. In another handwriting on the back of the sheet containing the original list is a recommendation to order Sir William Blackstone's four-volume *Commentaries on the Laws of England,* published in Oxford in 1765–69, which almost immediately became an essential text for every attorney and for every library of law books.

Published reports of English courts had a prominent place on Lee's list and included several recently published volumes, such as John Tracy Atkins's three-volume *Reports of Cases Argued and Determined in the High Court of Chancery* (1765–68); Mathew Bacon's five-volume *General Abridgement of Cases in Equity* (1732–56); Sir James Burrow's *Reports of Cases Adjudged in the Court of King's Bench,* for which a new five-volume edition was begun in 1771; Sir John Strange's two-volume *Reports of Adjudged Cases in the Court of Chancery* (1755); and Henry Home, Lord Kames's closely related *Principles of Equity* (1760). A less precise entry, "Wilson's Reports," probably referred to one or more of the editions Sergeant-at-Law George Wilson edited of the collected reports of such judges as Edward Coke, Robert Sylvester, 1st Baron Glenbervie, Sir Anthony Fitzherbert, Sir Matthew Hale, Sir Thomas Raymond, and William Salkeld. The appellate jurisdiction of the General Court required a comprehensive set of reported precedents.

In addition to books on English law, Lee's list includes several historical volumes, perhaps to provide an enlarged and enriched context for understanding changes in laws and legal practices as well as operations of government and politics in Great Britain. Among them were David Hume's history of England, which the council had not obtained after ordering it in 1763, and other histories of England, several of them quite recent, by Thomas Carte, White Kennett, Catherine Macaulay, and James Welwood; William Robertson's two-volume *History of Scotland during the Reigns of Queen Mary and of King James VI* (1759); his three-volume *History of the Reign of Charles the Fifth* (1769), about the sixteenth-century king of Spain and Holy Roman Emperor; and editions of two works by Thomas Salmon, *The Chronological Historian* (1727) and *A New Geographical and Astronomical Grammar* (1767). The other titles in Lee's list are more wide-ranging intellectually. They include "Harringtons Works," probably referring to John Toland's 1700 edition of James Harrington's *Oceana* and other titles; some or all of the *Philosophical Transactions of the Royal Society of London,* published serially beginning in 1665; Thomas Leland's 1756 translations of Demosthenes's orations; and Conyers Middleton's 1741 edition of the *History of the Life of Marcus Tullius Cicero.*

Between the summer of 1770 and the summer of 1776 the library acquired new volumes containing laws of the English colonies of Barbadoes, Bermuda, the Leeward Island, and Nevis (perhaps they were the "English Laws in So. America" mentioned on Lee's amended list); Blackstone's *Commentaries,* Atkyns's *Reports* (of which the first three volumes of the second edition were printed in 1771), and Sir James Burrow's *Reports of Cases Adjudged in the Court of King's Bench;* as well as Robertson's *History of Scotland.* Because Lee did not include references to many of the standard legal reference works and case reports, it is likely that most of them were probably already in the library in 1770. In several instances the surviving volumes from the library confirm that deduction, as do, in a few other instances, lists compiled in 1791 and 1828.

Among the surviving law books, volume 2 of Atkyns's *Reports* (1767), volume 2 of Sir Matthew Hale's *Historia Placitorum Coronae: The History of the Pleas of the Crown* (1736), and volumes 5 and 6 of a complete six-volume, third edition of *A Complete Collection of State-Trials,* edited by Sollom Emlyn (1742), bear council bookplates. Volume 1 of William Nelson's three-volume *Abridgment of the Common Law* (1724–26), volumes 2 and 3 of William Salkeld's *Reports* (1717 and 1718), a 1712 second edition of *The Third Part of the Modern Reports,* and a 1742 English translation of Claude Joseph de Ferriere's *History of the Roman or Civil Law* all have the "Virginia Council Office 1742" stamping on the front cover. A copy of the 1668 two-volumes-in-one edition of Henry Rolle's *Un Abridgment des Plusieurs Cases et Resolutions del Common Ley* and the second or third volume of a second edition of William Peere Williams's *Reports of Cases Argued and Determined in the High Court of Chancery* (1746–49) were in existence as recently as 1933 and bore evidence of council ownership.

During the American Revolution, when the executive and legislative archives of the colony were largely destroyed, the library also suffered severe losses.[21] In 1783 the attorney general of the state informed the president of the Court of Appeals that from the "scattered remains of the Public Library" he could find no more than about "fifty dissorted Volumes" of law books, which had been "exposed to great Injury from the Want of proper Presses and an Apartment for their Reception."[22] Nine years later, Edmund Pendleton, the president of the court, complained that the loss of legal reference works had been so severe that judges oftentimes had to postpone making decisions on important cases "until they can Consult the Books in their private repositories in the Countrey, to the delay & injury of Suitors." He compiled a list of the remnants "of the Books of the former Government" that had "escaped the Ravages & derangements of the War" and recommended that the General Assembly purchase an adequate new reference library for the use of the judges and other government officials.[23]

Pendleton's list of law books matches almost exactly, right down to the very edition, many of the short-title entries in the printed library catalog Secretary of the Commonwealth William H. Richardson compiled and published in

1828. Richardson correctly deduced that most or all the pre-1776 imprints then in the library had originally "belonged to the Colonial Council." He also noted that "some of the sets are broken. Many of them however are said to be scarce and valuable."[24] The two lists allow us with confidence to conclude that the library at the time of the American Revolution contained a complete or nearly complete set of parliamentary statutes, as well as a very large and comprehensive collection of published court reports and most of the standard legal reference works. Editions of almost every important compiler or commentator were in that library.

Along with its collection of acts of Parliament, the library almost certainly contained a full set of the printed laws of Virginia, beginning with *Acts of Assembly Now in Force,* which William Parks printed in Williamsburg in 1733, the first volume of laws published in the colony, as well as printed copies of the acts of each legislative session beginning with that of 1732 and no doubt the printed journals of the House of Burgesses, begun in the same year. It also very likely contained copies of three early printed volumes of the colony's laws: Francis Moryson's *The Lawes of Virginia Now in Force* (1662), John Purvis's *Complete Collection of all the Laws of Virginia Now in Force* (1684), and Robert Beverley's *Abridgement of the Publick Laws of Virginia, In Force and Use, June 20, 1720* (1722); and the library definitely contained a copy of John Mercer's 1737 *Exact Abridgment of All the Public Acts of Assembly, of Virginia, in Force and Use.*

Purvis's 1684 edition is of more than ordinary interest. He had compiled and published it without authorization, and for that reason, and because the General Assembly deemed it "very false and Imperfect," the legislators ordered it suppressed.[25] Several copies that once belonged to Virginia attorneys still exist, and the edition evidently remained useful to colonial attorneys and judges. Few of them could have had ready access to all the early and unpublished laws, even though a complete or nearly complete set probably existed in the capitol or in the office of the secretary of the colony. It is likely that the council library contained a copy of Purvis's unauthorized edition of the laws. Attorneys on both sides of an important case cited it in arguments before the General Court during the April session of 1772,[26] and when William Waller Hening compiled and published the seventeenth- and eighteenth-century Virginia statutes early in the nineteenth century, he referred to Purvis's edition several times when comparing variant texts.

It is also very likely that the library contained a copy of George Webb's Virginia replacement for Dalton's manual for justices of the peace. Webb's 1736 *Office and Authority of a Justice of Peace* was the first legal reference book published in Virginia and the first manual useful to both magistrates and lawyers and incorporating references to Virginia laws. If the library had one or more copies of Webb's guide during the final forty years of the colonial period, it probably also had for the last two years a copy of Richard Starke's 1774 less thorough sequel of the same title. Moreover, the known presence in the library of several reference works and histories of England and Scotland and the desire of some council members to enlarge that part of the collection strongly suggest that the library also included histories of Virginia, although no surviving volumes or records document the presence in the library of any of them. In addition to Captain John Smith's several volumes dating from the first years of the colony and other early writers' shorter books, the library probably contained copies of Robert Beverley's 1705 *History of Virginia* or its revised 1722 edition; Hugh Jones's 1724 *The Present State of Virginia;* Henry Hartwell, Edward Chilton, and James Blair's *The Present State of Virginia, and the College,* published in 1727; and William Stith's 1747 Williamsburg imprint, *The History of the First Discovery and Settlement of Virginia: Being an Essay Towards a General History of This Colony.*

The library of the Council of State as represented by the volumes that still exist and by the list of pre-1776 imprints in the 1828 catalog was overwhelmingly legal and political in nature, which is scarcely surprising. That is what Josiah Quincy observed in 1773. The books were in English, Latin, and law French, and they ranged from highly theoretical to severely practical. Acts of Parliament, records of the House of Commons, and collected reports of the Court of Common Pleas, the Court of King's Bench, and the Court of Queen's Bench formed the heart of the collection.

Two branches of law, admiralty and ecclesiastical, appear to have been neglected. As for admiralty law, the attorney general of the colony often served as judge of the provincial court of vice-admiralty after its founding in the 1690s.[27] The court had its own officers, and it may have had its own collection of books. For a time during and after the Revolutionary War the Commonwealth of Virginia had a court of admiralty,[28] but adoption of the US Constitution extinguished all state admiralty jurisdiction. Benjamin Waller, the longtime clerk of the General Court, was also advocate in the colonial court of vice-admiralty from 1742 to 1771, and he served as a judge of the Virginia Court of Admiralty during part of the Revolution. Whether he had anything to do with the fate of the books on admiralty law is not known. Those books may have remained in Williamsburg, where the court had held its sessions, after the court ceased to exist and after the state capital moved to Richmond.

With regard to ecclesiastical law, the list of the council's books surviving as of 1828 contains a few titles that touch on the subject, such as a copy of the 1705 third edition of Bishop Gilbert Burnet's *Exposition of the Thirty-Nine Articles of the Church of England,* but it is possible that the library had contained more. The Church of England was the established church in the colony, even though extant records indicate that the General Court seldom exercised any ecclesiastical jurisdiction. In some civil cases reference to applicable church law may have been required, as in the remarkable dower controversy of the virgin widow Catherine Eustace Blair in 1773,[29] but after the disestablishment of the church in January 1786, state courts would have had little or no need for reference works treating that branch of law. There is no way to know for certain which or how many books dealing with ecclesiastical law the library contained or what became of them.

In addition to statute books, court reports, and treatises on the law, the library contained an impressive collection of general reference works, many bearing directly on matters of British history, law, and public policy. It included a ten-volume 1735 English edition of Pierre Bayle's *Historical and Critical Dictionary* (the Library of Virginia still owns nine of the volumes); the three-volume *History of the Rebellion and Civil Wars in England,* by Edward Hyde, 1st Earl of Clarendon (which is also still in the Library of Virginia); multivolume collections of state papers compiled and published by John Thurloe, John Rushworth, and William Cecil, 1st Baron Burghley; Thomas Sprat's account of Monmouth's rebellion; William Guthrie's, Ralph James's, and Paul de Rapin-Thoyras's documentary histories; Charles-Louis de Secondat, Baron de La Brède et de Montesquieu's *De l'Esprit des Loix;* Francis Hutcheson's *System of Moral Philosophy;* and editions of the collected works of Francis Bacon, Robert Boyle, George Buchanan, John Locke, and John Milton.

Before and during the American Revolution, gentlemen other than attorneys also had access to the library and occasionally borrowed books from it, and some of them failed to return the books.[30] Later, James Innes, who was attorney general of Virginia from 1786 to 1796, somehow got into his private library the council's six-volume set of Sollom Emlyn's 1742 edition of *Complete Collection of State-Trials.* On 25 March 1800 St. George Tucker purchased the set from Innes's widow. The volumes are now in the Tucker-Coleman Collection, Earl Gregg Swem Library, College of William and Mary. Two of the volumes still wear the council bookplate. The Virginia Historical Society now owns John Bearer's English translation of Claude Joseph de Ferriere's *History of the Roman or Civil Law,* with the "Virginia Council Office 1742" stamping on the front. It was also removed from the library before preparation of the catalog in 1828. The University of Virginia Library owns volume 2 of the 1736 edition of Sir Matthew Hale's *Historia Placitorum Coronae* with the council bookplate, and it also has two detached boards with council stampings, suggesting that two unidentified original council volumes with twentieth-century covers are in the same library.

Together, Edmund Pendleton's 1791 list of law books and William H. Richardson's 1828 printed *Catalogue of the Library of the State of Virginia* provide nearly all that is now known about the contents of the council's library. Almost all the law books on Pendleton's list appear in Richardson's catalog, which enumerates 659 titles, encompassing a total of 1,582 volumes plus several maps. About half the titles—collections of British, US, colonial, and state statutes and reports of British and US court cases—are classified as law books. The rest are organized into broad categories: political economy; history and biography; agriculture and horticulture; miscellaneous subjects; and maps. Most of the books (555 of 659 titles) were printed after 1776. A large proportion of those volumes contained statutes and court reports from other states and were probably obtained through post-Revolutionary exchanges. Because the 1828 catalog lists volumes by short title, sometimes also by author or publisher, usually by place and date of publication, and almost always by size, it is possible to identify the editions of 121 titles representing 223 volumes from the library.

Two volumes bearing the council bookplate still belong to the Library of Virginia but were inexplicably omitted from the 1828 printed catalog even though Richardson included them in his preliminary manuscript list. One is a handsome 1717 edition of the Bible that is known as the Vinegar Bible, so called because of a typesetter's error in setting a running head for the Parable of the Vintner as "Parable of the Vinegar." The other is an elegant and unique Book of Common Prayer. Published in London in 1745, it has the royal coat of arms and the words "St. James's Chappell 1746" stamped in gold on the front cover. It probably belonged to the household of King George II. How it came into the council library is not known.

The library of the council evolved during the decades after the American Revolution into the Library of Virginia,[31] which still owns sixty-eight volumes representing twenty-five titles that show clear evidence of council ownership. Most of them contain, or once contained, the council's bookplate, but some have the inscription "Virginia Council Chamber" written inside the front cover. The oldest book identifiable as belonging to the library is volume 1 of Solomon Gesner's *Libri Quotor de Conciliis*, published in Wittenburg in 1601. It is one of the five volumes in the Library of Virginia bearing the "Virginia Council Office 1742" stamping. Eleven volumes of an incomplete *Collection of the Parliamentary Debates . . . 1688 to the Present Time* (1739–45) bear on their spines what appears to be a nineteenth-century stamping that reads, "GOVERNOR'S HOUSE," suggesting that for a time the books were in the governor's residence in Richmond.

Most of the volumes that were present in the library when the American Revolution began are now lost. Some may have been discarded as obsolete or worn out or been replaced with newer editions. In the 1830s, the General Assembly authorized the transfer of some of the law books to Lewisburg, in Greenbrier County, for the use of the Virginia Supreme Court of Appeals, which met there for one session each year.[32] Late in 1847 the court moved into the new state courts building in Richmond, and the assembly authorized the court to stock its library with law books from the state's library.[33] Between the publication of library catalogs in 1856 and 1877 all the old law books and more than half the other volumes left over from the council's library disappeared from the state's collection. No doubt a good many books were lost, destroyed, or stolen in April 1865, at the end of the Civil War, when the state courthouse burned and many books and public papers disappeared from the capitol. The assembly's Joint Committee on the Library reported in 1871 that "hundreds of volumes" had been removed from the library, "the most of these being portions of sets" of multivolume works.[34] The Library of Virginia now has only a small number of law books that were originally in the library, and it acquired all of them from private sources late in the twentieth century and early in the twenty-first. The court's law library now contains no volumes that had been in the council chamber library.

A collection of about sixteen law books, of which several were in the Supreme Court of Appeals library at one time and a few had been in the council library, was in existence as recently as 1933. Because some appear to have been scorched by fire, it is possible that they were in the state courthouse when it burned in 1865 and were either carried off by some person who had no authority to take them or were disposed of as damaged when the court began to rebuild its book collection in 1867. Dr. J. Henry Hoffmann, of Baltimore, Maryland, purchased the volumes when he spied a pile of old books on a sidewalk in Washington, DC, early in the twentieth century. He bought the lot without knowing what it contained from the people who were moving out of a building and had stacked the books on the pavement to get them out of the way. In the summer of 1933 he had the books on display at the Enoch Pratt Free Library in Baltimore. Hoffman offered to sell the collection to the state of Virginia for fifty thousand dollars, but the state had no funds available for the purpose at the time. One of the books had the "Virginia Council Office 1742" stamping on the front cover, and several others appear to have had that stamping removed.

The genuine council-library volumes then in Hoffmann's possession probably included a volume of Blackstone's *Commentaries on the Laws of England;* volume 1 of William Nelson's three-volume *Abridgment of the Common Law* (1724–26); Robertson's *History of Scotland;* Henry Rolle's *Un Abridgment des Plusieurs Cases et Resolutions del Common Ley* (1668); Sir Bartholomew Shower's *Second Reports of Cases in the Court of King's Bench* (1720); and William Peere Williams's three-volume *Reports of Cases in Chancery* (1746–49). All of them, with the exception of Robertson's *History* and Rolle's *Abridgment,* were in the state's library in 1828, and all but Nelson's and Rolle's abridgments were gone before publication of a catalog of the library in 1856. The location of Hoffmann's books is not now known.[35]

It is not wise to generalize too much from the admittedly limited knowledge we have about the contents of the library, but it is intriguing to observe that the one volume treating the subject of witchcraft known to have been in the library, John Webster's *Displaying of Supposed Witchcraft* (1677), argues that no pretense existed for punishing anyone whom ignorant or malicious persons might charge with possessing occult powers. This is consistent with the treatment of the few colonial Virginians who were suspected of witchcraft, unlike what occurred in some places in Great Britain, on the continent of Europe, or in the northeastern colonies.

The council's library met the needs of the lawyers and judges, and it was also suitable for the needs of statesmen. When news arrived in Williamsburg in May 1774 that Parliament had passed the Coercive Acts to put down colonial protests against British policies, several members of the House of Burgesses met to devise a plan of action. Thomas Jefferson, Patrick Henry, Richard Henry Lee, Francis Lightfoot Lee, and three or four others convened, Jefferson later recalled, "in the council chamber, for the benefit of the library in that room." Jefferson certainly knew where the best research library for the purpose was to be found. It was in the council chamber. He and the other burgesses also knew where in the library to look: they pulled down from the shelves some of the volumes of John Rushworth's *Historical Collections of Private Passages of State, Weighty Matters in Law, Remarkable Proceedings in Five Parliaments, Beginning the Sixteenth Year of King James, Anno 1618* and looked up parliamentary precedents from the seventeenth century in them. "With the help therefore of Rushworth," Jefferson continued, "whom we rummaged over for the revolutionary precedents & forms of the Puritans of that day, preserved by him, we cooked up a resolution ... for a day of fasting, humiliation & prayer, to implore heaven to avert from us the evils of civil war, to inspire us with firmness in support of our rights, and to turn the hearts of the King & parliament to moderation and justice." After the House of Burgesses adopted the resolution derived directly from English precedent, the royal governor dismissed the General Assembly. The burgesses reassembled in the Raleigh Tavern and called the meeting that issued the invitation for the assembling of the First Continental Congress in Philadelphia. That dramatic and important chain of events began in the council chamber where the books were located.[36]

The surviving books as physical relics, together with the other knowledge we have about the volumes known to have been in the council library, indicate what the political and legal elite of eighteenth-century Virginia believed was requisite for the well governing of the colony. The contents of the library reflected their interests and helped them protect their property and their liberty. The library demonstrates that those men lived in a sophisticated and complex legal and political culture and clearly understood the importance of legal reference works for the proper functioning of the government and the economy. The books served them well in the governing of their colony. Moreover, as a collection of reference works that guided Virginia's colonial statesmen as they perfected the arts of practical statecraft and as a research library for the Revolutionary generation the council library in Williamsburg also contributed directly to the creation of the American republic.

NOTES

1. Mark Antony De Wolfe Howe, ed., "Journal of Josiah Quincy, Junior, 1773," *Proceedings of the Massachusetts Historical Society*, 3d ser., 49 (1916): 465.
2. W. Hamilton Bryson, *Census of Law Books in Colonial Virginia* (Charlottesville, 1978).
3. John M. Jennings, "The First One Hundred Years of the Library of the College of William and Mary, 1693–1793" (master's thesis, American University, 1948), published in part in "Notes on the Original Library of the College of William and Mary in Virginia, 1693–1705," *Papers of the Bibliographical Society of America* 41 (1947): 239–67.
4. A very brief introduction is Henry R. McIlwaine, "Turning the Pages of the Past," *Richmond Magazine* 16 (Feb. 1930): 17–18, 42 and (Mar. 1930): 35–36, 41.
5. Edmund Pendleton to the Speaker of the House of Delegates, 2 Dec. 1791, with "List of Books" in Pendleton's handwriting and dated 29 Nov. 1791, Executive Communications, Record Group 78, Library of Virginia (the letter does not appear in *The Letters and Papers of Edmund Pendleton, 1734–1803*, ed. David John Mays, 2 vols. [Charlottesville, 1967]); [William H. Richardson, comp.], *A Catalogue of the Library of the State of Virginia, Arranged Alphabetically . . .* (Richmond, 1828).
6. Susan Myra Kingsbury, ed., *The Records of the Virginia Company of London*, 4 vols. (Washington, DC, 1906–33): 3:447.
7. Warren M. Billings, "English Legal Literature as a Source of Law and Legal Practice for Seventeenth-Century Virginia," *Virginia Magazine of History and Biography* 87 (1979): 403–16; Billings, "'Send us . . . what other Lawe books you shall thinke fitt': Books That Shaped the Law in Virginia, 1600–1860," ibid. 120 (2012): 314–39.
8. Warren M. Billings, "The Growth of Political Institutions in Virginia, 1634 to 1676," *William and Mary Quarterly*, 3d ser., 31 (1974): 225–42; Jon Kukla, "The Founding of Virginia Counties—1634?," *Magazine of Virginia Genealogy* 22 (Aug. 1984): 3–6.
9. Virginia, 1662–1702, Laws (Charles City Manuscript), 189, Thomas Jefferson Papers, ser. 8, vol. 9, Library of Congress; also found in Virginia, 1662–97, Laws (Peyton Randolph Manuscript), 80, ibid., vol. 8. When published in *The Statutes at Large; being a Collection of All the Laws of Virginia from the First Session of the Legislature in the Year 1619 . . .*, ed. William Waller Hening, 13 vols. (Richmond, 1809–23), 2:246, the title appeared as "An Act for Law Books," and the word *esteemed* appeared as *approved*.
10. *Virginia Magazine of History and Biography* 24 (1916): 400.
11. H. R. McIlwaine, Wilmer L. Hall, and Benjamin L. Hillman, eds., *Executive Journals of the Council of Colonial Virginia*, 6 vols. (Richmond, 1925–65), 3:47.
12. Robert Carter to John J. Maund, 10 Dec. 1792, Letterbook of Robert Carter, vol. 10,

Manuscript Department, Duke University Library. I thank John Barden for calling my attention to this letter.

13. H. R. McIlwaine, ed., *Legislative Journals of the Council of Colonial Virginia*, 3 vols. (Richmond, 1918–19), 3:1520. The final title was *Votes of the House of Representatives for His Majesties Province of New-York in America* (New York, 1698).

14. McIlwaine, Hall, and Hillman, *Executive Journals of the Council of Colonial Virginia*, 5:278, 488–89; John Pendleton Kennedy and H. R. McIlwaine, eds., *Journals of the House of Burgesses of Virginia*, 13 unnumbered vols. (Richmond, 1905–15), *1742–1747*, 235, and *1748–1749*, 319.

15. The bookplate of the House of Burgesses has sometimes been confused with the bookplate of the council. See Brent Tarter, "The Bookplate of the House of Burgesses," *Virginia Cavalcade* 37 (1988): 176–79.

16. Robert A. Brock, letter to the editor of the *Richmond Dispatch*, 17 Sept. 1893; McIlwaine, *Legislative Journals of the Council of Colonial Virginia*, 2:1055.

17. Hening, *Statutes at Large*, 4:360–62, 6:143.

18. The evolution of the separation of county court lawyers from the General Court bar is traced in Frank L. Dewey, "Thomas Jefferson's Law Practice," *Virginia Magazine of History and Biography* 85 (1977): 289–301. See also Anton-Hermann Chroust, *The Rise of the Legal Profession in America*, 2 vols. (Norman, OK, 1965), 1:282–93, for a list of the men who belonged to the General Court bar.

19. McIlwaine, Hall, and Hillman, *Executive Journals of the Council of Colonial Virginia*, 6:259n.

20. Edmund Jennings Lee Papers, Mss1 L5113 a27, Virginia Historical Society, Richmond.

21. Brent Tarter, "A Rich Storehouse of Knowledge: A History of the Library of Virginia," in *The Common Wealth: Treasures from the Collections of the Library of Virginia*, ed. Sandra Gioia Treadway and Edward D. C. Campbell Jr. (Richmond, 1997), 8–9.

22. Order of the Court of Appeals, 30 Apr. 1783, copy, together with Edmund Randolph to the president, 29 Apr. 1783, copy, in Executive Department, Office of the Governor, Letters Received, Record Group 3, Library of Virginia, printed in *Calendar of Virginia State Papers and Other Manuscripts*, ed. William P. Palmer and Henry W. Flournoy, 11 vols. (Richmond, 1875–93), 3:475.

23. Pendleton to the Speaker of the House of Delegates, 2 Dec. 1791.

24. William H. Richardson, comp., "Catalogue of Books belonging to the Executive Department of Va.," 7 Jan. 1828, enclosed in William Branch Giles to the Speaker of the House of Delegates, 7 Jan. 1828, Executive Communications, Record Group 78, Library of Virginia. I thank R. Neil Hening for calling my attention to this catalog.

25. Kennedy and McIlwaine, *Journals of the House of Burgesses, 1659/60–1693*, 201–3.

26. Thomas Jefferson, comp., *Reports of Cases Determined in the General Court of Virginia. From 1730, to 1740; and from 1768, to 1772*, ed. Thomas Mann Randolph (Charlottesville, 1829), 109–11, 121.

27. George Reese, ed., *Proceedings in the Court of Vice-Admiralty of Virginia, 1698–1775* (Richmond, 1983).

28. Hening, *Statutes at Large*, 9:103–5.

29. Frank L. Dewey, *Thomas Jefferson, Lawyer* (Charlottesville, 1986), 55–72.
30. Advertisement of clerk John Blair in William Rind's *Virginia Gazette* of Williamsburg, 12 Mar. 1772; Carter to Maund, 10 Dec. 1792; unnumbered leaf now tipped into the back of the Minute Book of the Council of State, 1781–82, Record Group 75, Library of Virginia, printed in McIlwaine, Hall, and Hillman, *Executive Journals of the Council of the State of Virginia*, 3:vii.
31. Tarter, "Rich Storehouse of Knowledge," 9–13.
32. *Acts of Assembly, 1830–31* (Richmond, 1831), 37–38; *Acts of Assembly, 1833–34* (Richmond, 1834), 27; *Acts of Assembly, 1834–35* (Richmond, 1835), 16; *Acts of Assembly, 1835–36* (Richmond, 1836), 8–9; *Acts of Assembly 1844–45* (Richmond, 1845), 17; MS Catalogue of Law Books at Lewisburg Library (ca. 1860), Record Group 35, Library of Virginia.
33. *Acts of Assembly, 1846–47* (Richmond, 1847), 1–16; order of 10 Dec. 1847, Virginia Court of Appeals Order Book No. 18, 135.
34. Jon Kukla, "Touches of Sentiment in the Affairs of Old Books," *Virginia Cavalcade* 28 (1978): 78–82; Report of the Joint Committee on the Library, 1872, printed as Document No. 15, *Journal of the Senate of Virginia, 1871–72;* Report of William P. Palmer, Relative to the Manuscripts in the State Library, 29 Nov. 1872, in *Journal of the House of Delegates of the State of Virginia, 1872–73* (Richmond, 1873), doc. 2, pp. 1–4. The history of the books and archival records from the colonial period to the twentieth century is recounted in Palmer and Flournoy, *Calendar of Virginia State Papers,* 1:iii–lxxi; Wilmer L. Hall, "The Public Records of Virginia; Their Destruction and Preservation," *Virginia Libraries* 4 (1931): 2–22; McIlwaine, "Turning the Pages of the Past"; and Tarter, "Rich Storehouse of Knowledge," 3–64.
35. *Baltimore Sun,* 2 July 1933, sec. 2, p. 4; H. R. McIlwaine to J. Henry Hoffman, 18, 20 July, 4, 10 Aug., 11 Sept., 11 Oct. 1933, and Hoffman to McIlwaine, 19, 27 July, 9 Aug., 10 Oct. 1933, all in Office of the State Librarian, General Correspondence, Record Group 35, Library of Virginia; Hoffman's list of books, with photostatic copies of some title pages, in the Rare Book Room, Library of Virginia.
36. *The Works of Thomas Jefferson,* ed. Paul Leicester Ford, 12 vols. (New York, 1904–5), 1:11–12.

ENGLISH STATUTES IN VIRGINIA, 1660–1714

John Ruston Pagan

A COLLECTION
OF THE
STATUTES
Made in the REIGNS of
King Charles the I.
AND
King Charles the II.

With the ABRIDGMENT of such as stand Repealed or Expired.

Continued after the Method of Mr. PULTON.

WITH

Notes of *References*, one to the other, as they now stand Altered, Enlarged or Explained.

TO WHICH ALSO ARE ADDED,

The Titles of all the *Statutes* and Private *Acts* of PARLIAMENT Passed by their said MAJESTIES, untill this present Year, M.DC.LXVII.

With a TABLE directing to the Principal Matters of the said STATUTES.

By THO: MANBY of *Lincolns-Inn*, Esq.

LONDON,

Printed by *John Streater*, *James Flesher*, and *Henry Twyford*, Assigns of *Richard Atkyns* and *Edward Atkyns* Esquires; *Anno Dom.* 1667.

Cum Gratia & Privilegio Regiæ Majestatis.

Virginia's county courts and its General Court enforced acts of Parliament in the colony and purchased editions of English laws. Thomas Manby, A Collection of the Statutes Made in the Reigns of King Charles the I. And King Charles the II. (London, 1667). (Courtesy Wolf Law Library, College of William and Mary)

V₁RGINIA HAD A GOVERNMENT OF dual legislative authorities in the seventeenth and early eighteenth centuries. Under the transatlantic constitution—an evolving framework of legal relations within England's empire—both the Crown and the General Assembly had jurisdiction to prescribe laws for the colony. The Crown occasionally required Virginians to enforce acts of Parliament, but for the most part the imperial government allowed colonists to deviate from the metropolitan model and enact legislation tailored to their own needs, provided they refrained from passing statutes contrary or repugnant to English law. Instead of delineating separate spheres of imperial and provincial legislative power, the transatlantic constitution struck a workable balance between local autonomy and central control. "If modern American law has longed for theoretical, logical, and conceptual consistency over doctrines and institutions," Mary Sarah Bilder has observed, "transatlantic legal culture valued a certain pragmatism and flexibility."[1]

This essay explores the principal ways in which the pragmatic makers of transatlantic legal culture introduced English statutes into Virginia's legal system during the later Stuart period (1660–1714). The first section discusses the *extension* of English statutes to Virginia, an exercise of the royal prerogative that projected particular acts of Parliament beyond the realm of England and imposed them on the king's subjects overseas. The second section examines the *accretion* of English statutes to Virginia's corpus juris, a voluntary process of adoption, incorporation, and application that gradually added a variety of parliamentary acts to the body of laws that Virginians willingly enforced.[2] The third section describes Virginians' efforts to acquire up-to-date parliamentary statute books to help them keep abreast of legal developments at "home" in England[3] and govern their colonial communities in conformity with current English law.

EXTENSION OF ENGLISH STATUTES TO VIRGINIA

The Englishmen who colonized Virginia retained their identity as a free people whose liberty rested on the rule of law.[4] King James I assured the Virginia Company's first settlers that they and their descendants would enjoy all the "liberties, franchises and immunities" they would have possessed if they had stayed in England.[5] He later instructed the company to come "as neere as convenientlie maie be" to operating a legal system "agreable to the laws, statutes, government, and pollicie" of England.[6] Writing in the 1650s, Sir Matthew Hale noted that "the English planters carry along with them those English liberties that are incident to their persons."[7] Hale did not mean that specific English legal doctrines accompanied Englishmen wherever they went, for English law as such operated only in England.[8] His point was that migrants to the king's dominions could expect to be governed there in conformity with customary English legal norms. Those norms included protection from arbitrary power; a prohibition against the deprivation of life, liberty, or property without due process of law; and an exemption from taxation without consent.[9] Denial of the colonists' inherited rights as Englishmen would be tantamount to a denial of their status as subjects of the English king.[10]

Some of the colonists' inherited liberties, such as those listed in Magna Carta, had roots in English statutes.[11] In the sixteenth century, statutes became the highest form of positive law in England.[12] As Robert Zaller has remarked, parliamentary legislation derived from the whole community of the realm, and not just from the Crown, making statutes "a collective and uniquely comprehensive expression of the will of all."[13] Statutes played a vital role in shielding Englishmen from oppressive governance. By the seventeenth century, Jeffrey Goldsworthy notes, "Parliament, rather than the ordinary courts, was regarded as the principal guardian of the liberties of subjects."[14] But despite the growing importance of statutes as a source of legal rights and constitutional principles, most acts of Parliament did not operate automatically in the colonies, because they lay outside the realm of England, the territory over which Parliament had legislative jurisdiction. The colonies belonged to the Crown and were "part of its Royalty,"[15] which meant that the king held *imperium* (sovereignty) and *dominium* (the right to possess and rule) there.[16] The king had the prerogative to prescribe laws for his dominions, and therefore the Crown's approval was a prerequisite to extending English statutes to the colonies.[17]

The procedural formalities of extension depended on whether the statute in question expressly included the colonies in its territorial ambit.[18] If a statute did not refer to the dominions, its ambit was implicitly limited to England and Wales, but the monarch could extend it to the colonies simply by ordering his officials to enforce it there. The royal command effectively negated the presumption that acts of Parliament applied only inside the realm.[19] Extending a statute that "particularly named"[20] the colonies involved the king's use of his power to approve or disapprove proposed legislation. No bill could become law without the monarch's assent, a step in the legislative process that still had real significance in the later Stuart period.[21] Assent simultaneously exercised both the monarch's legislative power as the king in Parliament and his prerogative power to prescribe laws for his overseas possessions. Extending statutes to the colonies by assent made colonial administration a collaborative venture between the king and the houses of Parliament. This arrangement would later attract harsh criticism from Americans who tried to draw a bright-line distinction between the king and Parliament,[22] but in the seventeenth century it provided a workable method of prescribing laws for the developing empire.

Parliament's role in legislating for the colonies began during the Interregnum. James I and Charles I had tried to prevent the Commons and the Lords from participating in colonial governance, but the temporary lapse of royal authority enabled Parliament to acquire a permanent voice in imperial policymaking.[23] Parliament passed two colonial trade laws early in the 1650s.[24] Although those measures were repealed when Charles II regained the throne in 1660, he and all subsequent monarchs used parliamentary legislation as an instrument for regulating commerce between England and the colonies. The Navigation Act of 1660[25] provides a good illustration of post-Restoration imperial cooperation between the king and the two houses of Parliament. The act applied to "any Lands Islelands Plantations or Territories to his Majesty belonging or in his possession . . . in Asia Africa or America."[26] The House of Commons passed the measure on 4 September 1660, and the House of Lords concurred three days later.[27] The clerk of the Parliaments, a royal appointee assigned to the Lords, read the bill before the Privy Council on 9 September, at which time it "passed his Majesties approbation."[28] On 13 September the members of both houses assembled in the Lords' chamber in the presence of Charles II. "Then His Majesty gave Command for the passing" of several bills, including the Navigation Act, "the Clerk of the Crown reading the Titles, and the Clerk of the Parliaments pronouncing the Royal Assent" in "these Words: *Le Roy le veult* [The King wills it]."[29]

Charles II's Navigation Act sought to increase customs revenues, drive the Dutch out of the colonial trade, and secure a monopoly for English merchants and mariners.[30] Section 1 stripped Virginians of the right to trade with foreigners by declaring that "noe Goods or Commodities whatsoever" were to be imported into or exported from the colonies except in English, Irish, Welsh, or colonial vessels "wherof the Master and three fourths of the Marriners at least are English."[31] Violators risked forfeiture of the ship and cargo, with a third of the proceeds going to the king, a third to the governor, and a third to "him or them who shall Seize Informe or sue for the same in any Court of Record."[32] Section 18 authorized condemnation of all ships carrying tobacco, sugar, and other enumerated colonial products to ports outside the British Isles or the English colonies. This part of the 1660 act attempted to ensure that colonial products were unloaded and taxed before being consumed domestically or re-exported to foreign countries.[33]

News of the Navigation Act's passage reached Virginia by late December 1660. Even before county magistrates had a chance to read the statute, they learned that the new law would complicate their lives. At the 31 December session of the Northampton County Court, Tunis Derickson and five other Dutch mariners complained that their ship's owners had fired them and dumped them on the Eastern Shore of Virginia "upon pretence of Submission to an Act of Parliament in England that their shall bee but one fourth part of Company upon any shipp that Shalbe Dutchmen." Finding himself "in a Strange Country and not knowing what to doe," Derickson sought help from the county magistrates. He found a sympathetic audience, for Virginians had long espoused free trade and cultivated good relations with the Dutch. The court ordered the shipowners to pay the Dutchmen their full wages for the period from the time they sailed from Europe until they were discharged in Virginia and also required the owners to finance the mariners' passage back to England or Holland.[34]

While the Northampton magistrates were getting a firsthand introduction to the burdens of the Navigation Act, the authorities in London were taking steps to enforce it. On 1 December the Crown instructed the new Council for Foreign Plantations to write the colonial governors and order them "to take special care and enquire into the strict execution" of the Navigation Act.[35] The council dispatched its letter to Virginia governor Sir William Berkeley on 17 February 1661, enclosing a copy of the act and instructing him "to prosecute the good provisions and intentions" of the statute.[36] The General Assembly, meeting in late March and early April, expressed concern about the possible revival of a monopolistic Virginia Company and the danger of "the losse of our liberties for want of such an agent in England as is able to oppose the invaders of our freedoms and truly to represent our condition to his sacred majestie."[37] The legislature appropriated two hundred thousand pounds of tobacco to send Governor Berkeley, a longtime advocate of free trade, to England to lobby for changes in commercial policy. He departed for England early in June, leaving Francis Moryson in charge as acting governor.[38]

In London Berkeley met with the Council for Foreign Plantations and appeared before the Privy Council, where he pressed for free trade in the face of stout opposition from London merchants.[39] About January 1662, he produced a printed brief in which he argued that the Navigation Act's restrictions injured Virginians and benefited neither the Crown nor the mother country. "[W]e cannot but resent," Berkeley complained, "that forty thousand people should be impoverish'd to enrich little more than forty Merchants, who being the only buyers of our *Tobacco,* give us what they please for it, and after it is here, sell it how they please."[40] Virginians tried to bolster Berkeley's credibility in government circles by vouching for his steady royalism. In March 1662 Moryson and the General Assembly prefaced their revision of the Virginia acts by praising Berkeley for having "retein'd us in an inviolated obedience to his Majesty, that we were the last of his Subjects that necessity enforc'd from our duty, which was an Act of approved Loyalty." They also boasted about their fidelity to English law, claiming that they had "endeavoured in all things, as near as the capacity and constitution of this Countrey would admit, to adhere to those Excellent, and often refined Laws of England, to which we profess and acknowledge all Reverence and Obedience."[41]

Berkeley promoted his economic program in government and commercial circles throughout the remainder of his stay in London, achieving a modest degree of success in his diversification efforts. The Crown refused to grant his request for free trade, however. The only sop the colonists received was a provision in the Customs Fraud Act[42] that clarified the Navigation Act's requirement that the master and three-fourths of the crew be English. "[I]t is to be understood," the 1662 statute declared, "that any of His Majesties Subjects of England Ireland and His Plantacons are to bee accounted English and no others."[43] When Berkeley returned to the colony in September 1662, he carried fresh instructions from Charles II ordering him to ensure the "severe prosecution and punishment" of those who transgressed the Navigation Act.[44]

To let Berkeley and his fellow governors know that the Crown was keeping a close eye on them, in June 1663 the Privy Council dispatched a sharply worded circular letter reminding the governors of the severe penalties they would incur if they allowed violations of the Navigation Act. The Privy Council had been informed by shipmasters trading in Virginia, Maryland, and other colonies "of many neglects or rather contempts of his Majesties Commands for the true observance" of the Act "through the dayly practices and designes sett on foote, by trading into forrain parts," especially Manhattan and European countries such as Holland and Spain. These violations resulted from the governors' failure to check ships' certificates and take the required bonds, "of which neglect and contempt his Majestie is sensible." If a governor failed to administer the act properly, the Privy Council threatened, "His Majesty will interpret it a very greate neglect in you," and the governor could expect to be punished and dismissed from office.[45]

Charles and Parliament tightened the screws further in the Staple Act of 1663.[46] Enacted "by the Kings most Excellent Majestie with the Advice and Consent of the Lords Spirituall and Temporall and the Commons in this present Parliament assembled,"[47] this statute governed trade with any of the Crown's territories in Asia, Africa, or America. The statute aimed to foster the employment of English ships and mariners, promote the sale of English woolens and other manufactured goods, and make the "Kingdome a Staple not onely of the Commodities of those Plantations but alsoe of the Commodities of other Countryes and Places for the supplying of them."[48] The Staple Act supplemented the Navigation Act by prohibiting European commodities from being imported into English colonies except directly from England, Wales, or Berwick-upon-Tweed in English-built ships of which the master and at least three-fourths of the crew were English. Although Irishmen were considered honorary Englishmen for purposes of the crew-composition rule, the terms of the act deemed Irish ports foreign.[49] Under section 4 of the Staple Act, violators faced forfeiture of their goods and cargo, with the proceeds being divided equally among the king, the governor, and the informer. The measure emphasized colonial courts' obligation to enforce the new law by authorizing informers to bring their condemnation suits "in any of His Majesties Courts" in the place where the offense was committed or in any court of record in England.[50]

Like the Navigation Act, the Staple Act was designed to drive England's greatest commercial rivals, the Dutch, out of the lucrative transatlantic carrying trade. The legislation exacerbated tensions between the two nations, who also struggled for control of trade with Africa. In January 1664, English forces attacked Dutch posts on the African coast, and in August the Dutch settlement at New Amsterdam surrendered. Dutch reprisal raids in Africa soon followed, and the English responded in December by attacking a Dutch merchant fleet off Gibraltar. On 27 January 1665, Charles II wrote Berkeley to warn him that a Dutch attack on Virginia might be imminent. The governor should build forts, seize Dutch ships, and do whatever was necessary to protect the colony and the "Navigation of our merchants."[51]

Charles formally declared war against Holland on 4 March 1665. This conflict, the Second Anglo-Dutch War, has been called "the clearest case in [English] history of a purely commercial war."[52] Governor Berkeley learned about the Anglo-Dutch War early in June[53] and immediately began organizing the colony's defense.[54] He called the General Assembly into session in October to appropriate funds for the construction of a fort,[55] which Berkeley decided to locate at Jamestown. As the fort neared completion, Berkeley received instructions from Charles II to abandon the Jamestown project and build another fort at Point Comfort. Berkeley considered the king's order unwise, because a fort at Point Comfort would be virtually worthless. Nevertheless, "that we may be found rather to pay a ready obedience to all his majesties commands" than "demur to any of them at this distance," Berkeley issued an order on 29 March 1666 telling Virginians to follow Charles's foolish instructions to the letter.[56] The Crown's decision was wasteful and probably dangerous, Berkeley told the Earl of Arlington on 13 July 1666, "But the Command was soe possetive wee durst not disobey it."[57]

Berkeley's prediction of a military disaster proved accurate. In June 1667 a Dutch naval squadron sailed up the James River flying false English colors and captured the frigate Charles II had sent to protect the colony. The Dutch then seized the tobacco fleet, which was preparing to sail for England, and carried off their prizes "without a blow" thanks to the cowardice of the English merchant mariners, who refused to transport Berkeley's forces into battle. As they departed, the Dutch burned five or six of the tobacco vessels plus the royal frigate, wounding the governor's pride and forcing him to write a groveling apology to the king.[58]

England's inability to meet the costs of war forced Charles to agree to a peace treaty with the Dutch on 21 July 1667.[59] The Treaty of Breda allowed England to keep New Netherland but granted some commercial concessions to the Dutch, including relaxation of the Navigation Act's ban on Dutch ships' importation of German goods into England. Economic warfare in the colonial trade continued unabated, however. On 20 January 1669 the king in council ordered the commissioners of the customs to send an officer to each plantation to inspect ships' papers and take the governor's oath that he would faithfully execute the trade laws.[60] Berkeley, in turn, leaned on the colonial judiciary to help him carry out the Crown's instructions.

Although most colonists probably favored free trade and resented Parliament's regulations, self-interest encouraged members of the General Court of Virginia to enforce the Navigation Act and the Staple Act. The informers in these cases tended to be the court's own members, who had used their influence as councillors to win lucrative gubernatorial appointments as customs collectors and naval officers.[61] When councillors caught an illegal trader, they brought forfeiture proceedings and sought a share of the proceeds. In October 1669, for example, Councillor Theoderick Bland, a customs collector and prominent Charles City County politician,[62] obtained a General Court order seizing the *Hope,* allegedly of Amsterdam, "on behalf of his majestie for that the said Ship was a Dutch ship and navigated contrary to Act of parliament."[63] The vessel turned out to be the *Hope* of Accomack County, Virginia, however, and its Virginian owner strenuously denied that the ship had come to the colony directly from Amsterdam.[64] The outcome of the condemnation suit is unknown. The ship's owner, Colonel Edmund Scarburgh, did not have a punctilious attitude toward the trade laws. In 1663, while serving as the customs collector in Accomack County, he had allowed an English ship coming directly from Holland with a cargo of merchandise to load tobacco and sail directly back to the Netherlands.[65] In another instance, Thomas Ballard, a James City County politician who soon joined the Council of State,[66] brought a condemnation action in the General Court in April 1670 against the *Dolphin,* of Dartmouth, on the ground that it "belongeth to Dutch owners and is manned contrary to Act of parliament."[67] Ballard lost the suit when the shipmaster produced proof of English ownership and lading. The ship "had but two Dutchmen aboard that were Seamen," which brought the vessel within the Navigation Act's requirement that three-fourths of the crew be English, but the General Court made the master pay hefty litigation costs for failing to record his documents properly.[68]

County courts shared the General Court's duty to enforce Parliament's trade laws. Composed of justices of the peace, Virginia county courts handled the same kinds of criminal and administrative matters that came before English justices of the peace, and they also functioned as the colonial equivalents of the central courts at Westminster and the church courts. Most noncapital criminal cases began and ended in the county courts, as did the majority of civil suits. The General Assembly required county magistrates to swear that they would administer justice "after the laws and customes of this colony, and as neere as may be after the laws of the realme of England and statutes thereof made."[69] This command to conform to English law obliged colonial judges to pay close attention to the intricacies of commercial legislation.

In *Rex ex rel. Spencer v. the Ship Constant Matthew*,[70] for instance, the Northumberland County Court had to try a difficult condemnation suit brought under the Staple Act in March 1678. Councillor Nicholas Spencer, the king's collector for the Potomac River, sought the forfeiture of a fifty-ton Irish vessel because the ship's papers showed that it had sailed directly from Londonderry to Virginia with a load of Irish-made goods. The jury found that the ship's master had broken the law by failing to stop in England and enter the goods with the customs officers there. The court ordered forfeiture of the ship and its cargo. The shipmaster, on behalf of himself and his ten-man crew, asked the court to pay their wages from the proceeds of the condemnation sale so that they could return home to Londonderry. The merchant who had hired them to make a round-trip journey to Virginia had paid the king's duties in Ireland and had said nothing about a mandatory stop in England along the way. The Northumberland County justices of the peace accepted the mariners' claim that they had been ignorant of the statute's requirements and awarded them their wages, an act of compassion toward men who found themselves marooned by the workings of an exceedingly complicated regulatory regime.

Rex ex rel. Stringer v. the Ship Katherine of London,[71] tried by the Accomack County Court in April 1685, provides another example of a county court's execution of England's demanding trade laws. Acting on a tip, Colonel John Stringer, the king's collector for the Eastern Shore of Virginia, seized the *Katherine* for importing "diverse uncustomed goods."[72] The Crown's lawyer alleged that the ship's master had imported goods illegally and had neglected to furnish the information that the Staple Act required. Section 6 of the act prohibited ships from unloading until the master had informed the governor or his deputy of the ship's name and the master's name; shown that the ship was English-built and English-owned; proven that the vessel was navigated by an English commander and a crew that was at least three-quarters English; and produced an inventory of the cargo showing where the ship was laden. Two of the *Katherine*'s crew members testified that six months earlier they had seen "a very small" bundle of "Scotch linnen Cloth" brought on board after sunset while contrary winds detained the ship in a Scottish harbor. The cloth, which had been consigned to the ship's Scottish merchant, had then been transported directly from Scotland to Virginia without being entered at an English customs house. The twelve jurors found the *Katherine* "to be lyable to Condemnation," and the court confirmed the verdict, ordering the ship to be appraised and then disposed of as the governor saw fit.[73]

The draconian penalty imposed in this case no doubt pleased the Crown and Governor Francis Howard, 5th Baron Howard of Effingham, because it put money in their pockets. The decision also redounded to the benefit of a couple of Eastern Shoremen. Three weeks after the trial, one of the justices of the peace who heard the case, Major Charles Scarburgh, bought the *Katherine* for £65 18s. 3d. A third of this sum went to the king, a third to Effingham, and a third to the twenty-year-old informer, Hugh Montgomerie.[74] The young man's share of almost £22 must have seemed like a fortune, for the sum was roughly equivalent to four or five years' wages for a hired servant on the Eastern Shore.[75] Scarburgh's deal turned sour in June 1687, however, when the *Katherine* was seized for importing European goods without proper customs documents.[76] The Eastern Shore collector, council member John Custis, won a jury verdict that the *Katherine*'s customs cocket was inaccurate. The deputy attorney general who handled the case for Custis, Charles Holden, an experienced Eastern Shore lawyer, produced the Customs Fraud Act and the Staple Act in support of his motion for judgment. The "said Lawes being read and considered by the Court," the Accomack justices condemned both the ship and its cargo.[77]

Parliament strengthened its commercial regulations in the Plantation Trade Act of 1696,[78] which required stricter customs enforcement, ship registration, and other measures designed to prevent circumvention of the mercantile system. To underscore colonial judges' duty to respect the supremacy of English law, Parliament declared that any and all colonial laws "which are in any wise repugnant" to English statutes that "relate to and mention" the plantations "are illegall null and void to all Intents and Purposes whatsoever."[79] The 1696 act authorized penalties and forfeitures to be recovered in vice-admiralty courts held in the colonies.[80] The Crown established its vice-admiralty court in Virginia in 1698,[81] and that tribunal took a leading role in enforcing the navigation and trade laws. The regular colonial courts retained concurrent jurisdiction, giving plaintiffs the option of litigating in either forum.[82]

Surviving court records from the later Stuart period contain numerous examples of Virginians' enforcement of parliamentary trade laws.[83] This evidence contradicts a scholar's recent assertion that condemnation actions "routinely resulted in an acquittal."[84] The cases support Lawrence Harper's conclusion that colonial juries' alleged opposition to implementing England's commercial regulations "has been very much exaggerated."[85] Colonists wished to remain in the monarch's good graces, and therefore they generally tried to obey parliamentary mandates even when they disagreed with the laws' underlying rationale, especially if obedience coincided with an opportunity to gain a windfall.

ACCRETION OF ENGLISH STATUTES TO VIRGINIA'S BODY OF LAWS

Besides enforcing statutes at the king's command, Virginians sometimes voluntarily adopted or incorporated certain "municipal laws of England," Sir William Blackstone's term for acts of Parliament that applied in the mother country but not in the colonies.[86] Creating an entire body of law would have been next to impossible in the early decades of settlement, so selective introduction of English statutes by the General Assembly was a quick and easy way to build an effective legal system in the American wilderness. In 1632, for instance, the colonial legislature declared that the 1563 and 1604 English statutes regulating artificers and workmen were "*thought fitt* to be published in this colony."[87] The assembly also ordered that the Tudor laws against engrossing commodities and forestalling the market "be made known and executed in this colony"[88] and declared that Parliament's 1606 statute punishing drunkards was "*thought fitt,* to be published and dulie put in execution."[89] In 1658 the assembly directed that English laws against bigamy were to "be putt in execution in this countrie."[90] The English statute that prescribed capital punishment for bigamy literally applied only to "persons within his Majesties Domynions of England and Wales," but this reference to the act's territorial scope did not deter the assembly from adopting it for use in Virginia. A 1699 colonial act exempted Protestant dissenters from penalties for failing to attend Church of England services if they would have qualified for an exemption under Parliament's Toleration Act of 1689.[91] And in 1705 the assembly ordered that the 1696 English statute allowing Quakers to testify by affirmation was to be "to all intents and purposes, in full force within this dominion."[92]

Adopting English statutes by reference presented a significant notice problem. How were colonists supposed to comply with an act of Parliament if they knew only its title and general topic? William Waller Hening criticized the General Assembly for adopting an English statute "by a mere *general reference,* when not one person in a thousand could possibly know its contents."[93] This was a valid criticism, and the colony's principal method of promulgating legislation, scribal publication, probably offered little help.[94] At the conclusion of each session of the assembly, county courts purchased manuscript copies of the acts and published them locally by reading each new law aloud during a court session.[95] If rigorously followed, scribal publication informed the community that the assembly had decided to introduce certain acts of Parliament into Virginia's legal system, but the practice did not tell people what those laws required them to do. County magistrates could not enforce the adopted acts unless they had access to the English statutes at large and could look up the relevant texts. As we will see, several county courts addressed this need by purchasing sets of English law books.

Virginians viewed adopted English statutes as equivalent to the laws the king had explicitly ordered them to enforce. Thus, when a Stafford County mill owner brought suit in 1691 against a laborer who had left his work unfinished, the plaintiff grounded his claim directly on the adopted English Statute of Artificers[96] and did not even bother to mention the 1632 act of assembly that had integrated the Elizabethan statute into Virginia's body of laws. Closely tracking the act of Parliament in this instance, the owner sought a penalty of £5 and one month's imprisonment, plus common-law damages and costs. The county court submitted the debt action to a jury, which rendered a verdict in the defendant's favor.[97]

The General Assembly sometimes adopted English statutes wholesale. A 1692 act of assembly empowered the governor to commission a court of oyer and terminer to try without a jury any slave accused of committing a crime "which the law of England requires to be satisfied with the death of the offender or loss of member." The special court, usually made up of the local justices of the peace, had authority to pass judgment "as the law of England provides in the like case."[98] In 1693 the Northampton County justices, sitting as a court of oyer and terminer, tried a slave under a 1532 act of Parliament imposing capital punishment for willfully burning down a dwelling house.[99] They sentenced the defendant to hang for violating "the Knowne Lawes of England"[100]—known to the justices and their forebears, perhaps, but one wonders whether or how the slave acquired knowledge of that law.[101]

The assembly employed a somewhat different technique—incorporation—when it wished to borrow language from an English statute rather than put the statute itself into effect.[102] Of course, all colonial laws had to comport with English law,[103] but occasionally the governor, burgesses, and councillors went beyond mere concordance by copying passages from English statutes and inserting them into their own legislation, tweaking the language if necessary to fit local circumstances. The bill then had to pass both houses of the assembly, survive gubernatorial scrutiny, and avoid disallowance by the imperial bureaucracy in London.[104] When completed, this process of selective incorporation resulted in a Virginia law that received its "obligation, and authoritative force, from being the law of the country."[105]

Virginia's 1710 statute of limitations for certain actions to recover real property provides a good example of incorporation.[106] The colonial statute borrowed wording from a 1624 act of Parliament requiring writs of formedon in descender, formedon in remainder, and formedon in reverter to be sued within twenty years after the cause of action accrued.[107] The Virginia law also included some language from a 1540 English statute prescribing limitation periods for assizes of mort d'ancestor and several other property actions.[108] Unlike some other acts of assembly adopting English statutes, the 1710 measure did not identify the source from which the legislature derived its text, much less purport to give effect to an otherwise inapplicable act of Parliament.[109] However, the committee that compiled a comprehensive collection of Virginia's statutes that the Williamsburg printer William Parks published in 1732 "added Many useful Marginal Notes, and References," including citations to the 1624 and 1540 English statutes that served as models for parts of the 1710 colonial legislation.[110] A comparison of the texts confirms that the Virginia law was simply a cut-and-paste job, an act of imitation, not activation.

Judicial accretion offered another way to add English statutes to Virginia's body of laws. This occurred when colonial judges decided on their own to apply English municipal statutes on an ad hoc basis. Judges presumably derived their authority to apply acts of Parliament from royal instructions such as Charles I's 1641 commission to Governor Berkeley, which declared that Virginia was to be governed "according to the lawes and statutes of our Realme of England, Which Wee propose to have established there."[111] This vague command, coupled with the governor's commissions to justices of the peace empowering them "to act according to the laws of England, and of this country,"[112] led Virginia judges to view the English statutes at large as something akin to a "brooding omnipresence in the sky"[113] that offered a vast selection of fallback rules they could apply interstitially when other types of law left gaps.

Fallback rules were useful in situations in which a quartet of circumstances converged: (*a*) the king had not expressly ordered the colonies to enforce a particular rule; (*b*) the Virginia General Assembly had not enacted a law covering the subject; (*c*) customary law, including the colonial version of the common law, seemed inadequate because of pleading technicalities or for other reasons; and (*d*) a municipal law of England prescribed a rule that colonial judges found well suited to local conditions. Presettlement English statutes made attractive candidates for ad hoc application because they did not raise fairness concerns. Englishmen who migrated to Virginia had received constructive notice—that is, were presumed to have knowledge—of all statutes in force in England at the time of their departure. Emigrants had been represented, actually or virtually, in the Parliaments that enacted those laws. The first settlers brought their imputed knowledge of English law with them on the *Susan Constant,* the *Godspeed,* and the *Discovery* and then passed it along to later generations together with the rest of their cultural baggage.

Virginians frequently had occasion to apply pre-1607 criminal statutes on an ad hoc basis.[114] In 1681, for instance, an informer brought a prosecution in the Accomack County Court based on an alleged violation of a 1563 perjury statute. The county court dismissed the prosecution because the information failed to specify, as required, the time when the act had been committed.[115] When smallpox appeared on the Eastern Shore in 1668, the local authorities ordered infected people to stay home or risk being "severely punished according to the Statute of the First of King James,"[116] a 1604 quarantine law aimed primarily at preventing the plague from spreading through cities and towns. The English statute authorized the death penalty for anyone who ventured outside his home with "any infectious sore upon hym uncured." The law empowered authorities to have others who broke quarantine whipped like vagabonds.[117] And when fourteen "seditious & rude people" met in 1673 to discuss ways of protesting Surry County's high taxes, the magistrates arrested and interrogated them under a 1411 statute that prohibited riots and unlawful assemblies.[118]

County courts applied pre-1607 English statutes in civil litigation as well. In 1663 the owner of a Northampton County shoemaking business who became frustrated by a currier's failure to deliver hides on time haled him into court under a 1604 act of Parliament. The law required curriers to process leather within eight days in summer and sixteen days in winter. Noncompliance entitled the customer to receive ten shillings for every hide and piece of leather not dressed within the prescribed period.[119] To make sure the tardy currier understood his obligations, the magistrates ordered the sheriff to "cause the Statute to be produced" to the defendant "that hee may not pretend Ignorance." The plaintiff, Colonel Edmund Scarburgh, a former Speaker of the House of Burgesses and longtime justice of the peace on the Eastern Shore, had received some legal training in England. He skillfully used his knowledge of the law to his own benefit.[120] In 1685 a Northumberland County property owner successfully invoked a 1429 act of Parliament[121] to win an award of treble damages "according to the Statute of England in the like case provided" against a tenant who had forcibly resisted demands that he leave the plaintiff's house.[122] No one seemed to care that the General Assembly of Virginia had not formally adopted these statutes. They fit the problems at hand, so judges used them to fill interstices in the colony's framework of laws.

If a provision in an English municipal statute conflicted with Virginia law, the latter prevailed. Illustrations of this principle can be found in freedom suits that illegitimate children filed after being bound into servitude under the poor laws. The English Poor Law of 1601[123] authorized justices of the peace to bind males until the age of twenty-four and females until the age of twenty-one. The General Assembly adopted the English statute in 1672, ordering county courts to "put the laws of England against vagrant, idle and desolute persons in strict execution" and authorizing magistrates to bind into servitude all children whose parents were not able to support them. The assembly changed the age of emancipation to twenty-one for males and eighteen for females.[124] In *Morgan v. Bally*,[125] a 1698 case in the Accomack County Court, a twenty-one-year-old servant sued his master, claiming that the 1672 Virginia law entitled him to his freedom. The master relied on the 1601 act of Parliament and produced a copy of the English statute for the court to read and consider. After comparing the two laws and hearing oral argument, the justices of the peace ruled in the servant's favor, holding that the act of assembly "was bindeing to us in this Country."[126] Other county courts reached the same conclusion.[127] Inasmuch as the House of Burgesses was made up largely of men who served concurrently as county magistrates,[128] the county benches had no qualms about deferring to the wisdom of the colonial legislature.

For most of the seventeenth century, Virginia judges applied even post-1607 English statutes if they perceived a need for a ready-made rule. To prevent infanticide, for example, colonial courts enforced a 1624 act of Parliament aimed at women suspected of killing their newborns.[129] If a woman concealed the death of her illegitimate child, the statute created a rebuttable presumption that the baby had been born alive and murdered by the mother. The woman faced the death penalty unless she could prove by at least one witness that the child had been stillborn. The county courts and the General Court tried defendants under the 1624 English act even though it did not mention the colonies.[130] In 1689 in the General Court case *Rex v. Lewis,* Elizabeth Lewis "was convicted for the Murder of a Bastard Child upon the Stat. 21. Jac. 1 and Sentenced to dye." She petitioned for mercy, claiming that "the Child was born dead." The council granted a reprieve until the next General Court, but because of the loss of the court's records, the final outcome is unknown.[131]

Early in the 1680s, however, the General Court's decision in *Griffin and Burwell v. Wormeley*[132] cast doubt on the propriety of applying postsettlement English statutes without express authorization from either Parliament or the General Assembly. The case involved the question whether the Statute of Frauds,[133] enacted by Parliament in 1677, applied to wills executed in Virginia after that date. The Statute of Frauds required that "all Devises and Bequests of Land or Tenements" be in writing, signed by the testator, and attested in his presence "by three or fower credible witnesses."[134] The act did not mention the colonies. Prior to its passage, Virginia courts had deemed two witnesses sufficient to authenticate a will devising land.

In January 1681, Lieutenant Colonel John Burnham, of Middlesex County, a justice of the peace and member of the House of Burgesses, executed a deathbed will before only two witnesses. Burnham's would-be executors, Colonel Leroy Griffin and Major Lewis Burwell, were also the devisees of the 2,250 acres of land bequeathed in the will. They presented the will for probate in the Middlesex County Court on 7 February 1681. Councillor Ralph Wormeley objected, contending that the will was invalid because Burnham had not been in his right mind when he made it. Wormeley argued that Burnham's property therefore escheated to the Crown. The county court referred the case to the General Court because it involved "a matter of greate Consequence & wherein the Kings majestie hath a Right."[135] Depositions that the county court took later at the General Court's direction demonstrated that Burnham had moved in and out of consciousness when dictating the purported will, and a bystander had had to hold his hand while he made his mark on it. At some stage of the judicial proceedings, a jury found the will valid, indicating that Burnham had had testamentary capacity.[136] The verdict eliminated all the factual issues in the case, leaving the outcome to be determined by the General Court's ruling on the legal question of whether the English Statute of Frauds operated in Virginia. If the statute applied, the will was invalid, and the property escheated to the Crown for lack of heirs. If the act of Parliament did not apply, however, the property passed as Burnham had intended.

Representing Wormeley, who hoped to profit from the escheat by buying the property from the Crown, the lawyer William Fitzhugh advanced several reasons for presuming that the Statute of Frauds and other general acts of Parliament applied in Virginia. He argued that it would have been highly impractical to force settlers to create a completely new legal system the moment they stepped ashore at Jamestown. Besides the numerous precedents in which county courts and the General Court had applied postsettlement English statutes, Fitzhugh pointed to the colonists' land patents as evidence that Virginia was joined "to the Realm of England as parcel thereof," and "if we are a Part & branch of Engld. then consequently, we have a Right to, & benefit of the Laws of England."[137]

Griffin and Burwell argued against the applicability of the Statute of Frauds on what amounted to due process grounds. They invoked the emerging principle of the rule of law, a doctrine developed in the seventeenth century to protect liberty and property by preventing the arbitrary exercise of government power.[138] At the heart of the rule of law lay the concept of adherence to established and predictable norms. Authorities had to announce those norms publicly prior to enforcing them in particular cases.[139] Griffin and Burwell contended that "it would be not only unreasonable but inhuman to require Obedience and observation of a Law of which we have no means to take notice." Nobody had proclaimed the Statute of Frauds to be in effect in Virginia, nor had any metropolitan official sent copies of the act to the colony so that settlers could familiarize themselves with its contents. Therefore, Burnham had been incapable of conforming his conduct to the 1677 law's three-witness requirement, and it would be unjust to upset his legitimate expectations after his death.[140]

Griffin and Burwell's lack-of-notice argument raised serious questions about the fairness of applying the Statute of Frauds to Burnham's will. On 30 September 1681, the General Court, "not being satisfyed whether the Lawes & Statutes of England ought to be binding to the People of this Countrey before Publick Proclamacon & Promulgacon thereof," referred the case to the General Assembly, which not long thereafter lost its jurisdiction to hear and determine appeals from the General Court.[141] Meanwhile, across the Atlantic, the English attorney general, Sir William Jones, weighed in with an opinion on 22 September 1681. Governor Thomas Culpeper, 2d Baron Culpeper of Thoresway, who was in England at the time, had sought Jones's guidance. The three-witness requirement of the Statute of Frauds did not apply in Virginia, the attorney general concluded, because the statute did not mention the colony and the General Assembly had not adopted or incorporated it. Jones asserted that "an Act of Parliament made in England doth bind Virginia or any other of the English Plantations where they are expressly named," but "a new law or Statute made in England, not naming Virginia or any other Plantation, shall not take Effect in Virginia or the other Plantation, 'till received by the General Assembly or others who have the Legislative Power in Virginia or such other Plantation."[142]

Jones's reasoning reflected the same fairness concerns that Griffin and Burwell's lawyers had raised. When Parliament enacted a law "without naming more Places than England as the Extent to which it shall relate," Jones explained, the lawmakers were "not to be presumed to have Consideration of the particular Circumstances and Conditions of the Plantations, especially considering no Member come from thence to the Parliament of England." Moreover, an act of Parliament normally took effect soon after passage, and "it is commonly so short a Time as no Notice can arrive to the Plantations" before people became obliged to obey the new law. People should not be bound "by Law of which they are, or may be reasonably supposed necessarily & invariably ignorant."[143] Culpeper showed the attorney general's opinion "to all the then Judges of England, Who declared the same to be Law."[144]

The governor took Jones's opinion with him when he returned to Virginia about November 1682. Heeding the attorney general's advice, the General Court entered judgment for Griffin and Burwell, apparently on the ground that the Statute of Frauds did not apply in Virginia.[145] The Burnham will case probably served as a precedent for the Richmond County Court's decision in *Hayberd v. Hawksford*,[146] an ejectment suit brought in 1701. The plaintiff claimed land as the heir by intestate succession; the defendant claimed by devise in a will that complied with Virginia customs but not with the Statute of Frauds. The Richmond County Court ruled for the defendant, holding that the statute "doth not reach or is pleadable in this Colony."[147] In 1748 the General Assembly enacted its own version of the Statute of Frauds and borrowed some of the language in the 1677 English statute but jettisoned the three-witness requirement in favor of Virginia's traditional rule requiring that all devises and bequests of land be in writing, be signed by the testator, and be attested "by two or more credible witnesses" unless wholly written in the devisor's own hand.[148]

Were other postsettlement English statutes "pleadable" in Virginia? No one could say for sure. In 1705 the Virginia historian Robert Beverley claimed that Sir Edmund Andros, when he was governor from 1693 to 1698, "caused the Statutes of England to be allowed for Law there; even such Statutes, as were made of late time, since the grant of the last Charter."[149] Henry Hartwell, James Blair, and Edward Chilton complained to the Board of Trade in 1697, "It is none of the least Misfortunes of that Country, that it is not clear what is the Law whereby they are govern'd." Virginians understood that English statutes and acts of the General Assembly were the highest forms of law, "but how far both or either of these is to take place, is in the Judge's Breast, and is apply'd according to their particular Affection to the Party."[150] This trio of colonial politicians had an axe to grind, and their allegations may have exaggerated the confused state of Virginia jurisprudence at the end of the seventeenth century. Nevertheless, the hybrid character of early Virginia law—a blend of the metropolitan and the provincial—undoubtedly caused headaches for those who had to operate the system or represent clients. As another Virginian wrote about the same time, "[W]e are too often obliged to depend upon the Crooked Cord of a Judge's Discretion."[151]

The distinction between pre- and postsettlement English statutes became clearer in 1710 as a consequence of an infanticide case tried by the General Court. A woman was indicted under the 1624 English statute that created a presumption of murder if an unwed mother concealed her newborn's corpse. The defendant's lawyer moved to dismiss on the ground that "being a penal statute made since the Settlement of this Country, and wherein the plantations are not named," the law did not operate in Virginia. According to Lieutenant Governor Alexander Spotswood, the judges consulted "the ablest Lawyers here" and acquitted the defendant on the ground that the 1624 English statute was ineligible for ad hoc application. "But lest that Judgement should give encouragement to such wicked practices," in 1710 the General Assembly passed its own act, which incorporated "the Very terms of the Act of Parliament with some small variation adopting it to the Circumstances of this Country."[152] The main "variation" was a clause providing that the statute applied only to white women or other females who were not enslaved,[153] a candid acknowledgment that indentured servants were the people most likely to commit infanticide and hide babies' corpses.[154] Those women knew only too well that Virginia law would lengthen their terms of servitude if they were caught bearing children out of wedlock. To remind women of the penalty for infanticide, the 1710 statute required ministers to read the law in church every May.[155]

The conclusions reached in 1710 by the bench and bar of Williamsburg coincided, for the most part, with the views of early eighteenth-century English jurists.[156] In 1720 Richard West, counsel to the Board of Trade, opined that "all statutes in affirmance of the common law, passed in England, antecedent to the settlement of a colony, are in force in that colony, unless there is some private act to the contrary, though no statutes, made since those settlements, are there in force, unless the colonies are particularly mentioned."[157] Virginians probably would have qualified West's statement by saying that presettlement statutes were in force only if they suited local conditions,[158] but most would have agreed with his summary of the rule governing postsettlement statutes.[159] The master of the rolls, Sir Joseph Jekyll, reported in 1722 that the Privy Council had drawn the same distinction between pre- and postsettlement statutes. In newly settled colonies "inhabited by the *English,* acts of parliament made in *England,* without naming the foreign plantations, will not bind them," and therefore the Statute of Frauds did not apply in dominions such as Barbados and, by implication, Virginia.[160] Sir Philip Yorke, the English attorney general, rendered an opinion to the same effect in 1729. Responding to a query about the status of English statutes in Maryland, Yorke said that acts of Parliament made since the colony's settlement did not apply there unless (*a*) they expressly referred to the colonies in general or to Maryland in particular; (*b*) the provincial assembly had adopted them; or (*c*) they had been "received there by long uninterrupted usage, or practice, which may import a tacit consent of the lord proprietor, and the people of the colony" that they should have the force of law.[161]

Presettlement English statutes went unmentioned by George Webb when he wrote his influential handbook for Virginia justices of the peace in 1736. His distillation of the general rule implied, however, that he understood the principle behind the General Court's 1710 infanticide decision. "All Acts of Parliament made in *England,* expressly declaring, That they shall extend to *Virginia,* or to His Majesty's *American* Plantations, are of full Force in this Dominion, tho' not Enacted here," Webb wrote. "Divers other Statutes are Enacted here, and Declared to be of Force in this Colony, by our Acts of Assembly."[162] Webb's restatement of current doctrine left no room for the ad hoc application of postsettlement English statutes that neither referred to the colony nor bore the General Assembly's imprimatur. Nevertheless, the issue remained controversial for the rest of the century. As late as 1798, two prominent Virginia jurists, St. George Tucker and John Tyler, could still disagree about whether the 1677 Statute of Frauds's liberalization of the rules of descent for leaseholds pur autre vie (for the life of another) applied to a Virginia will executed before the Revolution.[163] Tyler thought the English statute applied, contending that "it was not doubted in this Country till the Revolution that the General Statutes of England posterior to our Colonization were in force here. That we claimed the Benefit of them all."[164] Tucker denied that the statute had anything to do with the case, insisting that "even the most zealous advocates for the supremacy of the British parliament went no further than to say, that we were bound by all acts of parliament made after the establishment of the colonial legislatures *if therein* especially and particularly *named*." Because the 1677 act did not name the colonies, Tucker argued, the Virginia will was governed by presettlement English law, which prohibited a testator from devising a leasehold pur autre vie.[165] Although Tucker greatly exaggerated the number of conflicts that would have arisen from Tyler's theory, most eighteenth-century Virginia lawyers probably would have shared Tucker's view that only presettlement English statutes were eligible for ad hoc application.

ACQUISITION OF ENGLISH STATUTE BOOKS

Extension and accretion introduced scores of English statutes into Virginia's legal system. To interpret and apply those laws, colonial judges needed reliable, up-to-date statute books. In August 1661, soon after learning about the passage of the Navigation Act, the York County justices of the peace announced that they found it "very necessary that a Statute booke be provided for the Courts use." They ordered that "the Statutes att Large" be sent to them "out of England the next shipping."[166] The magistrates evidently wanted a book containing the full, authoritative texts of acts of Parliament rather than abridged versions.[167] As Edmund Wingate, the author of a popular abridgment candidly acknowledged, an abridgment "is but an extract of the Statutes at large; when any doubt shall arise in the Text (as you shall finde it here abridged) relie not wholly hereupon, but (in such case) repair to the Statutes at large."[168] Various works with the phrase *statutes at large* in the title appeared in the late sixteenth and early seventeenth centuries,[169] but no book with that precise phrase in the title would have been current enough to serve the York County justices' purposes. The most useful collection from their standpoint would have been the 1661 edition of Ferdinando Pulton's *A Collection of Sundry Statutes, Frequent in Use*, a comprehensive compilation first published in 1618.[170] The massive, 1,511-page work contained the statutes at large from Magna Carta (conveniently translated into English, as all the other statutes were) through the laws passed by Charles II's most recent Parliament, which adjourned on 30 July 1661.

The General Assembly of Virginia passed a law in the fall of 1666 instructing every county court to buy "all the former statutes at large and those made since the beginning of the raigne of his sacred majestie that now is," meaning King Charles II.[171] The Lancaster County Court complied in January 1670 by asking the commander of the ship *Duke of Yorke* to bring some law books with him on his return voyage, promising to reimburse him out of the next year's tax levy.[172] The volumes arrived in due course, and in November 1671 the justices appropriated funds to pay for them.[173] In October 1671 the York County Court, citing the 1666 Virginia statute, ordered a couple of legal treatises plus a compilation of the statutes of Charles II's reign.[174] The books were later "dispersed in severall Persons hands," prompting the justices of the peace to order the clerk to launch a search for the missing volumes and "secure the same for the use & benefitt of the Court."[175]

Another spate of book buying occurred at the beginning of the eighteenth century. In July 1700 the Essex County Court asked one of its members to order law books from England "as the Law directs for the use of the County."[176] In May 1701 the Richmond County Court ordered that its clerk "forthwith send to England for all the Statutes at large being two Volumes and that the name of the County be sett in Letters of gold on the Covers."[177] The justices may have had in mind the two-volume edition of Joseph Keble's *The Statutes at Large in Paragraphs and Sections or Numbers*,[178] which was published in London in 1695 and contained all the statutes enacted through May of that year. The clerk, William Colston, died early in the fall of 1701,[179] and either he failed to place the county's book order or his successor discovered that Keble's two-volume edition was outdated because it omitted the Plantation Trade Act of 1696,[180] the most recent English statute requiring colonists to enforce England's commercial policies. The Richmond County justices placed another book order in November 1703, after they received a directive from Governor Francis Nicholson and the Council of State telling Virginia magistrates to purchase copies of any acts of Parliament "as are now wanting in their Courts" and to "continue the like care for the future that the Courts be duly provided with the Laws & Statutes of England as from time to time they come out."[181] The Richmond justices acknowledged the importance of staying current when they "ordered that the Statutes and acts of Parliament to the Latest date now Extant be sent for."[182] The books apparently went astray, for in May 1705 the justices of the peace lamented "the Great Inconvenience of not haveing the Laws and Statutes and other necessary Law books," and they accepted a magistrate's offer to order them from England.[183]

Keeping up with Parliament's growing output of legislation proved expensive. In November 1703 the Middlesex County Court announced that it would comply with the governor and council's order and purchase "what Laws and Statutes of England are wanting ... with what convenient speed may be."[184] The records do not reveal which books they acquired in the next four years, but we do know that in April 1707 the court authorized two of its members "to get one good Chest with lock and key to Hold the Court bookes etc., to be set in the Jury Roome."[185] The following November, the court appropriated three thousand pounds of tobacco—almost 36 percent of that year's entire county budget—"to buy Law books for the Court."[186] In June 1709 Harry Beverley, the justice of the peace to whom that task had been assigned, "produced the Statutes at Large in five volumes which he bought with the Tobacco raised by the County," and the court ordered that the expensive tomes "be carefully Lodged amongst the County records."[187] The five books were probably the three-volume edition of Keble's *Statutes at Large*, published in 1706 and current through the session of Parliament that ended on 14 March 1704;[188] the *Supplement to the Statutes at Large*, published in 1706 and containing acts passed between 1696 and 1704;[189] and the *Addenda to the Third Volume of the Statutes at Large*, published in 1708 and current through the session of Parliament that ended on 1 April 1708.[190] These weighty compilations brought the Middlesex justices completely up to date on potentially applicable English legislation.

As Gordon Wood has argued, colonial adjudication "was not simply a matter of applying some kind of crude, untechnical law to achieve common-sense 'frontier' justice." He found "much evidence to suggest that even as early as the late seventeenth century in new back-country counties the quality of legal procedures was remarkably sophisticated."[191] Virginians' frequent and varied use of English statutes in the later Stuart period supports Wood's claim. Although the mixed nature of early Virginia jurisprudence occasionally caused confusion, settlers still managed to construct a legal regime that coherently blended imported and indigenous legislation.

The makers of early Virginia's legal culture drew upon acts of Parliament often and for three principal reasons: to obtain the instructions they needed to carry out imperial commands; to identify useful legislation they could transfer from the mother country's advanced legal system to their own emerging polity; and to find suitable rules of decision to help them determine the outcome of individual cases. English statute books served as essential guides for men who had to fathom the complexities of the Navigation Act, the Staple Act, and all the other metropolitan legislation that touched their lives. Integrating English statutes into colonial jurisprudence proclaimed Virginians' fidelity to the rule of law and reaffirmed their ethnocultural identity. As members of the English nation, colonists took pride in having what Sir William Berkeley described as "the best Lawes in the World for the security of the subject."[192] The presence of English statute books in the courthouses of colonial Virginia both symbolized and perpetuated this legacy.

NOTES

1. Mary Sarah Bilder, *The Transatlantic Constitution: Colonial Legal Culture and the Empire* (Cambridge, MA, 2004), 7. For a discussion of the origins and development of dual legislative authorities in English America, see Bilder, "English Settlement

and Local Governance," in *The Cambridge History of Law in America,* ed. Michael Grossberg and Christopher Tomlins, 3 vols. (New York, 2008), 1:63–103. On the prohibition against passing colonial statutes that were repugnant to English law, see Bilder, "The Corporate Origins of Judicial Review," *Yale Law Journal* 116 (2006): 535–41.

2. I have borrowed the term *accretion* from Robert M. Bliss, who referred to "the accretion of precedent and custom" in seventeenth-century Virginia. Bliss, *Revolution and Empire: English Politics and the American Colonies in the Seventeenth Century* (Manchester, 1990), 63. *Accretion* is an equally apt term for Virginians' gradual addition of English statutes to their corpus juris.

3. For an example of a longtime Virginia resident's reference to England as "home," see the nuncupative will, dated 22 Jan. 1671, of William Mellinge, who directed that two hogsheads of tobacco "bee sent home for England to buy a silver Tankard of five pound price" as a bequest to his friend and executor Lt. Col. William Waters. Northampton Co. Order Book (1664–74), 97. Mellinge served at various times as a burgess, justice of the peace, sheriff, and clerk in Northampton County. Except for a brief trip to London in the early 1660s, Mellinge resided continuously in Virginia from about 1636 until his death almost thirty-five years later, yet he still considered England his "home."

4. On the link between law and English identity, see Jack P. Greene, *The Constitutional Origins of the American Revolution* (New York, 2011), 5–8.

5. First Charter from James I to the Virginia Company, 10 Apr. 1606, in *The Three Charters of the Virginia Company of London with Seven Related Documents; 1606–1621,* ed. Samuel M. Bemiss (Williamsburg, 1957), 9. The Second Charter, dated 23 May 1609, contained a similar provision. Ibid., 51.

6. Second Charter, ibid., 52.

7. Sir Matthew Hale, *The Prerogatives of the King,* ed. D. E. C. Yale, Selden Society 92 (London, 1976), 43–44.

8. Christopher Tomlins, *Freedom Bound: Law, Labor, and Civic Identity in Colonizing English America, 1580–1865* (New York, 2010), 88–89.

9. For discussions of the colonists' understanding of the basic liberties that they brought with them from England to America, see Jack P. Greene, *Peripheries and Center: Constitutional Development in the Extended Polities of the British Empire and the United States, 1607–1788* (New York, 1986), 25; and John Phillip Reid, *Constitutional History of the American Revolution,* abr. ed. (Madison, WI, 1995), 23, 58–59. For an analysis of Sir Edward Coke's suggestion that "there were core English liberties—property rights and consent—that the king had to respect whenever Englishmen traveled to his non-English dominions," see Daniel J. Hulsebosch, "The Ancient Constitution and the Expanding Empire: Sir Edward Coke's British Jurisprudence," *Law and History Review* 21 (2003): 466–69.

10. Ken MacMillan, *Sovereignty and Possession in the English New World: The Legal Foundations of Empire, 1576–1640* (New York, 2006), 37.

11. Magna Carta, which originated in an agreement between King John and the barons in 1215, was enacted into a statute by King Edward I in 1297. Chapter 29 provided:

"No Freeman shall be taken or imprisoned, or be disseised of his Freehold, or Liberties, or free Customs, or be outlawed, or exiled, or any other wise destroyed; nor will We not pass upon him, nor [condemn him,] but by lawful judgment of his Peers, or by the Law of the Land. We will sell to no man, we will not deny or defer to any man either Justice or Right." 25 Edward 1, c. 29 (1297). See also the Petition of Right, in which King Charles I agreed not to compel his subjects "to make or yeild any Guift Loane Benevolence Taxe or such like Charge without common consent by Acte of Parliament." 3 Charles 1, c. 1, § 8 (1628). All quotations from acts of Parliament come from *The Statutes of the Realm,* 12 vols. (London, 1810–25), a compilation of laws enacted between 1235 and 1713.

12. David L. Smith, *The Stuart Parliaments, 1603–1689* (London, 1999), 178.
13. Robert Zaller, *The Discourse of Legitimacy in Early Modern England* (Stanford, CA, 2007), 476.
14. Jeffrey Goldsworthy, *The Sovereignty of Parliament: History and Philosophy* (Oxford, 1999), 106.
15. *Craw v. Ramsey,* Vaughan 274, 300, 124 Eng. Rep. 1072, 1084 (C.P. 1670).
16. MacMillan, *Sovereignty and Possession,* 6.
17. Hale, *Prerogatives of the King,* 42–44. Some English jurists asserted that the law applicable to a newly acquired territory depended on whether the king of England conquered it from a Christian king, conquered it from an infidel king, or inherited it. See Joseph Henry Smith, *Appeals to the Privy Council from the American Plantations* (New York, 1950), 467–73, discussing *Calvin's Case,* 7 Coke Rep. 1, 17b, 77 Eng. Rep. 377, 397–98 (Exch. Ch. 1608), and its progeny. These jurists viewed the American colonies as conquered countries for which the king could prescribe whatever laws he saw fit. See William Blackstone, *Commentaries on the Laws of England,* 4 vols. (Oxford, 1765–69), 1:105. But the issue remained unresolved, and "[n]o clear acceptance of the doctrine of the adjudged English cases appears in the colonies." Smith, *Appeals to the Privy Council,* 473. On the debate over the status of the colonies and the scope of the king's power to determine which English statutes applied there, see Greene, *Peripheries and Center,* 23–28. For a discussion of the applicability of English statutes to the colonies, see Elizabeth Gaspar Brown, *British Statutes in American Law, 1776–1836* (Ann Arbor, MI, 1964), 1–22. On the theoretical and historical origins of the king's absolute prerogative to prescribe laws for his overseas territories, see MacMillan, *Sovereignty and Possession,* 37–41.
18. *Territorial ambit* refers to the parts of the world where the law applies. Michael Hirst, *Jurisdiction and the Ambit of the Criminal Law* (Oxford, 2003), 2.
19. For example, when the exiled Charles II issued his commission to Virginia governor Sir William Berkeley and the Council of State on 3 June 1650, the king ordered his appointees to take the oath of allegiance prescribed by 3 James I, c. 4, § 9 (1606). *The Papers of Sir William Berkeley, 1605–1677,* ed. Warren M. Billings, with the assistance of Maria Kimberly (Richmond, 2007), 94. See also ibid., 551, on the 1676 proclamation by Charles II promising a pardon to participants in Bacon's Rebellion who took the oath of allegiance prescribed by the 1606 English statute.
20. A colony was "particularly named" if it was expressly mentioned or "included un-

der general words," such as "American plantations." See Blackstone, *Commentaries*, 1:101, 105.

21. The last royal veto occurred on 11 Mar. 1708, when Queen Anne, on the advice of her ministers, withheld her assent to the Scottish Militia Bill, An Act for settling the Militia of that Part of Great Britain called Scotland. With the queen seated on her throne in the House of Lords, "adorned with Her Crown and Regal Ornaments," the clerk informed the assembled peers and Commons that "La Reine se avisera [*sic*]" (The Queen will consider it), a euphemistic way of expressing her disapproval. The queen herself then offered an explanation. That morning she had learned that a French fleet bearing Charles Francis Edward Stuart, "the Old Pretender," had sailed from Dunkirk, presumably headed for Scotland. She assured the Lords and Commons that she would "continue to take all proper Measures for disappointing the Enemy's Designs." *Journals of the House of Lords,* 39 vols. (London, 1767–1830), 18:506. Anne and her ministers evidently suspected that the militia might prove disloyal, so they decided to leave the Scottish force "unsettled."

22. Thomas Jefferson, for example, argued in 1774 that colonists owed a duty of obedience to the monarch but not to the British legislature, "a body of men foreign to our constitutions, and unacknowledged by our laws." Jefferson, "A Summary View of the Rights of British America," in *The Papers of Thomas Jefferson,* ed. Julian Boyd et al. (Princeton, NJ, 1950–), 1:129. See also the preamble to the Virginia Constitution of 1776, dismissing Parliament as "a foreign jurisdiction." William Waller Hening, ed., *The Statutes at Large; Being a Collection of All the Laws of Virginia, from the First Session of the Legislature,* 13 vols. (Richmond, Philadelphia, and New York, 1809–23), 9:113. The Declaration of Independence alleged that George III had tried to "subject us to a jurisdiction foreign to our constitution, and unacknowledged by our laws."

23. For a discussion of the early Stuarts' claim that the colonies belonged to the king alone and therefore could not be regulated by parliamentary legislation, see Eric Nelson, *The Royalist Revolution: Monarchy and the American Founding* (Cambridge, MA, 2014), 39–50, 257n47, 264n102. On the emergence of Parliament's role in colonial governance, see Ian K. Steele, "The British Parliament and the Atlantic Colonies to 1760: New Approaches to Enduring Questions," in *Parliament and the Atlantic Empire,* ed. Philip Lawson (Edinburgh, 1995), 35–38.

24. An Act for Prohibiting Trade with the Barbadoes, Virginia, Bermuda and Antego, enacted 3 Oct. 1650, and An Act for Increase of Shipping, and Encouragement of the Navigation of this Nation, enacted 9 Oct. 1651. C. H. Firth and R. S. Rait, eds., *Acts and Ordinances of the Interregnum, 1642–1660,* 3 vols. (London, 1911), 2:425–29, 559–62. The background and purposes of the 1650 and 1651 acts are analyzed in Robert Brenner, *Merchants and Revolution: Commercial Change, Political Conflict, and London's Overseas Traders, 1550–1653* (Princeton, NJ, 1993), 592–628; and J. E. Farnell, "The Navigation Act of 1651, the First Dutch War, and the London Merchant Community," *Economic History Review,* 2d ser., 16 (1964): 439–54.

25. An Act for the Encourageing and Increasing of Shipping and Navigation, 12 Charles 2, c. 18 (1660), confirmed by 13 Charles 2, c. 14 (1661).

26. 12 Charles 2, c. 18, § 1.
27. *Journals of the House of Commons,* 12 vols. (London, 1802–3), 8:151; *Journals of the House of Lords* (London, 1830), 11:160.
28. W. L. Grant and James Munro, eds., *Acts of the Privy Council of England, Colonial Series,* 6 vols. (London, 1906–12), 1:298–99.
29. *Journals of the House of Lords,* 11:171.
30. For more about the commercial rivalry that led to the Navigation Act, see John R. Pagan, "Dutch Maritime and Commercial Activity in Mid-Seventeenth-Century Virginia," *Virginia Magazine of History and Biography* 90 (1982) 485–501; and Victor Enthoven and Wim Klooster, "The Rise and Fall of the Virginia-Dutch Connection in the Seventeenth Century," in *Early Modern Virginia: Reconsidering the Old Dominion,* ed. Douglas Bradburn and John C. Coombs (Charlottesville, 2011), 90–127. For discussions of the act's background, purpose, and effects, see Charles M. Andrews, *The Colonial Period of American History,* 4 vols. (New Haven, CT, 1934–38) 4:60–90; Lawrence A. Harper, *The English Navigation Laws, a Seventeenth Century Experiment in Social Engineering* (New York, 1939), 50–58; and J. M. Sosin, *English America and the Restoration Monarchy of Charles II: Transatlantic Politics, Commerce, and Kinship* (Lincoln, NE, 1980), 49–55.
31. 12 Charles 2, c. 18, § 1. The Navigation Act permitted ships belonging to the people of Berwick-upon-Tweed to trade with the colonies but banned Scottish vessels.
32. Ibid.
33. Two other sections also affected Virginians. Section 3 banned the importation into the British Isles of any colonial products not carried in the type of ship defined in § 1. Section 19 required ships going from England, Ireland, Wales, or Berwick-upon-Tweed to the colonies to post bond guaranteeing that they would carry enumerated colonial products such as tobacco only to ports in England, Ireland, Wales, or Berwick-upon-Tweed. Other lawful vessels, such as colonial ships, had to post bond with the governor ensuring that they would carry enumerated colonial products only to another English colony or to England, Ireland, Wales, or Berwick-upon-Tweed.
34. *In re Derickson* (1660), Northampton Co. Order Book (1657–64), 86–87.
35. *Papers of Sir William Berkeley,* 143.
36. Ibid., 148.
37. Hening, *Statutes at Large,* 2:17.
38. Warren M. Billings, *Sir William Berkeley and the Forging of Colonial Virginia* (Baton Rouge, 2004), 132–35, 140–41.
39. Ibid., 136–62.
40. Thomas R. Stewart, ed., *A Discourse and View of Virginia by Sir William Berkeley* (Norwalk, CT, 1914), 6–7. Berkeley wrote the pamphlet sometime between August 1661 and January 1662, when he had it printed. Billings, *Sir William Berkeley and the Forging of Colonial Virginia,* 277. The quotation in the text comes from Stewart's facsimile reprint of the printed version of Berkeley's *Discourse.* For a slightly different version, see *Papers of Sir William Berkeley,* 164–65.
41. *The Lawes of Virginia Now in Force* (London, 1662), ii, 2; Hening, *Statutes at Large,* 2:43.

42. An Act for preventing Frauds and regulating Abuses in His Majesties Customes, 14 Charles 2, c. 11 (1662). Charles assented to the act on 19 May 1662. *Journals of the House of Lords,* 11:471–72.
43. 14 Charles 2, c. 11, § 5.
44. Instructions from Charles II to Berkeley, 12 Sept. 1662, in *Papers of Sir William Berkeley,* 179.
45. *Papers of Sir William Berkeley,* 198–99; Grant and Munro, *Acts of the Privy Council,* 1:365–67.
46. An Act for the Encouragement of Trade, 15 Charles 2, c. 7 (1663). The act received the royal assent on 27 July 1663. *Journals of the House of Lords,* 11:579.
47. 15 Charles 2, c. 7, § 1.
48. Ibid., § 4.
49. The Staple Act explicitly mentioned the 1662 Customs Act and evidently incorporated the latter's definition of "English" crewmen as including Irish and colonial subjects. 14 Charles 2, c. 11, § 5. The Staple Act required that European goods bound for the American colonies be "laden and shipped in England Wales and the Towne of Berwicke upon Tweede and in English built Shipping." 15 Charles 2, c. 7, § 4. If an Irish merchant wished to send Irish-made goods to America, he had to ship them to England first and then reship them to the colonies.
50. 15 Charles 2, c. 7, § 4.
51. Charles II to Berkeley, 27 Jan. 1665, in *Papers of Sir William Berkeley,* 243.
52. Sir George Clark, *The Later Stuarts, 1660–1714,* 2d ed., Oxford History of England (Oxford, 1956), 63.
53. *Papers of Sir William Berkeley,* 256, 291.
54. See "Orders for the defense of Virginia," 21 June 1665, in *Papers of Sir William Berkeley,* 255–56. For a detailed account of Berkeley's conduct during the Second Anglo-Dutch War, see Billings, *Sir William Berkeley and the Forging of Colonial Virginia,* 204–8.
55. See act of 9 Oct. 1665, in Hening, *Statutes at Large,* 2:220–21.
56. "Order-in-council to fortify Old Point Comfort," 29 Mar. 1666, in *Papers of Sir William Berkeley,* 273–75.
57. Berkeley to Henry Bennet, 1st Earl of Arlington, 13 July 1666, ibid., 289.
58. Berkeley to Charles II and the Privy Council, ca. 24 June 1667, ibid., 319–20.
59. See N. H. Keeble, *The Restoration: England in the 1660s* (Oxford, 2002), 104 (attributing the Treaty of Breda to financial pressures).
60. Commissioners of the customs to Berkeley, 3 Feb. 1669, in *Papers of Sir William Berkeley,* 352.
61. On the councillors' ability to secure plum appointments that enabled them to profit from enforcing England's trade laws, see Emory G. Evans, *A "Topping People": The Rise and Decline of Virginia's Old Political Elite, 1680–1790* (Charlottesville, 2009), 10–12, 42.
62. For a brief sketches of Bland's career, see *Papers of Sir William Berkeley,* 118n1; and John T. Kneebone et al., eds., *Dictionary of Virginia Biography* (Richmond, 1998–), 2:14.

63. *Rex ex rel. Bland v. the Ship Hope* (1670), in *Minutes of the Council and General Court of Colonial Virginia*, ed. H. R. McIlwaine, 2d ed. (Richmond, 1979), 216; *Papers of Sir William Berkeley*, 369.
64. Petition of Edmund Scarburgh, ca. 30 Mar. 1670, in *Papers of Sir William Berkeley*, 369–70.
65. Philip Alexander Bruce, *Economic History of Virginia in the Seventeenth Century*, 2 vols. (New York, 1895), 1:358n1.
66. Ballard joined the Council on 22 June 1670. McIlwaine, *Minutes of the Council and General Court*, 223. He served until 1679. He represented James City County in the House of Burgesses in 1666. Kneebone et al., *Dictionary of Virginia Biography* 1:307–8.
67. *Rex ex rel. Ballard v. Ship Dolphin* (1670), in McIlwaine, *Minutes of the Council and General Court*, 212.
68. Ibid., 214.
69. Hening, *Statutes at Large*, 1:169. Clauses demanding that magistrates conform their rulings to English law became standard features of judicial commissions. See, e.g., Susie M. Ames, ed., *County Court Records of Accomack-Northampton, Virginia, 1640–1645* (Charlottesville, 1973), 178 (commission issued 1642); Warren M. Billings, ed., *The Old Dominion in the Seventeenth Century: A Documentary History of Virginia, 1606–1700*, rev. ed. (Chapel Hill, NC, 2007), 98 (commission issued 1652); *Papers of Sir William Berkeley*, 435 (commission issued 1673); and *The Papers of Francis Howard, Baron Howard of Effingham, 1663–1695*, ed. Warren M. Billings (Richmond, 1989), 98 (commission issued 1684).
70. Northumberland Co. Order Book (1666–78), 344–46.
71. Accomack Co. Wills, Etc., Orders (1682–97), 60–61.
72. Effingham to George Nicholas Hack, 23 Mar. 1685, in ibid., 60–60a; *Papers of Francis Howard, Baron Howard of Effingham*, 187. For a 1675 condemnation suit brought by Stringer, see the account of *Rex ex rel. Stringer v. the Ship Phoenix* in *American Slavery, American Freedom: The Ordeal of Colonial Virginia*, by Edmund S. Morgan (New York, 1975), 202–3.
73. Accomack Co. Wills, Etc., Orders (1682–97), 60a–61.
74. The indenture of sale, dated 25 Apr. 1685, is recorded in Accomack Co. Wills and Deeds (1676–90), 403–4. Montgomerie was twenty years old at the time he gave a deposition in a different case on 11 Feb. 1685. Accomack Co. Wills, Etc., Orders (1682–97), 62a.
75. The farm price of Chesapeake tobacco in 1685 was one penny sterling per pound. Russell R. Menard, "The Tobacco Industry in the Chesapeake Colonies, 1617–1730: An Interpretation," *Research in Economic History* 5 (1980): 159. Thus, Montgomerie's informer's fee equaled 5,273 pounds of tobacco. In the mid-1680s, male hired servants on the Eastern Shore earned around 1,000 to 1,200 pounds of tobacco per year plus food, washing, and lodging. John Ruston Pagan, *Anne Orthwood's Bastard: Sex and Law in Early Virginia* (New York, 2003), 142, 191n59.
76. *Rex ex rel. Custis v. the Ship Katherine*, Accomack Co. Wills, Etc., Orders (1682–97), 114–15.

77. Accomack Co. Wills, Etc., Orders (1682–97), 114a.
78. An Act for preventing Frauds and regulating Abuses in the Plantation Trade, 7 & 8 William 3, c. 22 (1696). The act received the royal assent on 10 Apr. 1696. *Journals of the House of Commons* 11 (1693–97): 555.
79. 7 & 8 William 3, c. 22, § 8 (1696).
80. Ibid., § 6.
81. George Reese, ed., *Proceedings in the Court of Vice-Admiralty of Virginia, 1698–1775* (Richmond, 1983), 6.
82. Michael Garibaldi Hall, *Edward Randolph and the American Colonies, 1676–1703* (Chapel Hill, NC, 1960), 184–85; Andrews, *Colonial Period of American History*, 4:258–59; David R. Owen and Michael C. Tolley, *Courts of Admiralty in Colonial America: The Maryland Experience, 1634–1776* (Durham, NC, 1995), 106; Steven L. Snell, *Courts of Admiralty and the Common Law: Origins of the American Experiment in Concurrent Jurisdiction* (Durham, NC, 2007), 148–49.
83. For additional cases involving county courts' enforcement of English trade statutes, see *Rex ex rel. Spencer v. Lynes* (Westmoreland Co. Court, 1685), in Billings, *Old Dominion in the Seventeenth Century*, 113–16 (jury verdict and judgment for king's collector in forfeiture action against ship's merchant who carried tobacco out of Maryland without paying customs duties on part of his cargo); *Rex ex rel. Crofts v. the Ship Crown of London* (1686), Middlesex Co. Order Book (1680–94), 275 (jury verdict and judgment for collector in condemnation action under the Staple Act); *Rex ex rel. Custis v. the Barque Fortune of Boston, Lincolnshire* (1687), Northampton Co. Order Book & Wills (1683–89), 278–79, 286 (jury verdict and judgment for collector in action to condemn vessel and cargo under the Staple Act for importing cloth not listed on the ship's customs cocket); *Rex ex rel. Cole v. the Sloop Katherine of New York* (1686), York Co. Deeds, Orders, Wills (1684–87), 153–54 (judgment for collector in bench trial of action to condemn ship and cargo under the Staple Act for bringing European goods from New York to Virginia without passing through a port in England, Wales, or Berwick-upon-Tweed).
84. Claire Priest, "Law and Commerce, 1580–1815," in Grossberg and Tomlins, *Cambridge History of Law in America*, 1:414.
85. Harper, *English Navigation Laws*, 195. William E. Nelson likewise concluded that Virginia courts "succeeded in enforcing Parliament's Navigation Acts." Nelson, *The Common Law in Colonial America*, vol. 3, *The Chesapeake and New England, 1660–1750* (New York, 2016), 28.
86. Blackstone, *Commentaries*, 1:105–6.
87. Hening, *Statutes at Large*, 1:167. This 1632 act referred to "statutes" but cited only 1 James 1, c. 6 (1604). Using the plural made sense, though, because the 1604 law clarified magistrates' powers under an earlier statute, 5 Elizabeth 1, c. 4 (1563).
88. Hening, *Statutes at Large*, 1:172. This 1632 act did not cite particular English statutes, but evidently the lawmakers had in mind An Acte against Regratours Forestallers and Engrossers, 5 & 6 Edward 6, c. 14 (1552), amended by 5 Elizabeth 1, c. 12 (1563), and made perpetual by 13 Elizabeth 1, c. 25 (1571). At later sessions, the assembly defined engrossing and forestalling and tailored the laws to Virginia cir-

cumstances. See Act 31 of Sept. 1632, Act 6 of 1633, Act 6 of 1643, and Act 8 of 1655, in Hening, *Statutes at Large,* 1:194–95, 217, 245, 412. In 1662 the assembly purported to repeal "all acts concerning ingrossing," an apparent reference to the colonial versions. Ibid., 2:124.

89. Hening, *Statutes at Large,* 1:167. In this 1632 act, the assembly cited the English Acte for repressinge the odious and loathsome synne of Drunckennes, 4 James 1, c. 5 (1606), but did not cite the later statute making the 1606 law perpetual and relaxing its standards of proof, 21 James 1, c. 7 (1624).

90. Hening, *Statutes at Large,* 1:434. This 1658 act seems to refer to An Acte to restrayne all persons from Marriage until their former Wyves and former Husbandes be deade, 1 James 1, c. 11 (1604).

91. Hening, *Statutes at Large,* 3:171. This 1699 act required Virginians to attend Church of England services at least once every two months and prescribed penalties for failing to do so. The assembly excused Protestant dissenters from paying the penalties if they were "every way qualified" for an exemption under An Act for Exempting their Majestyes Protestant Subjects dissenting from the Church of England from the Penalties of certaine Lawes, 1 William & Mary, c. 18 (1689). This English statute, generally called the Toleration Act of 1689, allowed freedom of worship by Protestant nonconformists who were willing to take certain oaths of allegiance and leave their church doors unlocked during services.

92. Hening, *Statutes at Large,* 3:298, the 1705 act adopting "so much" of 7 & 8 William 3, c. 34 (1696), "as relates" to allowing Quakers to testify by affirmation. For yet another example of adoption, see the 1726 Virginia law declaring that a 1691 act of Parliament prohibiting fraudulent devises was "to be in force in this colony and dominion." Hening, *Statutes at Large,* 4:164, adopting An Act for Relief of Creditors against Fraudulent Devises, 3 William & Mary, c. 14 (1691).

93. Ibid., 3:171n.

94. On the shortcomings of scribal publication of statutes, see David D. Hall, "The Chesapeake in the Seventeenth Century," in *A History of the Book in America,* vol. 1, *The Colonial Book in the Atlantic World,* ed. Hugh Amory and David D. Hall (New York, 2000), 61–62.

95. See, e.g., Northampton Co. Orders, Wills, Etc. (1698–1710), 304. The county court spent four days in November 1706 reading aloud the comprehensive revisal of 1705.

96. 5 Elizabeth 1, c. 4, § 10 (1563).

97. *Gibson v. Blande* (1691), Stafford Co. Orders (1689–93), 160–61. For another example of an action based on the Statute of Artificers, see *Brent v. Dunne* (1690), ibid., 48.

98. Hening, *Statutes at Large,* 3:102–3. On the role of oyer and terminer courts for the trial of slaves, see Peter Charles Hoffer and William B. Scott, eds., *Criminal Proceedings in Colonial Virginia: Fines, Examination of Criminals, Trials of Slaves, Etc., from March 1710 to 1754* (Athens, GA, 1984), xliv–lii.

99. 23 Henry 8, c. 1, § 1 (1532).

100. *Rex v. Tom Cary* (1693), Northampton Co. Orders and Wills (1689–98), 237–39.

101. The homeowner obtained restitution under a 1529 statute, 21 Henry 8, c. 11. For an-

other case in which a slave was sentenced to hang for arson in violation of 23 Henry 8, c. 1, and 4 & 5 Philip and Mary, c. 4 (1558) (accessory to arson punishable without benefit of clergy), see *Regina v. Sarah* (1705), Northampton Co. Orders, Wills, Etc. (1698–1710), 244–47.
102. For a discussion of the General Assembly's use of English statutes as models for colonial legislation, see Warren M. Billings, *A Little Parliament: The Virginia General Assembly in the Seventeenth Century* (Richmond, 2004), 134, 193, 210–11. For examples of the mix-and-match approach to adoption and incorporation, see St. George Tucker's list of the postsettlement English statutes that made their way into the acts of assembly via one route or the other. St. George Tucker, *Blackstone's Commentaries: with Notes of Reference, to The Constitution and Laws, of the Federal Government of the United States; and of the Commonwealth of Virginia,* 5 vols. (Philadelphia, 1803), 1: appendix, 396. For another list, see *A Collection of All the Acts of Assembly, Now in Force, in the Colony of Virginia* (Williamsburg, 1733), 603.
103. This requirement dated back to the creation of the Virginia legislature. See the Virginia Company's Instructions to the Governor and Council of State in Virginia, 24 July 1621, in *The Records of the Virginia Company of London,* ed. Susan Myra Kingsbury, 4 vols. (Washington, DC, 1906–35), 3:484, requiring the General Assembly and Council of State to "imitate and followe the policy" of the form of government, laws, customs, and manner of administering justice "used in the Realme of England as neere as may bee." The Crown retained the requirement when it assumed control of the colony. See King Charles I's Instructions to Governor Sir William Berkeley, Aug. 1641, in *Papers of Sir William Berkeley,* 29, empowering the General Assembly to make laws for the colony "correspondant as near as may be to the laws of England."
104. Colonial legislation had to conform to imperial policies and the fundamental principles of English law. See Philip Hamburger, *Law and Judicial Duty* (Cambridge, MA, 2008), 261–62; Elmer Beecher Russell, *The Review of American Colonial Legislation by the King in Council* (New York, 1915); and Gwenda Morgan, "'The Privilege of Making Laws': The Board of Trade, the Virginia Assembly and Legislative Review, 1748–1754," *Journal of American Studies* 10 (1976): 1–15.
105. Blackstone, *Commentaries,* 1:105.
106. An act for settling the Titles and Bounds of Lands: and for preventing unlawful Shooting and Ranging thereupon (1710), in Hening, *Statutes at Large,* 3:521–22.
107. An Acte for lymytacon of Accons, and for avoyding of Suits in Lawe, 21 James 1, c. 16, § 1 (1624).
108. Lymitacon of Prescription, 32 Henry 8, c. 2, §§ 1–3 (1540).
109. See An Act for settling the Titles and Bounds of Lands, and for preventing unlawful Shooting and Ranging thereupon, Act 13 of 1710, in *Acts of Assembly, Passed in the Colony of Virginia, from 1662, to 1715* (London, 1727), 341–42.
110. *Collection of All the Acts of Assembly, Now in Force,* title page, 259–60, 603. For a discussion of this volume's importance, see W. Hamilton Bryson, *Virginia Law Books: Essays and Bibliographies* (Philadelphia, 2000), 14–15.
111. Commission from King Charles I to Sir William Berkeley, 10 Aug. 1641, in *Papers*

of Sir William Berkeley, 25. Another version of the 1641 commission used the word *purpose* instead of *propose.* Evarts Boutell Greene, *The Provincial Governor in the English Colonies of North America* (New York, 1907), 215. Berkeley's 1650 commission from King Charles II said that Virginians were to be regulated "according to the laws and Statutes of the Realm of England which wee purpose to Establish there." *Papers of Sir William Berkeley,* 91. Berkeley's 1660 commission reverted to *propose.* Ibid., 124.

112. Hening, *Statutes at Large,* 2:70.
113. The phrase "brooding omnipresence in the sky" comes from *Southern Pacific Co. v. Jensen,* 244 U.S. 205, 222 (1917) (Holmes, J., dissenting).
114. See Arthur P. Scott, *Criminal Law in Colonial Virginia* (Chicago, 1930); and Hoffer and Scott, *Criminal Proceedings in Colonial Virginia.*
115. *Rex ex rel. Sandford v. Kennet,* Accomack Co. Wills, Deeds & Orders (1678–82), 230, alleging violation of 5 Elizabeth 1, c. 9 (1563).
116. Northampton Co. Deeds and Wills (1666–68), 19a, enforcing 1 James 1, c. 31. The quarantine order, issued by the county's militia commander, concluded with a flourish: "God Save the King!"
117. An Acte for the charitable Reliefe and orderinge of persons infected with the Plague, 1 James 1, c. 31, § 2 (1604).
118. Surry Co. Deeds, Wills, Etc. (1671–84), fol. 40, citing 13 Henry 4, c. 7 (1411). I owe this reference to Brent Tarter. For his analysis of the broader social and political significance of this prosecution, see Tarter, *The Grandees of Government: The Origins and Persistence of Undemocratic Politics in Virginia* (Charlottesville, 2013), 72–73.
119. An Acte concerninge Tanners Curriers Shoomakers and other Artificers occupyinge the cuttinge of Leather, 1 James 1, c. 22, § 21 (1604).
120. *Scarburgh v. Bradford* (1663), Northampton Co. Order Book (1657–64), fol. 153. For biographical sketches of Scarburgh, see Susie M. Ames, ed., *County Court Records of Accomack-Northampton, Virginia, 1632–1640,* American Legal Records 8 (Washington, DC, 1954), xxvii; and Ames, ed., *County Court Records of Accomack-Northampton, Virginia, 1640–1645* (Charlottesville, 1973), xv–xvi.
121. 8 Henry 6, c. 9 (1429).
122. *Byram v. Johnson* (1685), Northumberland Co. Order Book (1678–98), pt. 1, 287. The jury found that the plaintiff had sustained five hundred pounds of tobacco in actual damages. The relevant statute was 8 Henry 6, c. 9. The record does not reveal whether the court relied on the statutes at large or on an abridgment. The statute's treble-damages provision was abstracted in a chapter titled "Forcible Entry," in Edmund Wingate's *An Exact Abridgment of All Statutes In Force and Use, upon the 4th day of January, in the Year of our Lord 1641/42,* 2d ed. (London, 1655), 219, a work that was well known in Virginia. See W. Hamilton Bryson, *Census of Law Books in Colonial Virginia* Charlottesville, 1978), xvii, 156; *Rex v. Smith* (1670), Accomack Co. Orders (1666–70), 174, 180, citing p. 225 of the 1655 edition of Wingate's *Abridgement.*
123. An Acte for the Releife of the Poore, 43 Elizabeth 1, c. 2, § 3 (1601).

124. Hening, *Statutes at Large,* 2:298.
125. Accomack Co. Orders (1697–1703), 34a.
126. Ibid.
127. See the discussion of *Morgan v. Bally* and a couple of similar cases in Pagan, *Anne Orthwood's Bastard,* 136–44. Arthur P. Scott cites a 1692 case in which the Henrico County Court held that the 1672 Virginia act, rather than the English Poor Law, determined a girl's age of emancipation. Scott, *Criminal Law in Colonial Virginia,* 30n40.
128. See Warren M. Billings, "The Growth of Political Institutions in Virginia, 1634 to 1676," in *Magistrates and Pioneers: Essays in the History of American Law* (Clark, NJ, 2011), 35–36, noting that between 1662 and 1676 "no man sat in the House of Burgesses who was not simultaneously a justice of the peace."
129. An Acte to prevent the murthering of Bastard Children, 21 James 1, c. 27 (1624).
130. See, e.g., *Rex v. Carter* (1680), Accomack Co. Wills, Deeds & Orders (1678–82), 160–67 (woman presented to the county court under 21 James 1, c. 27, indicted by the grand jury, and bound over to the General Court for trial); and *Rex v. Anderson and Mikell* (1681), ibid., 218, 233–36 (prosecution of mother and her male accomplice under 21 James 1, c. 27). See also Scott, *Criminal Law in Colonial Virginia,* 33, 200–201 (discussing trals in the General Court under 21 James 1, c. 27).
131. H. R. McIlwaine et al., eds., *Executive Journals of the Council of Colonial Virginia,* 6 vols. (Richmond, 1925–67), 1:522. See also ibid., 1:314, a 1694 order by the council that "Elizabeth Lewis a person Condemned and reprieved until the next Generall Court" was to be kept "in Close Custody in the Comon Goal of James City as a Condemned person."
132. *Griffin and Burwell v. Wormeley* (1683), in McIlwaine et al., *Executive Journals,* 1:479–85, 492; Richard Beale Davis, ed., *William Fitzhugh and His Chesapeake World, 1676–1701* (Chapel Hill, NC, 1963), 88–89, 151–59; Robert T. Barton, ed., *Virginia Colonial Decisions: the Reports by Sir John Randolph and by Edward Barradall of Decisions of the General Court of Virginia, 1728–1741,* 2 vols. (Boston, 1909), 2:B1–B2.
133. An Act for prevention of Frauds and Perjuryes, 29 Charles 2, c. 3 (1677). The act received the royal assent on 16 Apr. 1677. *Journals of the House of Lords* 13 (1675–1681): 120. It applied to wills executed on or after 24 June 1677.
134. 29 Charles 2, c. 3, §5.
135. Middlesex Co. Order Book (1680–94), 11.
136. Ibid., 47, 48, 55; depositions in Middlesex Co. Deeds, Etc. (1679–94), 28–33; William Fitzhugh to Ralph Wormeley, n.d., in Davis, *William Fitzhugh,* 153.
137. Davis, *William Fitzhugh,* 154.
138. For an account of the struggle to define legal restraints and constitutional boundaries in early seventeenth-century England, see James S. Hart Jr., *The Rule of Law, 1603–1660: Crowns, Courts and Judges* (Harlow, England, 2003).
139. John Phillip Reid, *Rule of Law: The Jurisprudence of Liberty in the Seventeenth and Eighteenth Centuries* (DeKalb, IL, 2004), 5.

140. See "The Replication of Lewis Griffin and Lewis Burwell," in McIlwaine et al., *Executive Journals*, 1:481.
141. Middlesex Co. Deeds, Etc. (1679–94), 27. In October 1683, Charles II instructed the new governor, Lord Howard of Effingham, that he was "not for the future to admit or allow of any Appeals whatsoever to bee made from the Governor and Council unto the Assembly." Billings, *Papers of Francis Howard, Baron Howard of Effingham*, 25. Litigants who were dissatisfied with the decisions of the General Court could appeal to the king in Council provided the amount in controversy exceeded the prescribed minimum. Smith, *Appeals to the Privy Council*, 83–84.
142. Barton, *Virginia Colonial Decisions*, 2:B1.
143. Ibid., 2:B2.
144. Ibid.
145. Ibid., noting that Jones's opinion had been "affirmed in open Court" in Jamestown; Davis, *William Fitzhugh*, 88n2; McIlwaine et al., *Executive Journals*, 1:492; Hening, *Statutes at Large*, 2:564; "The Randolph Manuscript," *Virginia Magazine of History of Biography* 18 (1910): 130n. Wormeley was slow to obey the judgment. In April 1684, Griffin and Burwell were still trying to gain possession of Burnham's land. Middlesex Co. Order Book (1680–94), 166.
146. *Hayberd v. Hawksford* (1701), Richmond Co. Order Book (1699–1704), 82–83.
147. Ibid., 83.
148. Hening, *Statutes at Large*, 5:456.
149. Robert Beverley, *The History and Present State of Virginia*, ed. Susan Scott Parrish (Chapel Hill, NC, 2013), 204.
150. Henry Hartwell, James Blair, and Edward Chilton, *The Present State of Virginia, and the College*, ed. Hunter Dickinson Farish (Williamsburg, 1940), 40. Although the report was written in 1697, it was not published until 1727.
151. Louis B. Wright, ed., *An Essay Upon the Government of the English Plantations on the Continent of America* (San Marino, CA, 1945), 23.
152. Spotswood to the Council of Trade, 6 Mar. 1711, in *The Official Letters of Alexander Spotswood*, ed. Robert A. Brock, 2 vols. (Richmond, 1882–85), 1:57–58. The bill was prepared pursuant to a request made by the council on 31 October 1710 and was amended by both the House of Burgesses and the council as it wound its way through the legislature. See H. R. McIlwaine, ed., *Legislative Journals of the Council of Colonial Virginia*, 2d ed. (Richmond, 1979), 493, 494, 495, 497–98; John Pendleton Kennedy and H. R. McIlwaine, eds., *Journals of the House of Burgesses of Virginia,1619–1776*, 13 unnumbered vols. (Richmond, 1905–15), *1702/3–1705, 1705–1706, 1710–1712*, 259, 261, 262, 264, 265, 268. Spotswood assented to the bill on 9 December 1710. Ibid., 298.
153. Hening, *Statutes at Large*, 3:516.
154. Hugh F. Rankin, *Criminal Trial Proceedings in the General Court of Colonial Virginia* (Williamsburg, 1965), 138. For discussion of Virginia laws extending the terms of servants who bore children out of wedlock, see Pagan, *Anne Orthwood's Bastard*, 84–85.

155. Hening, *Statutes at Large*, 3:516–17.
156. For a thorough examination of the views of English jurists on the applicability of English statutes to the American colonies, see Smith, *Appeals to the Privy Council*, 464–522.
157. George Chalmers, *Opinions of Eminent Lawyers, on Various Points of English Jurisprudence, Chiefly Concerning the Colonies, Fisheries, and Commerce, of Great Britain*, 2 vols. (London, 1814), 1:195.
158. Few Virginians probably would have endorsed the Reverend Hugh Jones's claim in 1724 that "[a]ll the laws and statutes of England before Queen Elizabeth are there in force, but none made since; except those that mention the plantations, which are always specified in English laws, when occasion requires." Hugh Jones, *The Present State of Virginia*, ed. Richard L. Morton (Chapel Hill, NC, 1956), 94. Jones erroneously excluded the presettlement statutes of James I from Virginia's body of laws, and he incorrectly claimed that pre-Elizabethan statutes always applied in the colony whether or not the colonists found them suitable to colonial conditions.
159. The constitutional crisis of the 1760s and 1770s would cause some Virginians to repudiate the rule articulated by West. Thomas Jefferson, for instance, claimed that "the rule, in our courts of judicature was, that the common law of England, and the general statutes previous to the 4th of James, were in force here; but that no subsequent statutes were, *unless we were named in them*, said the judges and other partisans of the crown, but *named or not named*, said those who reflected freely." Jefferson, *Notes on the State of Virginia*, ed. William Peden (Chapel Hill, NC, 1982), 132.
160. *Anonymous*, 2 Peere Williams 75, 24 Eng. Rep. 646 (Chan. 1722).
161. Chalmers, *Opinions of Eminent Lawyers*, 1:197. For a discussion of controversies over the applicability of English statutes in Maryland, Pennsylvania, South Carolina, and Jamaica, see St. George Leakin Sioussat, "The Theory of the Extension of English Statutes to the Plantations," in *Select Essays in Anglo-American Legal History*, ed. Association of American Law Schools, 3 vols. (Boston, 1907–9), 1:416–30.
162. George Webb, *The Office and Authority of a Justice of Peace* (Williamsburg, 1736), 324.
163. The Statute of Frauds changed English law by allowing a tenant pur autre vie to devise his interest by will. 29 Charles 2, c. 3, § 12 (1677).
164. *Mercer v. Hedgman* (Staunton District Court, 1798), in *St. George Tucker's Law Reports and Selected Papers, 1782–1825*, ed. Charles F. Hobson, 3 vols. (Chapel Hill, NC, 2013), 1:430n39. This quotation is Tucker's summary of Tyler's position.
165. Ibid., 1:430–31.
166. York Co. Deeds, Orders, Wills (1657–62), 125. In October 1661 the county court appropriated 450 pounds of tobacco to Lt. Col. William Barbar "to procure a Statute booke for the Court." The same amount was appropriated for copies of the acts of assembly and six orders. Ibid., 134.
167. On the distinction between statutes at large and abridgments, see William S. Holdsworth, *A History of English Law*, 2d ed., 17 vols. (Boston, 1922–72), 4:307–13.
168. Wingate, *Exact Abridgement of All Statutes in Force and Use*, ii.

169. See W. Harold Maxwell and Leslie F. Maxwell, eds., *A Legal Bibliography of the British Commonwealth of Nations,* 2d ed., 7 vols. (1955–64), 1:553–56.
170. Ferdinando Pulton, *A Collection of Sundry Statutes, Frequent in Use* (London, 1661). Holdsworth called Pulton's work "an advance upon all former editions of the statutes," setting a new standard "to which subsequent editors made at least an attempt to conform." Holdsworth, *History of English Law,* 4:309–10. Pulton (1536–1618) began the work in 1611. Following its initial publication in 1618, revised editions appeared in 1628, 1632, 1635–36, 1640, 1661, and 1670. Maxwell and Maxwell, *Legal Bibliography,* 1:555–56; Virgil B. Heltzel, "Ferdinando Pulton, Elizabethan Legal Editor," *Huntington Library Quarterly* 11 (1947): 77–79. Pulton's works were listed in several colonial Virginians' estate inventories. Bryson, *Census of Law Books,* 20. For an example of a compilation by an editor who imitated Pulton's method, see Thomas Manby, *A Collection of the Statutes Made in the Reigns of King Charles the I. and King Charles the II.* (London, 1667).
171. Hening, *Statutes at Large,* 2:246.
172. Lancaster Co. Orders (1666–80), 133. The county court also asked the captain of the *Duke of Yorke* to obtain weights and measures, as required by a 1662 statute. Hening, *Statutes at Large,* 2:89.
173. The county court appropriated 2,688 pounds of tobacco for both the law books and the weights and measures. Lancaster Co. Orders (1666–80), 211.
174. York Co. Deeds, Orders, and Wills (1665–72), 361.
175. York Co. Deeds, Orders, and Wills (1677–84), 331, order of 24 Aug. 1681.
176. Essex Co. Order Book (1699–1702), 53. The justice, Capt. Jonathan Battaile, was also asked to acquire a set of weights and measures for the county's use. At the next court of levy, in December 1700, the justices appropriated 7,525 pounds of tobacco to Battaile "for Law Books, Weights & Measures, etc." Ibid., 73.
177. Richmond Co. Order Book (1699–1704), 104.
178. Joseph Keble, *The Statutes at Large in Paragraphs and Sections or Numbers, from Magna Charta to the End of the Reign of King Charles II ... In this impression are added all the Statutes made in the reigns of King James II, King William and Queen Mary to the end of the last session of Parliament, May, 3, 1695,* 2 vols. (London, 1695). The first edition of Keble's *Statutes at Large* was published in 1676, and the last edition appeared in 1736. Maxwell and Maxwell, *Legal Bibliography,* 1:554. Some Virginia lawyers possessed their own copies of Keble's collection. Godfrey Pole, who practiced in Northampton County in the early eighteenth century, owned "Keebles Statutes at large to the End of Charles 2d [1685]." "Miscellaneous Colonial Documents," *Virginia Magazine of History and Biography* 17 (1909): 147n1; Bryson, *Census of Law Books,* 19.
179. See Richmond Co. Order Book (1699–1704), 118–19.
180. An Act for preventing Frauds and regulating Abuses in the Plantation Trade, 7 & 8 William 3, c. 22 (1696).
181. McIlwaine et al., *Executive Journals,* 2:336, order of 27 Aug. 1703.
182. Richmond Co. Order Book (1699–1704), 297. English statute books could be

updated by "publishing" (reading) new laws during county-court sessions. In June 1702, for example, the Northumberland County Court read a royal proclamation concerning piracy and published An Act for the more effectuall Suppression of Piracy, 11 William 3, c. 7 (1700). Northumberland Co. Order Book (1699–1713), pt. 1, 206. In May 1709 the Middlesex County Court published An Act for ascertaining the Rates of Foreign Coins in Her Majesties Plantations in America, 6 Anne, c. 57 (1708), and An Act for the Encouragement of the Trade to America, 6 Anne, c. 64 (1708). Middlesex Co. Order Book (1705–10), 228.

183. Richmond Co. Order Book (1704–8), 60.
184. Middlesex Co. Order Book (1694–1705), 538.
185. Middlesex Co. Order Book (1705–10), 96.
186. Ibid., 202. The total Middlesex budget for November 1707 to November 1708 was 8,384 pounds of tobacco.
187. Ibid., 240.
188. Joseph Keble, *The Statutes at Large, in Paragraphs, and Sections or Numbers, from Magna Charta, to the End of the Session of Parliament, March 14, 1704, In the Fourth Year of the Reign of Her Majesty Queen Anne*, 3 vols. (London, 1706). Volume 1 contained 963 pages; volume 2 had 1,037 pages; and volume 3 had 1,005 pages.
189. *A Supplement to the Statutes at Large, Beginning with the Seventh and Eighth Years of the Reign of King William III, And Continued to the End of the Last Session of Parliament, March 14, 1704, in the Fourth Year of the Reign of Her Majesty Queen Anne* (London, 1706), 731 pages.
190. *Addenda to the Third Volume of the Statutes at Large, Beginning with the Fourth Year of the Reign of Queen Anne, and Continued to the End of the Last Session of Parliament, April 1, 1708, in the Seventh Year of Her Majesties Reign* (London, 1708), 270 pages.
191. Gordon S. Wood, *The Creation of the American Republic, 1776–1787* (Chapel Hill, NC, 1969), 297; Nelson, *Common Law in Colonial America*, 3:37–38, 50.
192. Berkeley to Francis Moryson, 11 Feb. 1677, in Billings, *Papers of Sir William Berkeley*, 583.

JOHN MERCER

MERCHANT,
LAWYER,
AUTHOR,
BOOK COLLECTOR

Bennie Brown

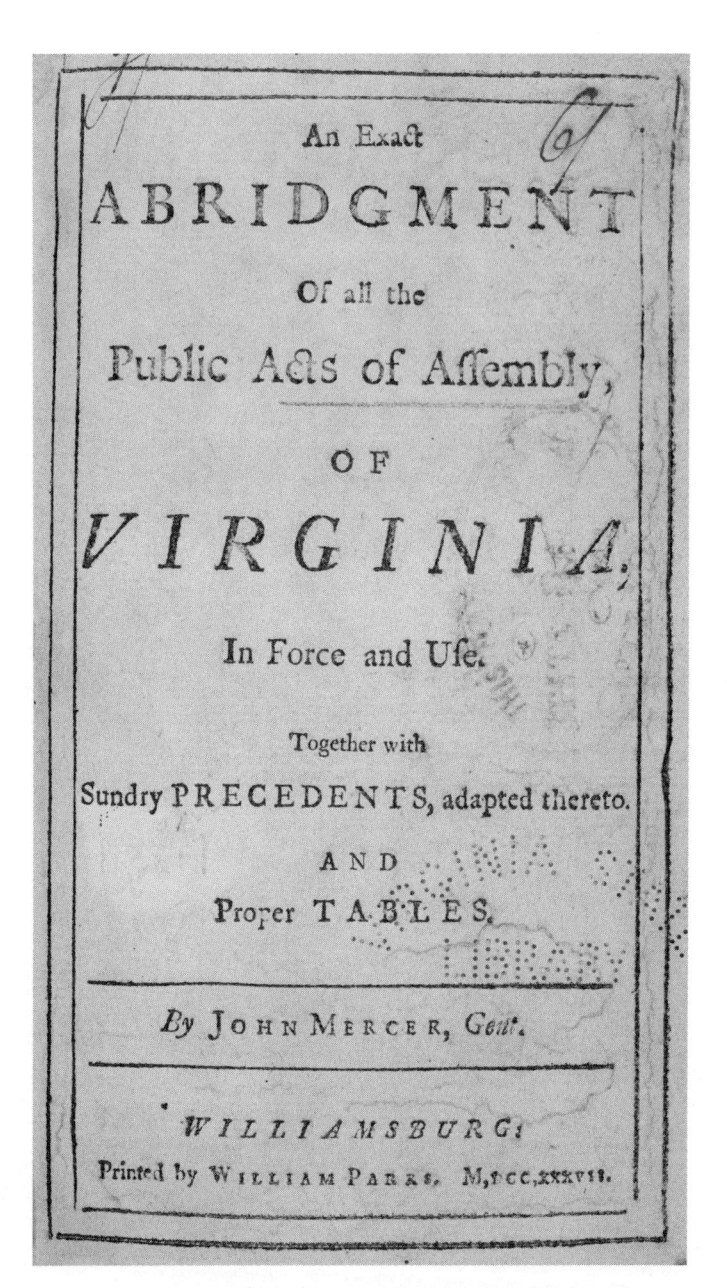

An Exact
ABRIDGMENT
Of all the
Public Acts of Assembly,
OF
VIRGINIA,
In Force and Use.

Together with
Sundry PRECEDENTS, adapted thereto.
AND
Proper TABLES.

By JOHN MERCER, Gent.

WILLIAMSBURG:
Printed by WILLIAM PARKS. M,DCC,XXXVII.

John Mercer's 1737 abridgement of Virginia laws aided judges, lawyers, and laymen. John Mercer, Exact Abridgment of all the Public Acts of Assembly, of Virginia, In Force and Use (Williamsburg, 1737). (Courtesy the Library of Virginia)

Soon after John Mercer died in Stafford County in the autumn of 1768, the author of an unsigned obituary printed in the *Virginia Gazette* in Williamsburg wrote that "he had practiced the law with great success in this colony upward of forty years. He was a Gentleman of great natural abilities, improved by an extensive knowledge not only in his profession, but in several branches of polite literature."[1] The writer took no notice that Mercer had also been an abiding bibliophile who assembled one of the largest law libraries in colonial Virginia. The library reflects his extensive background in both law and literature, but that was only one facet of his involvement with books. That involvement fell into three broad categories: as collector of the books he acquired for his personal library and use; as a contributor to books for which he acted as editor, author, or patron; and as a dealer in books that he acquired through his business activities and sold or lent to neighbors, family members, and customers.

Mercer was born in 1705 into a family of merchants in Dublin, Ireland. John and Grace Fenton Mercer gave their inquisitive son a substantial dose of formal learning that may even have included attendance at Trinity College. Whatever its nature, his schooling deepened his bookishness and educated him soundly, but as he later remarked, except for that education, "I never got a shilling of my fathers or any other relation's estate, every penny I got has been by my own industry." His quest for those pennies started in earnest after he immigrated in 1720 to Virginia, where he rose to prominence starting as a merchant and then becoming a lawyer, author, and book collector.[2]

Mercer acquired a sloop and relied on his connections to the Dublin mercantile community to establish a thriving import-export business along the Potomac River that included not only the typical merchandise in clothing and other consumer goods but also books. He set himself up in Stafford County on the site of Marlborough. One of a string of port towns the General Assembly had earlier established to centralize commerce on the Potomac, Rappahannock, York, and James Rivers, Marlborough was essentially a ghost town when Mercer started acquiring vacant lots and purchasing others from their owners. He eventually gained exclusive possession of the entire defunct town after the assembly disestablished it and granted him the right to acquire the remaining public and private properties. The site became the most important part of his larger landholdings, for it was there that he built his primary residence, an impressive mansion that he called Marlborough, overlooking the Potomac River.[3]

Comfortably fixed as a prospering merchant, Mercer aimed higher. His business with and personal ties to Northern Neck elite families such as the Masons, the Custises, the Fairfaxes, the Roys, and the Washingtons eased his passage into the colony's great planter class. In 1725 he married Katherine Mason, who was the sister of his business associate George Mason. Settling in the region in the 1660s, Mason's forbears had become one of Stafford County's leading clans, and for Mercer, marriage into that family represented a considerable step upward. John and Katherine Mercer had five children before she died in 1750. Mercer later married Ann Roy, the daughter of the well-to-do Scots immigrant Dr. Mungo Roy, of nearby Essex County, and they also had five children.

The accidental drowning of George Mason in 1735 drew Mercer and the Mason family closer still. Mason left behind a widow and three small children, the eldest of whom was a ten-year-old namesake. Mercer became the boy's guardian. Because Mercer could not find tutors to his liking, he gave young George Mason the run of the library at Marlborough and acted as his principal mentor, providing the major part of the boy's education. Mercer probably did the same with George's younger brother Thomson Mason as he did with his own son, James Mercer. Thomson Mason and James Mercer took advantage of the law books in Mercer's library and well before the outbreak of the American Revolution became respected members of the distinguished General Court Bar. As an adult, George Mason was a regular client of his uncle, buying goods and books from him and actively partnering with Mercer in the Ohio Company, a politically potent group of men who formed a speculative venture to acquire western land. Mason went on to achieve renown as the revolutionary author of the Fairfax Resolves, the drafter of the Virginia Declaration of Rights, an architect of the Virginia Constitution of 1776, and an active delegate at the convention that produced the Constitution of the United States and also at the Virginia ratification convention, where he opposed adoption of the constitution in part because it lacked a bill of rights. Mason owed at least some of his political success and influence to the contents of Mercer's library, and to that extent his state and country owe a debt to that library too.[4]

Mercer was not afraid to get into the political fray himself. Edmund Randolph later credited him with being "the first in Virginia who distinctly elucidated upon paper the principles which justified the opposition to the Stamp Act. He showed them in manuscript to his friends. They spread rapidly so as to produce a groundwork for an uniformity of popular sentiment."[5] Unfortunately, no text of Mercer's paper has ever surfaced, but Randolph may have had in mind a lost document that Mercer supposedly sent to the former Williamsburg mayor John Holt, who edited the *New York Gazette* at the time. The Stamp Act crisis embroiled Mercer personally too. His son George, who was in London as an agent for the Ohio Company, accepted a royal commission as the distributor of stamps in Virginia. Soon after George Mercer arrived in Williamsburg, a large crowd roundly condemned him and threatened him with violence or death if he did not resign. Despite John Mercer's opposition to the Stamp Act, he defended his son publicly in the *Virginia Gazette*. Privately he continued to justify his son's acceptance of the position long after Parliament repealed the Stamp Act, and in one of his last letters he expressed continued support of George's decision to become a stamp distributor.[6]

Not long after John Mercer married Katherine Mason, he decided to improve his knowledge of the law in order to gain a license to practice. As a lawyer rather than an attorney, he would be qualified to litigate his business affairs and landholdings, as well as those of others, in the county and General Courts. At that time, the words *attorney* and *lawyer* were not synonymous as they later became. An attorney could be any adult who represented the interests of another person in a court of law, perhaps acting under a power of attorney, whereas a lawyer was a person who had studied at one of the Inns of Court and been admitted to the bar in London or in Williamsburg—who had become "learned in the law," as the phrase went.[7]

Mercer was in no position at the time to leave family and business for an extended period of study in Dublin or at one of the Inns of Court in London. Instead of going abroad, he did what other aspiring young Virginia attorneys and lawyers often did: he acquired books and taught himself. A quick study, he easily and swiftly won his law license and began assembling the rudiments of his law library. Mercer's flair for advocacy led to a lucrative practice that eventually grew into the largest of the day, stretching from Stafford County to the rest of the colony and to the General Court in Williamsburg. It is not too much to say that he may well have been the first early Virginia lawyer whose practice furnished a major source of his income.

Mercer was a vestryman at Aquia Church and gained a seat on the Stafford County Court and became its presiding judge, but he never served in the House of Burgesses. That was probably because of his personality. Not only was he iron-willed and outspoken, but his violent temper, rapier-sharp tongue, and high-handedness often landed him in trouble. In 1730, when he was barely into his law practice, he fell foul of the General Assembly for writing a biting diatribe against a law that exempted owners of ironworks from paying taxes on their establishments and also required that roads be built to foundries at taxpayer expense. The House of Burgesses condemned Mercer's paper for its "false and scandalous Reflections upon the Legislature and the Justices of the General Court and other Courts of this Colony" and ordered Mercer's arrest to the bar of the House, where it fined but released him after he apologized for his ill-considered words.[8] Four years later he temporarily lost his law license after the Council of State suspended him for hectoring the justices of the Prince William County Court and for "Divers Misdemeanors & Irregular Practices."

Even though Mercer returned to the bar after a six-month suspension, his new license contained a proviso forbidding him to appear before the Prince William magistrates, but that condition was later dropped. His punishment scarcely chastened him, for he was intermittently disbarred through the 1740s and into the 1750s. One of those disbarments even led to his removal from the Stafford County bench, although he subsequently regained his place as presiding judge.[9]

Mercer developed a keen interest in law books, probably while learning the law. His contributions as an editor and author of law books revealed a flair for scholarship that greatly enhanced his command of colonial and British law. That scholarly bent was evidenced early on when he assisted William Parks with the publication of a full-text edition of the Maryland statutes in force. Enticed from England to Annapolis, Parks became the Maryland public printer, and in 1727 he issued his edition under the title *The Complete Collection of the Laws of Maryland*.[10] One of Mercer's surviving account books records the large payments he received from Parks for "an Abridgment of the Laws of Maryland contained in the printed Volume £11.10.00, and to an index Tables & Abridgmt of the Laws of the two last Sessions above Agreement £11.10.00."[11] Payment of that sizable amount makes plain that Mercer had a major hand in the compilation and indexing of the *Complete Collection* as well as the acts published after each successive session of the legislature. Mercer's personal copy of the Maryland laws includes an alternate title page rarely seen.[12] Parks's compilation remained in use until Thomas Bacon published an entirely new edition in 1765.

Mercer also prepared legal works of his own for use in Virginia. During the first suspension from his law practice, and with the aid of his growing law library, he compiled and published a comprehensive digest of Virginia law. As a precaution, given his fraught relationship with the Council of State, he sought permission "to Print an Abridgement compil'd by him of all the Laws of this Colony & to have the benefit of the Sale thereof." The council granted his petition but stipulated that he "deliver the said Abridgement to be Examined by the Attorney General" of the colony, John Clayton, and two barristers trained at the Inns of Court, Sir John Randolph, then Speaker of the House of Burgesses, and Edward Barradall, who soon thereafter succeeded Clayton as attorney general. The council ordered "that they Report their Opinion whether the same be fitt to be Printed."[13] Armed with the council's authorization, Mercer turned to William Parks, who had become Virginia's first public printer and who in 1737 published the manuscript as *An Exact Abridgment of all the Public Acts of Assembly, of Virginia*.

In the preface to the volume, Mercer explained, "As the Alterations and Additions made to the book, by the Laws of the last Session, necessarily delayed the publishing of it, a considerable Time ... a great Number of my

Subscribers, who had also subscribed for the *Virginia Justice,* lately published by Mr. *Webb,* insisted on my adding some *Precedents,* adopted to the *Acts of Assembly,* which were omitted by him, which I have added at the end of the Book."[14] Mercer later explained that in organizing the entries in the *Abridgment,* he had turned to one of his law books for "the easiest and fullest Table I ever met with" to serve as the model for its table of authorities. "I was obliged to Mr. *Wingate's Abridgment of the English Statutes* for help."[15] His reference was to Edmund Wingate's *An Exact Abridgment of all the Statutes in Force and in Use from the Beginning of Magna Carta,* published in London in various impressions from 1642 to 1708.

A second suspension of Mercer's law license freed him to update the book with a slim volume Parks printed in 1739 as *A Continuation of the Abridgment of all the Public Acts of Assembly, of Virginia.* In the preface, Mercer again referred to George Webb's *Office and Authority of a Justice of Peace,* which Parks had published in Williamsburg in 1736. Those are the only surviving explicit indications that Mercer owned a copy of Webb's book, but considering the size and comprehensive nature of Mercer's library, he almost certainly obtained a copy immediately or very soon after Parks printed it.

The importance of Mercer's *Abridgement*s was in their compactness and handiness. In contrast to the folio full-text editions of the statutes at large, the *Abridgment*s were single octavo volumes that digested the acts and arrayed them alphabetically. The smaller size made them convenient traveling companions for county-court lawyers riding from courthouse to courthouse. Their main drawback, as the preface to the *Continuation* indicated, was that they were out of date almost as quickly as they came off the printing press. Full-text compilations could be supplemented after each session of the assembly with the laws it adopted. Notwithstanding that shortcoming, Mercer's *Abridgment*s made two important contributions to Virginia law and practice. The 1737 edition was the first of its species ever printed in the colony, and it provided a useful Virginia-specific tool for lawyers and laymen, who had nothing of the sort to rely on later than Robert Beverley's badly outdated *Abridgment,* printed in London in 1722.

Later, as the assembly worked to complete a wholesale revision of the colony's laws, Mercer put out a feeler by way of a notice published in the 8 August 1751 issue of the *Virginia Gazette* to discover whether an updated and corrected edition of his work would be of interest to many subscribers.[16] He did not produce a revision then, but at later times in his career when he was again suspended from practicing in the courts, he used the opportunities to follow through with his intention and compiled a new, updated edition, which he had published in Glasgow in 1759. This time, in an astute move on his part, he presented a petition to the General Assembly, which accepted it and agreed to purchase copies of his *Abridgment of the Public Acts of the Assembly of Vir-*

ginia, in Force and Use, January 1, 1758, Together with a Proper Table exclusively through him at twenty shillings a copy, to be given to all the county justices of the peace.[17] The assembly recognized the book as an important resource for local magistrates in their daily legal proceedings in the local county courts.[18] Mercer's two *Abridgment*s were major additions to the study and practice of law in the colony and to any Virginia lawyer's library. Mercer's attention to detail and to keeping his work updated is obvious. His personal copy of the 1759 Glasgow edition contains manuscript notations that he made as late as 1765 to allow him to update and correct the book. Apparently he intended to publish another updated edition, because he advertised in the *Virginia Gazette* in April 1765 that he was readying that new edition "for the press and to be independently printed," but for want of subscribers it never came to fruition.[19]

Unfortunately, neither edition of Mercer's *Abridgment* was the financial success he had hoped for. He was evidently obsessed with making his *Abridgment* as up to date as possible, causing him to delay sending the first manuscript to William Parks. That forced him to publish an advertisement in the *Virginia Gazette* to apologize to his subscribers for the delay. Mercer's first venture into the world of personal publishing proved to be a tough lesson in marketing because he and Parks overestimated the number of copies they could sell. Customarily, Parks seldom did a press run of more than five hundred copies; however, because Mercer assumed a much greater demand, he printed about fifteen hundred copies. Of these, Mercer still retained more than twelve hundred in 1751. After his death, his executor was still trying to sell the remainders of the 1737 and 1759 editions at half price.[20]

Mercer was also involved in the publication of other books as a subscriber. That is, he paid a sum in advance to reserve a copy for himself and to provide a subvention to enable the author and publisher to cover the expense of publication. On 30 October 1730 Mercer paid 13 shillings for "my subscription for the Laws of Virginia,"[21] referring to the edition of all the laws of Virginia then in force that Parks published in 1733, the first complete compilation of the laws printed in Virginia. Mercer also subscribed to the 1752 edition, which William Hunter finished for Parks's estate. Mercer's name appears on the subscriber lists of both editions. He probably also subscribed to the 1769 Rind edition and the Purdie and Dixon edition, for which they solicited subscriptions in the *Virginia Gazette* as early as 1767.[22]

Mercer also subscribed to several books unrelated to law, including the William Warburton edition of Shakespeare published in London and Dublin in 1747—10 shillings and 10 pence for "Warburton's Shakespeare subscrip."— which he ordered through his mother in Dublin.[23] Mercer subscribed to Griffith Hughes's *The Natural History of Barbadoes* (1750) and to a 1768 edition of Charles Churchill's *Poems*. The latter was once presumed to be a Williamsburg imprint, but later research supports a New York imprint.[24] Mercer probably also subscribed to the Baskerville edition of the Bible published in 1763. The subscriber list records, "From Virginia—George Mercer, Colonel, Virginia," suggesting that the son subscribed to it for the father. It is specifically listed among the books advertised in 1771 for sale from the Mercer library: "Baskerville's Royal Bible. Of the latest Edition, neatly gilt and lettered, and bound in red Morocco. Imported by a Subscriber, at six Guineas the first Cost."[25]

In addition to his contributions to Virginia legal works, Mercer has been identified as the author of several unpublished literary works, which he circulated anonymously because of the controversial or politically volatile nature of the writing. The best-known is a scathing political satire written in 1756 about Lieutenant Governor Robert Dinwiddie titled *Dinwiddianae,* composed at the time of General Edward Braddock's disastrous wilderness campaign and the resulting political backlash in the colony. A couple of lesser-known anonymous literary works published in the *Maryland Gazette* are also attributed to Mercer.[26]

As a bibliophile, Mercer stands apart from most of his contemporaries, whose libraries are known only through estate inventories that merely list the contents of a library at the time of the owner's death. Even though no full contemporary catalog of Mercer's library survives, other important documents about his library and his trade in books give a relatively complete overview of his book holdings. Mercer is that rare example of a colonial Virginian, apart from Thomas Jefferson, who left quite detailed records, papers, business accounts, and other documents from which we can learn how he built his library from the time of his entry into the legal profession to his death.

Mercer's personal and business correspondence is the most general of these sources. It consists mainly of letters to his eldest son, George, while he was lobbying for the Ohio Company at Whitehall. For the most part, their exchanges concerned the advancement of the company's interests, but they also contain family news that yields clues to Mercer's book purchases. They indicate that Mercer routed orders for books through his son, who was evidently one of his regular shoppers.[27]

Mercer also purchased books from William Parks, both while Parks operated out of Annapolis and later, after he established himself in Williamsburg. After Parks died in 1750, Mercer continued to buy from William Hunter, Parks's successor at the Williamsburg printing office, and afterward he turned to a subsequent Williamsburg printer, Joseph Royle. These sales are recorded in the two surviving *Virginia Gazette* daybooks, but the only law-book purchases noted in the daybooks are some copies of session laws that the General Assembly passed, a second edition of the *Grounds and Rudiments of Law and Equity, Alphabetically Digested,* published anonymously in London in 1751, and John Mallory's two-volume *Attorney's Pocket Companion: Or, a Guide to the Practisers of the Law* (1759).[28]

The most detailed primary documents are Mercer's two surviving business ledger books, which cover critical periods in his life. The ledger books are in the Mercer Library, Bucks County Historical Society, Doylestown, Pennsylvania. The first, Ledger Book B, spans the years 1725–31, when he was first building up his library and establishing and broadening his mercantile activities; and the second, Ledger Book G, embraces the years 1740–51, when he was well established as a merchant and lawyer in the colony. The ledgers also include much personal information about Mercer's interests and activities and a journal of travels and daily activities entered on unused pages in the back.[29] The ledgers give an excellent record of his personal loans, trades, and purchases from England, as well as references to his purchases of books from neighbors, and of his sales to neighbors and friends up and down the Potomac River basin. They also include references to books that he borrowed or lent. These ledgers provide many insights into the creation and evolution of Mercer's library, the broad range of interests on which he collected, and especially the law books he obtained for his study and practice, which made up the largest single portion of his library.

The most important item on Mercer's law books in the later period is the "Catalog of Books" in Ledger G. It fills three folio leaves with almost two hundred titles of law books, making up about half the list. Next to each title is a notation of the number of volumes, size, and price. This catalog has long been assumed to be a catalog of Mercer's personal library, but a closer examination of the list and various accounts recorded in the ledger book suggests that the catalog is a list of market stock instead of a catalog of his own law collection. The location of the catalog does not accord with the standard business practice of entering debits and credits on facing pages of a ledger book, as is the case elsewhere in the business ledgers. Furthermore, many of the enumerated books do not show up in the later compilations made when the library was put up for sale after Mercer's death. Elsewhere in Ledger G, books are counted as sale items, and a notation across the top of the page reads, "Prices are the first cost in sterling money exclusive of commission shipping or other charges." Then, too, alongside other titles initials are inscribed in the left margin. They appear to be the initials of people who borrowed those titles from the library. However, similar sets of initials appear beside the titles of many of the books that Mercer purchased directly from overseas factors or local citizens, which argues that Mercer intended them for sale too.[30]

Many of the sets of initials are difficult or impossible to identify, but Mercer's accounts with patrons whose names correlate with several of the sets of initials help verify the connection between the sets of initials and specific accounts. The easiest set of initials to identify is "G J," for Gabriel Jones, a Williamsburg-born lawyer who returned to Virginia in 1743 after studying law in England, lived and practiced in Fredericksburg for many years during this time, and later in the eighteenth century moved west to Rockingham County. He was a regular purchaser of books and other goods from Mercer until Mercer's death in 1768. One specific reference in the ledger book in February 1746 confirms that Jones bought books from Mercer and that the initials refer to him: "By Gabriel Jones for sundrys marked G J."[31] From this notation it is clear that "G J" was acquiring the law books from Mercer while developing his law practice and building up his own library. Regardless of its purpose, the catalog in Ledger G represents a major collection of law books comprising the most useful guides, manuals of practice, and reports of cases.

The other principal source is the estate-sale catalog that James Mercer published in the *Virginia Gazette* in August 1771.[32] Only two law books are enumerated there: George Turnbull's translation of Johann Heineccius's *Methodical System of Universal Law* (1741) and a multivolume set of Sir Charles Viner's *General Abridgment of Law and Equity* (1741–57).

Another important source is a transcription that a Mercer descendant, William Randolph Mercer, of Doylestown, Pennsylvania, made in 1879 from a lost catalog that James Mercer used when he drew up the auction catalog for the *Virginia Gazette* in 1771. The transcription is in three parts; one lists buyers and their purchases, another is labeled "Law Library," and the third itemizes miscellaneous domestic furnishings.[33] Among the titles were works by Matthew Bacon, Wyndham Beawes, Richard Burn, Giles Duncombe, Joseph Harrison, and James Parker and an English-language edition of Prussian law. Notably, not all the books in the "Law Library" part are associated with the name of a purchaser, which probably means that James Mercer turned to his father's library catalog as his primary source. Together, these documents indicate how John Mercer acquired his law library and what it contained.

Books that Mercer bought in the 1720s formed the foundation of the law library. The first precise reference is a 1726 entry in Ledger B of books he had lent out to his neighbor Moses Battaley. Because the titles are not noted elsewhere in Ledger B, Mercer may have recorded his acquisition of them in the now-lost Ledger A. Some of the titles included John March's *Actions of Slander and Arbitraments* (1674), Joseph Washington's *An Exact Abridgment of all the Statutes* (1708), and John Rastell's *An Exposition of Certain Difficult and Obscure Words, and Termes of Lawes* (1618).[34]

Ledger B identifies Jonathan Forward as one of the British factors who in 1730 sold Mercer a copy of an anonymous work, *Practick Part of the Law*, also popularly known by its subtitle, *Compleat Attorney* (1724). Two years later, Mercer purchased ten law books from another English factor, Mathew Stotham. That purchase, one of Mercer's largest to that date, included William Bohun's *Cursus Cancellariae* (1715), Samuel Carter's *Treatise concerning Trespasses Vi et Armis* (1705), Richard Francis's *Maxims of Equity* (1728), John Herne's *Pleader* (1658), Giles Jacob's *New Law Dictionary* (1729), John Lilly's two-volume *Practical Register: Or, an Abridgment of the Law* (1719), William Nelson's *Law of Evidence* (1717), the anonymously compiled *Law of Ejectments* (1713), and the reports of William Salkeld and Peyton Ventris. A comment at the bottom of the invoice indicates that the books by Herne, Lilly, and Nelson and the *Law of Ejectments* were "extraordinary scarce."[35]

One of the largest purchases of law books recorded in Ledger B was Mercer's acquisition of forty-four titles from Robert Beverley, of Newlands, in Spotsylvania County, in 1731. The books had probably belonged to Beverley's recently deceased father, Harry Beverley, a noted justice of the peace in that county and brother of Robert Beverley, who compiled the abridgment of Virginia laws printed in 1722. The younger Robert Beverley never held public office or practiced law, and his own estate inventory indicated that he had few law books of his own.[36] Mercer's purchase from the Beverley collection included many of the standards in English law, including Richard Brownlow's *Declarations, Counts, and Pleadings* (1654); Sir Edward Coke's *First Part of the Institutes of the Laws of England* (1719), plus Coke's "2d. 3d. & 4th Part of the Institutes" (1681), and late seventeenth-century editions of Coke's and Sir George Croke's reports, as well as Robert Gardiner's *Instructor Clericalis* (1721–27); a 1671 printing of Sir Thomas Littleton's *Tenures;* Charles Molloy's *De Maritimi et Navali* (1722); Henry Swinburne's *Briefe Treatise of Testaments and Last Wills* (1611); Thomas Wood's *Institutes of the Laws of England* (1720); and three sets of Edmund Wingate's *Exact Abridgment of all Statutes* (1708).[37] In addition to these English classics, Mercer also obtained from the Beverley estate "Laws of Virginia folio printed two, £1. 4. 0," which, judging from the date he purchased them, were probably two rare London imprints, undoubtedly John Purvis's unauthorized *Complete Collection of all the Laws of Virginia* (1684) and probably the anonymous *Acts of Assembly, Passed in the Colony of Virginia* (1727).

Beverley's library contained several titles necessary to practice in the county courts, Henry Swinburne's *Treatise of Testaments and Last Wills,* and a 1727 edition of Michael Dalton's *Countrey Justice,* one of the standard manuals for justices of the peace. Mercer may have desired a new copy of Dalton's *Countrey Justice* to replace his own copy, which he had lent to Peter Hedgman.[38] Of equal or greater importance was a large manuscript set of acts of assembly. It was the most expensive item in the Beverley horde. Mercer listed it as "Written Laws of Virginia £25.0.0."[39] In the days before easy local access to printing presses, the secretary of the colony, the clerks in the county courts, justices of the peace, and lawyers maintained files of manuscript statutes that they updated after each session of the General Assembly. Indeed, private ownership of statutes was prevalent among men like Mercer because the files of the secretary of the colony were available only in the capital, and files that county clerks compiled could easily be incomplete. Men frequently bought and sold manuscript copies of the colony's laws. In fact, Mercer sold his set (or probably a copy of the set) to the newly created Prince William County Court in June 1731 for five thousand pounds of tobacco, or about £25. If Jefferson had not noted on one of his manuscript sets of Virginia laws that "he copied from Mercer's MS," we would not know that Mercer retained a manuscript set.[40]

The best-known example of a Virginian who collected sets of manuscript laws is Thomas Jefferson, who acquired the largest number from sales of libraries like those of Peyton Randolph, Richard Bland, John Page, and others. Jefferson's set of manuscript laws also became one of the bases for William Waller Hening's monumental thirteen-volume edition of the *Statutes at Large: Being a Collection of all the Laws of Virginia* (1809–23), which to this day remains vital to any study of the early Virginia legal order.[41]

While Mercer was collecting law books, he was also selling or lending books to his neighbors. In 1731 Mercer sold his partner George Mason a set of five law books that included Richard Brownlow's *Declarations in English* (1652–54), Robert Gardiner's *1, 2, & 3 Instructor Clericalis* (1721–27), John Rastell's *Les Termes de la Ley* (1721), Edmund Wingate's *Abridgment of Statutes* (1708), and a *Compleat Attorney* (1724). The lot cost Mason £2 3s., a price suggesting that Mercer may no longer have needed them.[42] He may have lent some of the law books he acquired from the Beverley estate to Daniel Dulany, of Maryland. Mercer appears to have been quite generous in lending books, which was a common practice among Virginia planters, who regularly borrowed or lent books to their family, friends, and neighbors. For instance, Landon Carter, at Sabine Hall, received letters from his son-in-law, Ralph Wormeley, of Rosegill, requesting books not in his library, and a look at the various volumes extant in his library reveals that the squire of Sabine Hall was also a frequent borrower of books but that he did not always return them. Robert Carter, of Nomini Hall, Landon Carter's nephew and himself the owner of one of the largest postcolonial libraries in Virginia, often requested from neighbors and family books he could not find to purchase. He even borrowed volumes from the Governor's Council Library in Williamsburg, which he kept for fifteen years before returning them.[43]

Soon after Mercer's death, his frustrated son and executor, James Mercer, estimated that about four hundred of his father's books were missing because they had been loaned. He published an advertisement that "borrowers are hereby requested to return them" before 19 December 1768, "the day appointed for the appraising of the estate."[44] The executor published a second request in 1771. Some multivolume sets, he announced, "want so many Volumes as to make those on Hand unvaluable. It is hoped that common Honesty will persuade those who have them to return them by the Day of the Sale." The executor also cautioned that John Mercer's personal books bore his bookplate and therefore "may be known by my Father's Arms. The Crest a Greyhound's

Head, the Motto *per varios Casus* [i.e., "Please be patient"].[45] Just how many of the borrowed books he recovered remains a mystery.

Estimating the size of John Mercer's library is difficult not only because of the limitations of the data but also because the collection was never static. Mercer bought books, sold books, lent books, and got rid of obsolete books. The number of books in his collection was constantly changing. Estimates vary from a low of about twelve hundred to a high of eighteen hundred. In his 15 December 1768 advertisement in the *Virginia Gazette* James Mercer declared that "of more than 1200 volumes now at home, with which it is hoped may be reckoned upwards of 400 volumes which appear to be missing by the said Mercer's catalogue; as he never sold any, those wanting, are supposed to be lent out." James Mercer's figures excluded an unstated number of volumes "reserved for the use of his children."[46]

James Mercer's 1768 list of his father's library was probably based on John Mercer's original manuscript catalog, not a catalog printed for the estate sale. On 29 August 1771 Alexander Purdie and John Dixon announced in their *Virginia Gazette* the availability of a printed catalog of unsold volumes.[47] Careful examination of all the documents concerning John Mercer's books indicates that his library probably included at least 1,800 volumes and more than 950 titles. Of those, about 460 were law books.[48]

A systematic businessman, John Mercer organized his stock of books for sale by categories, and it is very likely that he organized his personal collection of law books in the same way. In Ledger G the stock of books for sale was broken down as "Miscellanies, Parliament, Readings, Reports, Sheriffs, Statutes, Tables, Abridgments, Conveyancing, Courts & Courtkeeping, Crown, Dictionaries, Entries, Justice of Peace, Maxims, Tithes & Laws of the Clergy, Will's Excrs &c. and Writs."[49]

John Mercer's great library fell victim to a familiar fate. Mercer died heavily in debt as a consequence of numerous failed business enterprises, bad investments, and his own inability to collect debts owed to him. That compelled his son and executor to round up all the remaining assets and sell them to pay off all the estate's obligations. Besides the family silver and a thoroughbred race horse, the primary assets included the books, which James Mercer proceeded to sell in a series of auctions from 1768 to 1771. The William Randolph Mercer transcription indicates how the books were disposed of and who bought some of them. The first section of the manuscript lists 116 titles in 168 volumes, plus 164 copies of the first edition of Mercer's *Abridgment* and 213 copies of the second edition. The second section accounted for 79 titles in 151 volumes from the "Law Library of Jno. Mercer of Marboro."

Surprisingly, considering the size of Mercer's library, few of his books have been found. The Gunston Hall library at Mason Neck, Virginia, where Mercer's celebrated nephew George Mason resided, owns Mercer's set of John

Houghton's *Husbandry* (1727–28). The Virginia Historical Society, in Richmond, owns his copy of the Duke of Buckingham's *Works of John Sheffield* (1752). The John D. Rockefeller Jr. Library at the Colonial Williamsburg Foundation owns several of Mercer's volumes of the *London Magazine,* published between 1732 and 1755, and his copy of Patrick Gordon's *Geography Anatomiz'd* (1741). The Valentine Richmond History Center, in Richmond, Virginia, holds several volumes of his collection of *Works of the Learned* (1739–43). Gabriel Jones purchased the five sets from Mercer's estate, all of them bearing Mercer's bookplate. The Albert J. and Shirley Small Library at the University of Virginia has Mercer's copy of Edward Moore's *The World* (1755–57) and a couple of volumes of Giovanni Marana's *Letters Writ by a Turkish Spy* (1753), which James Mercer kept. It also holds Geronimo de Uztariz's *Theory and Practice of Commerce and Maritime Affairs,* translated by John Kippax (1751), Mercer's octavo set of *An Universal History,* published in London in 1747–68, which his son-in-law Muscoe Garnett later owned, and the 1719 edition of Sir Edward Coke's *First Part of the Institutes of the Laws of England,* which Mercer probably purchased from the Beverley estate and later presented to his nephew George Mason. Mercer's marked-up copy of the 1759 edition of his *Abridgment* and two volumes of John Rushworth's *Historical Collections of Private Passages of State* (1721–22), which St. George Tucker subsequently acquired, belong to the Earl Gregg Swem Library at the College of William and Mary. The John Carter Brown Library, at Brown University, in Providence, Rhode Island, owns Mercer's copy of the 1727 edition of *The Complete Collection of the Laws of Maryland.* The Clements Library, at the University of Michigan, owns Cadwallader Colden's *History of the Five Indian Nations of Canada* (1755), previously owned by Hugh Mercer. Another of Mercer's books is recorded in a nineteenth-century auction catalog, the Wynne Catalog of 1880, which lists Edward Burt's *Letters from a Gentleman in the North of Scotland* (1759), which later belonged to Gabriel Jones.

John Mercer's library was not as large as the libraries of William Byrd of Westover or Thomas Jefferson of Monticello, but it was one of the largest and most diverse in eighteenth-century Virginia. The approximately eighteen hundred volumes made it larger than the libraries of any other of his contemporaries, and his collection of law books was probably larger and more distinguished than that of any other private library in colonial Virginia.

NOTES

1. *Virginia Gazette* (Rind), 27 Oct. 1768.
2. Louis Mulkearn, ed., *George Mercer Papers, relating to the Ohio Company of Virginia* (Pittsburgh, 1954), 204–5; Pamela C. Copeland and Richard K. MacMaster, *The Five George Masons: Patriots and Planters of Virginia and Maryland* (Charlottesville, 1975),

72; J. A. Leo LeMay, "John Mercer," in *American National Biography*, ed. John A. Garraty and Mark C. Carnes, 24 vols. (New York, 1999), 15:325–27.
3. C. Malcolm Watkins, *The Cultural History of Marlborough, Virginia* (Washington, DC, 1968), 5–14; "Petition of John Mercer," *Virginia Magazine of History and Biography* 5 (1898): 278–82; John Pendleton Kennedy and H. R. McIlwaine, eds., *Journals of the House of Burgesses of Virginia, 1619–1776*, 13 unnumbered vols. (Richmond, 1905–15), *1742–1747, 1748–1749*, 286–89.
4. Copeland and MacMaster, *Five George Masons*, chaps. 3–4; George H. S. King, "Notes from the Journal of John Mercer, Esquire (1704–1768), of Marlborough, Stafford County, Virginia," *Virginia Genealogist* 4 (1960): 99–102; *The Papers of George Mason*, ed. Robert A. Rutland, 3 vols. (Chapel Hill, NC, 1970), 1:3–10; LeMay, "John Mercer"; Brent Tarter, "George Mason," in Garraty and Carnes, *American National Biography*, 14:645–47.
5. Edmund Randolph, *History of Virginia*, ed. Arthur H. Shaffer (Charlottesville, 1970), 193.
6. J. A. Leo Lemay, "John Mercer and the Stamp Act in Virginia, 1764–1765," *Virginia Magazine of History and Biography* 91 (1983): 3–38, esp. 25; Mulkearn, *George Mercer Papers*, 186; Douglas Southall Freeman, *George Washington: A Biography*, 7 vols. (New York, 1948–57), 3:146–51.
7. On the distinction between the two as they were understood at the time, see Giles Jacob, *A New Law Dictionary: Containing, the Interpretation and Definition used in the Law* ... (London, 1739), s.vv. "attorney" and "lawyer." See also Warren M. Billings, "'Send Us ... what other Lawe books you shall thinke fitt': Books That Shaped the Law in Virginia, 1600–1860," *Virginia Magazine of History and Biography* 120 (2012): 316.
8. Kennedy and McIlwaine, *Journals of the House of Burgesses, 1727–1740*, 66, 70, 71.
9. H. R. McIlwaine, Wilmer L. Hall, and Benjamin L. Hillman, eds., *Executive Journals of the Council of Colonial Virginia*, 6 vols. (Richmond, 1925–66), 4:318, 328, 348; 5:269, 419, 484; 6:17, 42–43, 50, 120.
10. Lawrence C. Wroth, *A History of Printing in Colonial Maryland, 1686–1776* (Baltimore, 1922), 59–63. Earlier compilations of Maryland statutes had been published in London, Philadelphia, and Annapolis, for which see Early State Records Online, accessed 25 July 2014, msa.maryland.gov/megafile/msa/speccol/sc4800/sc4872/html/codes.html.
11. John Mercer, Ledger B, leaf [42], Mercer Library, Bucks County Historical Society, Doylestown, PA.
12. Mercer's copy is in the John Carter Brown Library, Brown University.
13. McIlwaine, Hall, and Hillman, *Executive Journal of the Council of Colonial Virginia*, 4:348.
14. John Mercer, *An Exact Abridgment of all the Public Acts of Assembly, of Virginia, In Force and Use. Together with Sundry Precedents, adapted thereto. And Proper Tables* (Williamsburg, 1737), vii–viii.
15. John Mercer, *Continuation of the Abridgment of all the Public Acts of Assembly, of Virginia* (Williamsburg, 1739), iii.

16. *Virginia Gazette* (Hunter), 8 Aug. 1751, 20 Feb. 1752.
17. The American Antiquarian Society Library owns a copy of Mercer's 1759 *Abridgment* that was owned by John Morton, who was appointed justice of the peace in Prince Edward County in 1759. It includes an inscription, "Gift of the Assembly."
18. Kennedy and McIlwaine, *Journals of the House of Burgesses, 1758–1761*, 136–39, 147; H. R. McIlwaine, ed., *Legislative Journals of the Council of Colonial Virginia*, 2d ed., rev. (Richmond, 1979), 1225, 1229.
19. Mercer's copy is in the Earl Gregg Swem Library, College of William and Mary; *Virginia Gazette* (Royle), 25 Oct. 1765 (supplement).
20. McIlwaine, Hall, and Hillman, *Executive Journals of the Council of Colonial Virginia*, 5:434; *Virginia Gazette*, 25 Feb. 1737, 14 July 1738; *Virginia Gazette* (Hunter), 8 Aug. 1751; *Virginia Gazette* (Purdie and Dixon), 13 June 1771; Lawrence C. Wroth, *William Parks Printer & Journalist of England & America* (Richmond, 1926), 66.
21. Mercer, Ledger B, leaf [42], Mercer Library.
22. *Virginia Gazette* (Purdie and Dixon), 3–17 Sept. 1767.
23. Mercer, Ledger G, leaf [203], Mercer Library.
24. Susan Stromei Berg, *Eighteenth-Century Williamsburg Imprints* (New York, 1986), no. 181; Roger Pattrell Bristol, *Supplement to Charles Evans American Bibliography and Index* (Charlottesville, 1970), no. B2911.
25. *Virginia Gazette* (Purdie and Dixon), 29 Aug. 1771.
26. Richard Beale Davis, "The Colonial Virginia Satirist: Mid-Century Commentaries on Politics, Religion, and Society," *Proceedings of the American Philosophical Society* 57, pt. 1 (1967); J. A. Leo Lemay, *A Calendar of American Poetry in the Colonial Newspapers and Magazines and in the Major English Magazines through 1765* (Worcester, MA, 1972), nos. 1202, 1381.
27. Mulkearn, *George Mercer Papers*, 216–19.
28. Joseph Royle, *Virginia Gazette* Daybook, leaves [33], [51], [183], Albert J. and Shirley Small Library, University of Virginia.
29. There are two major references on the personal and social aspects of Mercer's other material found in the ledger books. See King, "Notes from the Journal of John Mercer," 99–110, 152–62; and Sarah P. Stetson, "John Mercer's Notes on Plants," *Virginia Magazine of History and Biography* 61 (1953): 34–44.
30. Mercer, Ledger G, leaves [202–9], Mercer Library.
31. Ibid., leaf [203]. One recently discovered example is a law book that Gabriel Jones purchased through Mercer's business ledgers: *Baron and Feme, A Treatise of Law and Equity*, 3d ed. (London, 1738), which is owned by the Law Library of Congress—the only surviving example of a law book in Mercer's sale catalog that has been identified. Mercer, Ledger G, leaf [200], Mercer Library.
32. *Virginia Gazette* (Purdie and Dixon), 28 Aug. 1771.
33. In the Robert Alonzo Brock Collection, Huntington Library and Garden, Special Collections, San Marino, Cal.; see William Randolph Mercer to Robert Alonzo Brock, 4 May 1879, ibid.
34. The dates given for the books are not necessarily for the first editions but for the editions probably owned by Mercer, based on when he acquired them and on the de-

scription, size, number of volumes, and price of each title. The primary sources for identifying the English and American titles are taken from the *Eighteenth-Century Short Title Catalog (ESTC),* an electronic Internet catalog; and from John Worrall's *Bibliotheca Legum* (London, 1777), a copy of which (probably the 1746 edition) was listed in Mercer's library. Any other titles are identified through *OCLC* (Online Computer Library Center), an electronic Internet catalog.

35. Mercer, Ledger B, leaves [86], [98], Mercer Library.
36. William G. Stanard, "Major Robert Beverley and His Descendants," *Virginia Magazine of History and Biography* 3 (1896): 388–91.
37. Mercer, Ledger B, leaf [243], Mercer Library. The edition of Coke's *First Part of the Institutes of the Laws of England* cited in this account is probably the 1719 London edition that Mercer inscribed and gave to George Mason and that is now in the Small Library, University of Virginia.
38. Mercer, Ledger B, leaf [243], Mercer Library.
39. Ibid.
40. Ibid., leaf [123]; E. Millicent Sowerby, *Catalogue of the Library of Thomas Jefferson,* 5 vols. (Washington, DC, 1952–59), 2:241–42, no. 1826.
41. Sowerby, *Library of Thomas Jefferson,* 2:255–61, no. 1863.
42. Mercer, Ledger B, leaf [114], Mercer Library.
43. Ralph Wormeley to Landon Carter, 6 May 1771, Carter Papers, Small Library, University of Virginia. For other Sabine Hall examples, see Bennie Brown, "The Library of the Carters at Sabine Hall in Richmond County, Virginia," typescript (Williamsburg, 2014); and Robert Carter to Mr. Rose, 22 Apr. 1776, Carter to John J. Maund, 10 Dec. 1792, and Carter to James Gordon, 29 July 1778, all in Carter Papers, David M. Rubenstein Library, Rare Books and Manuscript Library, Duke University. For other Nomini Hall examples, see Bennie Brown, "The Library of Robert Carter of Nomini Hall, Westmoreland County, Virginia and Baltimore, Maryland," typescript (Williamsburg, 2009); and John R. Barden, "Reflections of a Singular Mind: The Library of Robert Carter of Nomini Hall," *Virginia Magazine of History and Biography* 96 (1988): 85.
44. *Virginia Gazette* (Rind), 15 Dec. 1768.
45. Ibid. (Purdie and Dixon), 29 Aug. 1771.
46. Ibid. (Rind), 15 Dec. 1768.
47. Ibid. (Purdie and Dixon), 29 Aug. 1771.
48. Bennie Brown, "The Book World of John Mercer of Marlborough: The Library collected by Mercer, and the Records of the Book Trade conducted by Him in Eighteenth-Century Virginia, 1720–1768," typescript (Williamsburg, 2010).
49. Mercer, Ledger G, leaves [200–202].

THE LIBRARY REVEALS THE MAN

GEORGE WYTHE, LEGAL AND CLASSICAL SCHOLAR

Linda K. Tesar

George Wythe owned a large and varied library and used his books in his work as law professor and judge. Bookplate of George Wythe. (Courtesy Earl Gregg Swem Library, College of William and Mary)

A LOVE OF READING AND LEARNing dominated the life of George Wythe. Benjamin B. Minor, the editor of the second edition of Wythe's case reports, wrote, "His learning was extensive both in his profession, and in general science and literature.... Not only was the father of poetry his intimate companion, but the philosophers, historians, and even dramatic poets of antiquity were as familiar to him in their original dress as were almost all of the meritorious works of the day in his vernacular tongue."[1] Stories come down to us of the young Wythe sitting at his mother's side learning to read the New Testament in Greek and Latin.[2] As an adult Wythe spent endless hours immersed in science, mathematics, literature, philosophy, Greek and Roman classics, and, of course, law. In describing Wythe's judicial decisions, one biographer wrote: "In the eight pages of one opinion, with its footnotes, Bracton and Justinian, Juvenal's *Satires,* and Quintilian, Euclid, Archimedes and Hiero, hydrostatic experiments and *Coke on Littleton, Tristam Shandy* and Petronius, Halley and Price and Prometheus, Don Quixote and Swift's *Tale of a Tub,* Locke's *Essay on Human Understanding,* and Turkish travellers, chase one another up and down to the bewilderment of all but the universal scholar."[3]

The books in Wythe's library deeply influenced every sphere of his life. His use of them and the very composition of his library set apart the man who owned them. Books dominated Wythe's political and legal careers. He used many sources as inspiration during the Revolution and quoted texts extensively in cases as a lawyer and in decisions as a judge. Although he had no children of his own, Wythe shared his passion for learning with younger generations, employing young gentlemen as his legal apprentices, teaching them in his capacity as a law professor, or serving as a Greek and Latin tutor. By the end of his life Wythe had acquired a substantial library that in some subjects rivaled the more renowned libraries of his Virginia peers. Unfortunately, Thomas Jefferson dispersed the contents of that library after Wythe's death, and fewer than one hundred volumes still exist. Recent scholarship has helped to identify the missing volumes and at last permits a detailed comparison with other eighteenth-century collections. Still, a library is a personal creation that both mirrors and molds the mind of its owner. Wythe's collection both reflected and shaped the unique qualities of the man himself.

At the outset, note should be made regarding the methodology for determining the contents of Wythe's collection and the sources for identifying specific volumes. Any catalog of his books that Wythe may have compiled has long since disappeared. The inventory that his executor, William DuVal, made following Wythe's death is lost.[4] In his will, Wythe bequeathed his books to his friend and former student Thomas Jefferson. Fortunately, a long-lost list in which Jefferson noted how he distributed the volumes resurfaced in 2008.[5] Regrettably, much like other library catalogs of the time, Jefferson's is inexact; in many cases it provides only vague clues about specific titles, and too frequently gives insufficient information to pinpoint precise editions.

Even before the discovery of the Jefferson inventory, researchers pondered the contents of Wythe's library and compiled bibliographies, the earliest being the one Mary R. M. Goodwin created in 1958 as part of her book *The George Wythe House: Its Furniture and Furnishings*.[6] She relied on knowledge of surviving volumes and order records from John Norton and Sons in London and the *Virginia Gazette* office in Williamsburg. In the 1970s, Barbara C. Dean expanded on Goodwin's work in a bibliographical research memorandum for the Colonial Williamsburg Foundation.[7] Dean used the commonplace books of Wythe's students, particularly those of Jefferson and John Marshall, to broaden the catalog of potential titles. After the discovery of the Jefferson inventory, Jeremy Dibbell, a librarian at the Massachusetts Historical Society, researched each entry and compiled a bibliography of Wythe's book collection, which he posted at LibraryThing.com in the group of legacy libraries.[8] At approximately the same time, Bennie Brown, an independent scholar and cataloger at The Book Press, Ltd., in Williamsburg, Virginia, began circulating his unpublished bibliography, "The Library of George Wythe of Williamsburg and Richmond."[9] Brown's bibliography contributed a few more highly significant sources from Wythe's references in his case reports and the works Wythe cited in a published rendition of *Bolling v. Bolling*, a case in which he and Jefferson served as opposing counsel.[10]

By combining these sources, a catalog of approximately 490 titles emerges, some conclusively proven, others less certain. No doubt Wythe owned many titles not included in any of the bibliographies. Wythe definitely lost items to theft and loans, and other circumstances may have whittled down the size of his collection. Without additional documentation, a truly definitive compilation of the contents of Wythe's library eludes us.[11]

Wythe was born in late 1726 or early 1727 and developed a love of books when he was growing up at the family home, Chesterville, in Elizabeth City County, Virginia.[12] The death of his father left his mother to guide his education, which may have included Greek and Latin lessons at home and grammar-school attendance at the College of William and Mary.[13] Sometime in the 1740s, Wythe moved to the vicinity of Petersburg to live with his uncle Stephen Dewey and serve as Dewey's legal apprentice. While Wythe later described the years there as drudgery, at the very least he would have had the opportunity to study the books of legal history and practice in Dewey's library.[14] Within four years of beginning his apprenticeship, Wythe qualified to practice law in 1746.[15]

Blessed with influential connections, the young lawyer embarked on a successful career in law and public service.[16] By the time of the Revolution, Wythe was a respected leader in Virginia, having served as acting attorney general of the colony twice and as the last clerk of the House of Burgesses. He had also contributed to the education of a number of young attorneys, including his most famous apprentice, Thomas Jefferson, as well as the future William and Mary law professor St. George Tucker and James Madison, the first Episcopal bishop of Virginia.

Wythe was a busy man throughout the years of the Revolution and the early republic. In addition to being a signer of the Declaration of Independence, he was a member of the committee that recodified Virginia's laws, a delegate to the Constitutional Convention of 1787 in Philadelphia, and chair of the committee of the whole in the Virginia Convention of 1788, which ratified the Constitution.[17] During those years, he also assumed the two roles for which he is most remembered, chancery judge in 1778 and law professor in 1779.[18] Wythe relinquished the professorship when he and his court moved to Richmond in 1789. He remained on the bench until his death.[19]

All the while, Wythe steadily added to his library. During the colonial years he sent frequent orders to John Norton and Sons in London and made occasional purchases at the Williamsburg office of the *Virginia Gazette*. Norton and Sons furnished case reports, venerated treatises of English legal history, and a few classical works in Greek. Wythe wrote at least four times requesting editions of the journals of the House of Commons.[20] The daybooks of the *Virginia Gazette* office also record a few purchases, among them "Franklin's Pamphlet,"[21] possibly Benjamin Franklin's *Cool Thoughts* or more likely his *The Interest of Great Britain Considered,* and Robert Nelson's *A Companion for the Festivals and Fasts of the Church of England*. In addition, Wythe's positions as a member and also clerk of the House of Burgesses would have given him ready access to session laws and the printed statutes of the colony. Wythe may have acquired a set for his personal library. He asked Norton and Sons to furnish him duplicate sets if his purchase could "be not made public."[22]

Wythe's popularity also contributed to the enlargement of his library. He received many books either as gifts or as purchases on his behalf. John Adams inscribed a copy of his influential 1776 pamphlet *Thoughts on Government Applicable to the Present State of the American Colonies* "From John Adams to George Wythe."[23] Similarly, Thomas Lee Shippen presented him with Hugh Blair's *Lectures on Rhetoric and Belles Lettres* inscribed, "For the Honorable George Wythe Esquire from his most affectionate friend and obliged humble servant Thomas Lee Shippen."[24] Daniel Call dedicated his edition of case reports to Wythe and gave him a copy inscribed, "From the Author, with the most affectionate regard and the profoundest respect, to the Honorable George Wythe Esquire."[25] While Thomas Jefferson was serving as minister to France, he searched the bookstalls of Europe and sent his mentor numerous books, among them *Code de l'Humanité,* by Fortuné Barthélemy de Félice, and his own *Notes on the State of Virginia.*[26]

By such means, Wythe amassed a library estimated at his death to be worth approximately £500.[27] Typical Virginia lawyers possessed more modest collections, such as those of Clement Read, clerk of Lunenburg County, and Henry Churchill, a Fauquier County attorney, which were assessed at £25 and £89, respectively. The average value of a county attorney's library in the eighteenth century was approximately £10.[28] Only lawyers who practiced in the General Court or wealthy planters would have maintained collections to rival Wythe's. For example, the library of Philip Ludwell was appraised at £250 in 1716, as was Peyton Randolph's in 1776.[29] One of the largest collections of the time, the 4,000 volumes owned by William Byrd II, of Westover, sold for £2,000 in 1777.[30] These examples suggest that the approximately 650 volumes Wythe bequeathed to Jefferson in 1806 constituted one of the more valuable eighteenth-century collections in Virginia.[31]

Until recently the bibliographic history of Wythe's library was so scant that comparing the library with others of the day was almost impossible. That is no longer the case. Even though our knowledge of his collection remains incomplete, we can now evaluate it in the light of what is known about the libraries of colonial attorneys in Virginia. The benchmark for comparison is W. Hamilton Bryson's 1978 *Census of Law Books in Colonial Virginia,* which Bryson compiled to "shed some light on the law which shaped the lawyers who shaped the nation."[32] Bryson's *Census* includes 612 titles, some of which are duplicates resulting from incomplete bibliographic citations in his sources. Of the works listed, 50 represent legislative material from England, Virginia, or other jurisdictions, such as Barbados, Maryland, or Scotland. Wythe may have owned none of the legislative records of other British colonies, but he probably owned most or all of the Virginia titles. His library also contained such copies of the *Journals of the House of Commons* that he was able to obtain from John Norton and Sons and probably one of the many versions of the British statutes at large. Wythe cited specific statutes in his second argument for the plaintiff in *Bolling v. Bolling,* but it is possible that he used a copy owned by someone else.[33] He also owned the *History and Proceedings of the House of Commons* and the *History and Proceedings of the House of Lords.*

Wythe probably owned only a few of the Continental works Bryson identified. We have evidence for seven of the thirty-six titles Bryson listed. Unsurprisingly, the Wythe library contained copies of most of the major works, such as George Harris's translation of *The Four Books of Justinian's Institutes,* Arnoldus Vinnius's *Institutes* in Latin, both Samuel von Pufendorf's

De Officio Hominis et Civis Juxta Legem and his *Of the Law of Nature and Nations,* a copy of *Corpus Juris Civilis,* and at least one work by Hugo Grotius, most likely *The Rights of War and Peace.* Notably missing from any compilation of Wythe's books (although perhaps not from his library) is *The Law of Nations,* the eighteenth-century classic by Emmerich de Vattel on the rights and obligations of citizens and states.

Bryson's *Census* recorded 399 legal treatises, the scholarly secondary sources that thoroughly addressed particular aspects of the law.[34] Wythe definitely owned at least 63 (16 percent) of all the treatises identified in the colony's private libraries, more than Bryson found in most of them. While Wythe's library does not appear to have included an exceptional number of treatises, he owned the most historically important titles, such as Ranulf de Glanville's *Tractatus de Legibus et Consuetudinibus Regni Angliae* (the earliest treatise on English law), Sir Robert Brooke's *La Graunde Abridgment,* Henry de Bracton's *De Legibus et Consuetudinbus Angliae,* and Sir Thomas Littleton's *Tenures.* He supplemented them with Sir Matthew Hale's *Historia Placitorum Coronae: The History of the Pleas of the Crown,* all four of Sir Edward Coke's *Institutes of the Lawes of England,* and when or soon after it came out in the 1760s, Sir William Blackstone's *Commentaries on the Laws of England.* Notably, while others of Wythe's generation purchased practical manuals in sizable quantities,[35] Wythe evidently acquired but few of the popular manuals for clerks and officials that dominate Bryson's *Census.* Notable exceptions that Wythe owned included William Brown's *Modus Intrandi Placita Generalia: The Entering Clerk's Introduction* and Michael Dalton's *Officium Vicecomitum: The Office and Authority of Sheriffs.*

Reports of cases represent by far the section of Bryson's compilation with the largest number of corresponding titles in Wythe's library. The chancellor may have owned as many as 61, nearly half of the 127 published reports of cases Bryson identified in the colony's private libraries, but he also owned 7 of the 11 other titles for which Bryson found no specific documentation.[36] These included Henry Blackstone's *Reports of Cases Argued and Determined in the Courts of Common Pleas and Exchequer Chamber* and Sir Michael Foster's *A Report of Some Proceedings on the Commission of Oyer and Terminer and ... of Other Crown Cases.* Although not the largest known collection of case reports in colonial Virginia, Wythe's collection, as far as it can be documented, was probably one of the best.

A comparison of the reporters in the Wythe library with those on Bryson's *Census* illustrates some of the differences between Wythe's collection and those of his contemporaries. John Mercer owned 97 copies of case reports, and William Byrd II owned 33,[37] but the average number of reports drops from 26 to 20 if Mercer's list of books is excluded. Wythe owned 70 copies of reports and 8 abridgments, not including 12 American reports published after the Revolution. Analyzing the titles Wythe may not have owned reveals that he probably preferred to purchase unabridged versions of reports and had limited interest in adding trial reports to his library. Some of the other reports missing from the catalogs of Wythe's books were among those least respected. For example, several of the lawyers, including John Mercer and Dabney Carr, owned John Fitzgibbons's *Reports,* yet John G. Marvin, a highly regarded nineteenth-century American legal bibliographer, wrote of Fitzgibbons's volume that "most of the cases ... are said to be incorrectly reported, and of no authority." Similarly, the reports of Sir Thomas Hetley were never "esteemed official," and William Murray, Lord Mansfield, forbade counsel ever to cite Thomas Barnardiston's chancery reports.[38]

A quick survey of the volumes of case reports owned by Wythe shows that the chancellor held Bartholomew Showers's *Cases in Parliament,* 15 different chancery reports, 22 reports of cases from the King's Bench, 6 Common Pleas reports, 2 Exchequer reports, and the works of 24 reporters covering multiple courts. Eight sets of abridgments and 12 other titles reporting cases in post-Revolutionary Virginia and other parts of the new nation rounded out this section of Wythe's library, for a total of 90 known titles.[39] Wythe owned books in English, law French,[40] and Latin, including different editions of some of the same reports, as in the case of Edmund Plowden's *Commentaries or Reports.* Wythe owned both the English version, *The Commentaries, or Reports of Edmund Plowden,* and *Les Commentaries, ou Reportes de Edmunde Plowden,* in law French. The Library of Congress has a copy of the English version believed to include Wythe's own manuscript notes and a copy of *Les Commentaries* that contains his bookplate. Wythe's library included highly respected reports, such as *The Reports of Sir Peyton Ventris* and George Andrews's *Reports of Cases Argued and Adjudged in the Court of King's Bench,* as well as reports that enjoyed a less stellar reputation, like John Latch's *Plusieurs Tres-Bons Cases* and *The Reports of Edward Bulstrode.*

Another useful study against which to measure Wythe's library and those of his contemporaries is Herbert A. Johnson's *Imported Eighteenth-Century Law Treatises in American Libraries, 1700–1799.* Johnson canvassed twenty-two libraries, including those of John Adams, William Byrd of Westover, Robert "King" Carter, John Jay, Thomas Jefferson, John Mercer, and St. George Tucker. Johnson limited the scope of his bibliography to treatises. He specifically excluded "works on political science or theory, philosophical tracts (except jurisprudence), and historical works not identifiable as legal history."[41] These choices eliminate numerous volumes from Wythe's library, namely, the case reports, histories, science books, literature, and the majority of his Greek and Roman titles.

From what we know, Wythe's library included approximately one-fifth of the 212 titles Johnson listed in two or more of the libraries he analyzed. Using Johnson's appendix A to break those titles out by subject provides a revealing glimpse of Wythe's choices for his collection. Much like his contemporaries, Wythe possessed several of the general abridgments, including Charles Viner's mammoth *A General Abridgement of Law and Equity*, Knightley D'Anvers's *A General Abridgment of the Common Law,* and Matthew Bacon's *A New Abridgment of the Law.* He also owned Bacon's *A General Abridgment of Cases in Equity.* While Wythe owned case abridgments and general abridgments, no evidence suggests that he held any of the statute abridgments that Johnson identified.

Wythe acquired four of the eight titles Johnson listed under commentaries and institutes, one or two of each type of practice manual (with one notable exception), one law dictionary, and one formulary. Perhaps most surprisingly given his position on the High Court of Chancery, the available evidence suggests that Wythe apparently owned no manuals of chancery practice. He did possess many of the more commonly held treatises, particularly in the areas of criminal law, natural law, and personal property. Thus, comparison with both Johnson's and Bryson's surveys confirms that Wythe held many of the same titles found in other eighteenth-century private libraries. But his library did not include a majority of the titles on Johnson's list, nor was it exhaustive in any one area. Wythe collected items from many fields of the law, but there are at least two glaring holes. He seems not to have owned a single work specifically devoted to maritime law, nor does he appear to have owned such popular works as Giles Jacob's *Every Man His Own Lawyer* or George Webb's 1736 *Office and Authority of a Justice of Peace,* the first legal reference work compiled and published in Virginia for Virginians.[42]

The legal portion of Wythe's library contained 123 titles of primary materials, including 81 case reporters, 8 abridgments, 10 legislative journals or reports, and 24 full-text compilations of statutes or individual session laws, as well as 89 treatises and legal dictionaries. These numbers suggest that Wythe's law library approached Mercer's in total number of volumes but was far smaller than the very large collection that Byrd assembled.

There is no doubt that Wythe's large, varied collection served him well as a lawyer and judge. Indeed, his familiarity with the works of multiple reporters and legal treatises peppers his arguments in *Bolling v. Bolling*[43] and flavors every case in his own published reports. But perhaps the primary reason for the size and breadth of this section of Wythe's library derived from his role as a teacher and his desire to provide his students with the broadest education that it was within his power to impart. If so, Wythe's efforts proved highly successful. For example, John Marshall managed to compile notations from at least thirty-five different case reports, four abridgments, and thirteen legal treatises in his three short months as Wythe's student.[44] Nevertheless, law books made up only 42 percent of the books known to have been in Wythe's library, which means that fewer than half of the titles that he owned directly related to his work as a teacher, lawyer, or judge. Yet, Wythe's knowledge was expansive, and he found ways to incorporate much from the other parts of his library into every aspect of his legal, political, and teaching careers.

The nonlegal subjects in Wythe's library actually provide a more illuminating commentary on the man and his thinking. One method of exploring this portion of his library is to compare it with George K. Smart's pioneering study "Private Libraries in Colonial Virginia," published in *American Literature* in 1938. Smart scoured library inventories published in early issues of the *William and Mary Quarterly* and the *Virginia Magazine of History and Biography* to locate the records of more than one hundred private libraries from seventeenth- and eighteenth-century Virginia. He noted the sizes of the various collections and identified popular titles.[45] There were no details about some libraries—no titles at all were given for about a quarter of them—but the contents of more than forty were completely or nearly completely enumerated. Smart discovered detailed information for 3,500 titles and partial entries for 5,000 more. Despite his findings, Smart's study limits our ability to go into the same depth as Bryson or Johnson because it includes no comprehensive list of titles, only broad categories.

Smart's conclusions were admittedly tentative, but his work enables an examination of the totality of Wythe's library in the context of his time. Smart analyzed both the entire group of libraries and particular characteristic collections. He divided the collections into seven categories: philosophy and law; science and practical arts; classics and languages; history, biography, and travel; religion; English literature; and doubtful, a catchall category for books with unrecognizable authors and titles.[46] Inserting Wythe into a version of Smart's chart of representative eighteenth-century libraries provides a quick glance at the overall comparison (see figure).[47] Among these libraries, Wythe's was second in size, the others ranging from the 102 titles that Edmund Berkeley owned to Robert Carter's 659. The figure demonstrates the unsurprising dominance of legal materials in Wythe's collection. It also substantiates the depth of Wythe's interest in the classics of Greece and Rome. Before discussing the latter, a brief tour of the other categories may help to give context to the unique qualities of Wythe's library.

Like his contemporaries, Wythe collected political and philosophical works of such noted thinkers as John Locke, Charles de Secondat, Baron de La Brède et de Montesquieu, David Hume, and Michel de Montaigne. He owned works of Desiderius Erasmus and Sir Francis Bacon, of Henry St. John, 1st Viscount Bolingbroke, and Henry Home, Lord Kames. A visitor to Wythe's

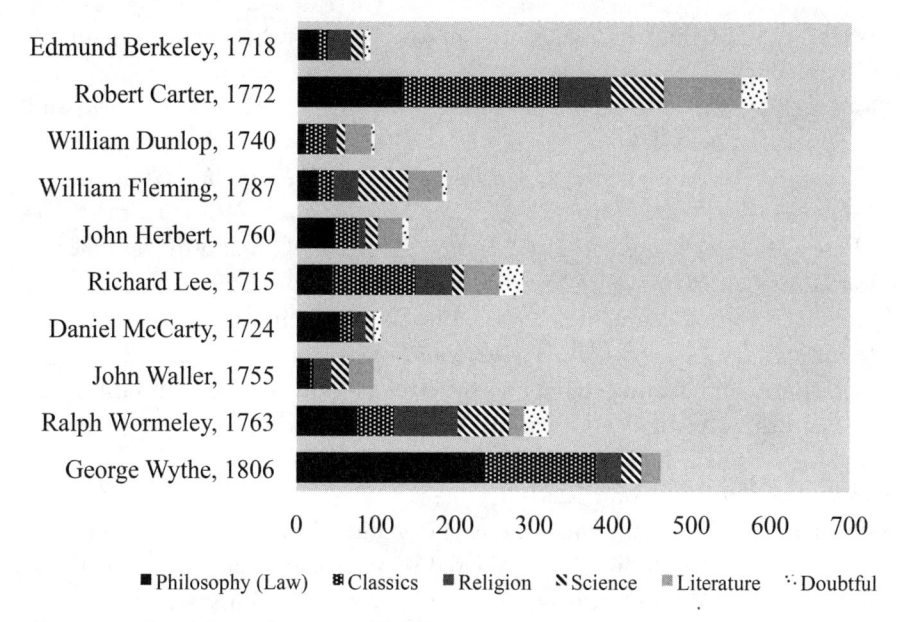

Library	
Edmund Berkeley, 1718	
Robert Carter, 1772	
William Dunlop, 1740	
William Fleming, 1787	
John Herbert, 1760	
Richard Lee, 1715	
Daniel McCarty, 1724	
John Waller, 1755	
Ralph Wormeley, 1763	
George Wythe, 1806	

■ Philosophy (Law)   ✪ Classics   ■ Religion   ⊠ Science   ■ Literature   ⋰ Doubtful

Representative eighteenth-century libraries

library would have found political titles such as Robert Filmer's *Patriarcha: Or the Natural Power of Kings* and *The Oceana* of James Harrington, as well as both parts of Thomas Paine's *Rights of Man*.

In the representative Virginia libraries, law and philosophy may have accounted for as many as half of the titles or as few as 7 percent, but the average was 23 percent, or roughly 48 titles.[48] Wythe's 21 philosophical and political titles account for little more than 4 percent of his total catalog, but when combined with his legal titles, as Smart did for the other libraries, the number soars to nearly 48 percent. Wythe's total of 238 titles outnumbers each of the other collections by more than 100.

As a lawyer, legislator, and judge, Wythe, as we might expect, owned a substantial collection of legal treatises, law reports, and works on philosophy and political science. These would also have been his primary tools in teaching his apprentices and law students. Unsurprisingly, given the role of precedent in common law and the momentous events in which he participated, Wythe supplemented his legal volumes with works of history, geography, and travel, particularly given the role of precedent in common law and the momentous events in which he participated.

Wythe favored English history, and his library included William Guthrie's *A General History of England,* David Hume's *The History of England, from the Invasion of Julius Caesar to the Revolution in 1688,* and *The History of the Rebellion and Civil Wars in England,* by Edward Hyde, 1st Earl of Clarendon.

Wythe did not limit himself to the mother country, however: he acquired George Buchanan's *Rerum Scoticarum Historia,* Samuel von Pufendorf's *An Introduction to the History of the Principal Kingdoms and States of Europe,* and Simon Pelloutier's *Histoire des Celtes, et Particulierement des Gaulois et des Germaines.* To these, Wythe added Filippo Mazzei's *Recherches Historiques et Politiques sur les États-Unis de l'Amérique Septentrionale,* William Stith's *The History of the First Discovery and Settlement of Virginia,* and the volumes of John Marshall's *The Life of George Washington,* curiously the only full-length biography to be documented as being in Wythe's collection. *Sandys' Travels Containing an History of the Original and Present State of the Turkish Empire,* by George Sandys, and geographies by William Guthrie and John Pinkerton, among others, testify to his curiosity about the world at large. Wythe may well have owned the *Geography and Navigation Completed,* by his maternal great-grandfather, George Keith.[49]

In total, Wythe obtained about thirty historical, biographical, or geographical titles, excluding books related to Greek or Roman history. These topics accounted for slightly more than 6 percent of his library, a smaller proportion than in the larger collections of Byrd and Mercer, but Wythe's collection compares favorably with the Virginia libraries included in Smart's overview. Works of this type formed about 15 percent of the separate collections, or an average of twenty-nine titles.[50]

Wythe's collection featured slightly fewer religious titles than did the representative eighteenth-century Virginia libraries in Smart's study, although it bears repeating that the libraries Smart analyzed were libraries of unusually wealthy or erudite men and therefore not necessarily typical of the educated class of Virginians. Those nine libraries contained an average of thirty-five religious books, or 15 percent of the whole number. The average for all the libraries Smart examined was twenty-nine titles, or 12 percent.[51] The size of Wythe's library makes the percentage of religious subjects, only 6 percent, much smaller than the average, but Wythe owned nearly thirty books demonstrating his interest in matters of faith and religion. This interest manifested itself in multiple editions of the Bible in Greek and English, as well as collections of the sermons of John Lightfoot, Laurence Sterne, William Stith, and John Tillotson. Wythe owned multiple copies of the Book of Common Prayer, Hugo Grotius's *De Veritate Religionis Christianae,* and *A New History of the Holy Bible,* by Thomas Stackhouse. Perhaps as a nod to the Quakers among his ancestors, Wythe's library also included Robert Barclay's *An Apology for the True Christian Divinity, Being an Explanation and Vindication of the Principles and Doctrines of the People called Quakers.*

Wythe enjoyed the classics from English and European literature. He owned three different sets of the works of William Shakespeare, as well as John Milton's *Paradise Lost* and *Paradise Regain'd* and a complete collection of

Milton's historical, political, and miscellaneous works. Wythe expanded this section of his library with *The Dramatick Works of John Dryden,* the poems of Erasmus Darwin, and the works of Alexander Pope, Joseph Addison, François Rabelais, and Jonathan Swift. He referenced *Don Quixote* in one of his case reports, so it is reasonable to conclude he may have owned Miguel de Cervantes's masterpiece as well, probably, but not certainly, one of the English translations. Despite owning some of these gems, Wythe devoted less than 5 percent of his library to English and European literature. By comparison, literature accounted for between 2 percent and 30 percent of the books in eighteenth-century Virginia libraries.[52] Robert Carter owned the most, 99, Daniel McCarty the fewest, only 2, with the average number of literary titles 34.

Gentlemen such as Wythe also studied the sciences and mathematics. Consequently, Wythe owned Sir Issac Newton's *Arithmetica Universalis* and algebra treatises by William Emerson, Thomas Simpson, and Colin MacLaurin. Wythe's scientific interests were varied. His library contained *The Description and Use of Nairne's Patent Electrical Machine,* Richard Helsham's *A Course of Lectures in Natural Philosophy,* and *An History of the Earth, and Animated Nature,* by Oliver Goldsmith. He also owned Matthew Dobson's *A Medical Commentary on Fixed Air,* in which Dobson proposed the use of carbon dioxide, or "fixed air," as an external disinfectant against putrid diseases.[53] These mathematical and scientific books accounted for 5 percent of Wythe's total collection, in contrast to the average of 13 percent in other eighteenth-century Virginia libraries.[54] In this instance, as with the religious subjects, the percentages are deceptive in part because of the above-average size of his library. Wythe owned twenty-five titles in this category. The average for the other libraries was thirty-one, but only Robert Wormley, William Fleming, and Robert Carter owned more scientific or mathematical works than Wythe.

According to Smart, dictionaries and books on language were "extremely common" in the typical seventeenth- and eighteenth-century libraries of Virginia.[55] Like his fellow Virginians, Wythe owned grammars, philological studies, and multiple dictionaries. In addition, his library included standard reference works of the day, including *Encyclopaedia, or, A Dictionary of Arts, Sciences, and Miscellaneous Literature,* the first American version of the *Encylopaedia Britannica,* Malachy Postlethwayt's *The Universal Dictionary of Trade and Commerce,* and the *New and Complete Dictionary of Arts and Sciences: Comprehending All the Branches of Useful Knowledge,* by the Society of Gentlemen.

Taking Smart's study as a whole, it appears that Wythe collected the typical subjects for a man of his time. A well-rounded gentleman was expected to be familiar with the historical, literary, religious, and political works of the type he owned. None of these areas stands out as unique to Wythe, nor was his collection, as we know it, exhaustive in any of these nonlegal subjects. Rather, what is most striking is the comparatively smaller percentages of these subjects in Wythe's library, the relatively averageness, or typical nature, of his holdings. This analysis of Wythe's collection, excluding the "classics and languages" category, shows nothing particularly special beyond his law books.

Considering his various legal roles, few would find the fact that Wythe owned a substantial legal collection peculiar or, perhaps, even notable. Instead, it is the section of the library devoted to the classics that most clearly distinguishes Wythe from his contemporaries. That he should have accumulated the writings of classical authors, both in translation and in the original languages, comes as no surprise given his love for and command of those works. The Wythe biographer Alonzo Dill noted that Wythe "thirsted like a living Tantalus for the refreshing springs of the ancient authors," but before the discovery of the Jefferson inventory, historians could only guess at how Wythe's passion influenced the character of his library.[56] Nevertheless, his holdings did not rival the massive collections of William Byrd of Westover or Thomas Jefferson, nor that of James Logan, of Philadelphia, credited with owning the best classical library in colonial America.[57] Still, the size and scope of Wythe's Greek and Latin selections substantiate the long-standing reputation of their owner. For a library of fewer than one thousand volumes, the sheer number and variety of classical authors in their original languages may not have been duplicated in eighteenth-century Virginia.

Familiarity with the Greek and Roman authors was common among Wythe's contemporaries, particularly among the Revolutionary leaders. Not every speaker or pamphleteer could claim extensive knowledge of classical sources, but the men who most strongly shaped Revolutionary sentiment used frequent allusions from a wide array of Greek and Roman authors to justify their rhetoric. One study of the classical influences on American revolutionaries includes enumerated references from 14 Greeks and 22 Romans in pamphlets, speeches, letters, and discourses.[58] Wythe owned at least 71 copies of the works of 32 of those 36 authors and orators and multiple titles or copies from several of them, including 9 by Homer, 5 each by Horace and Virgil, 4 by Lucretius, and 3 each by Euripides, Cicero, and Xenophon. The authors whose works may not have been represented in his library were the Greek poet Dio and the Roman philosophers Lucan, Seneca, and Marcus Aurelius.[59] Wythe did, however, own works by an additional 41 authors from antiquity, as well as Pieter Burmann's *Poetae Latini Minores* and a five-volume work that combined the works of Aeschine with those of Demosthenes.[60]

Wythe owned at least 118 titles from Greek and Roman authors, 122 if the compilation includes the parts of *Corpus Juris Civilis,* and an additional 23 titles that supported that collection in the form of dictionaries, thesauri, grammars, histories, and geographical studies. These account for nearly a third of Wythe's entire library. The classical scholar Meyer Reinhold noted that the average classical holdings in eighteenth-century "college libraries, other large libraries, and those of more educated Americans" made up about 10–12 percent of the whole.[61] In the Virginia libraries that Smart studied, on the other hand, classics accounted for 26 percent of the total collection.[62] However, Smart's survey represents libraries of varying sizes, with the number of classical titles ranging from 5 to 198. Even in Virginia, the libraries of only a few men, such as Robert Carter or Richard Lee, rivaled Wythe in their accumulation of classical authors and titles.[63]

Despite their familiarity with the classics, most eighteenth-century Americans read the Greek and Latin authors in English translation. True, many young men devoted countless hours in grammar school and college to the study of Greek and Latin, but few "read the Classical languages with ease."[64] George Wythe's mother may have been exceptional among colonial women in her ability to teach her son Latin and Greek, even as he became exceptional for his erudition among colonial and Revolutionary American men. What one can also lose sight of when considering the references to classical authors during the Revolutionary period is that the plethora of allusions and citations created a misleading facade. The display of rhetoric often disguised a generally superficial knowledge of the subject.[65] Many people relied on shortcuts such as Charles Rollin's *Ancient History,* which digested the material for widespread appeal.[66] The typical Virginian of the age was no different. Greek and Roman literature formed a significant part of a gentleman's education, but that education produced few men with a penetrating knowledge of the classics or true scholars of the languages.[67] It is the depth of his study and his intellectual approach to the material that most firmly set Wythe apart from his contemporaries.

Wythe did not merely delve into the works of classical authors for show; he rigorously devoured them and emulated their precepts. His biographer W. Edwin Hemphill described the study of Greek and Latin classics as Wythe's "chief intellectual interest," stating that Wythe "plunged deeply into a discriminating absorption of the classics."[68] His contemporaries noticed and commented on his erudition, often invoking the classics in their descriptions. Jefferson considered Wythe "the best Latin and Greek scholar in Virginia" and called him "the Cato of his country."[69] William Wirt regarded Wythe's knowledge of ancient literature as "rarely equaled in this country"[70] and proclaimed him "a man of Roman stamp, in Rome's best age."[71] Henry Clay, who studied law with him when Wythe was an old man, wrote that Wythe was "one of the purest, best, and most learned men in classical lore that I ever knew."[72]

Wythe's love of the classical languages also led him to collect and compare translated versions with the originals. Of the 122 classical titles in his library, 48 were in Latin, 7 in Greek, and 34 in a combination of the two. For his favorite authors, he acquired multiple versions in multiple languages. For example, Wythe owned one copy of Homer's *Iliad* and two copies of his *Odyssey* in Greek, one copy of the *Iliad* and two of the *Odyssey* in English, and two copies of the *Iliad* in both Greek and Latin and another that included the *Odyssey* in both languages. He also owned a Latin volume enumerating the errors in Homer. Similarly, Wythe's five copies of Horace included one in English, three in Latin, and one a dual side-by-side version in French and Latin. Wythe acquired the writings of Anacreon, Euripides, Theocritus, and Thucydides in Greek, Latin, and English, and works of Demosthenes and Isocrates in Greek, Latin, and French.

To augment his collection and deepen his study of the classics, Wythe collected a variety of volumes detailing aspects of the ancient world, particularly Greece. These included James Stuart's *The Antiquities of Athens,* David Le Roy's *Ruins of Athens, with Remains and Other Valuable Antiquities in Greece,* Jean-Jacques Barthélemy's *Travels of Anacharsis the Younger in Greece,* John Potter's *Archæologia Græca or the Antiquities of Greece,* and Pierre Augustin Guys's *Voyage Littéraire De La Grèce.* Not surprisingly, Wythe owned multiple Latin and Greek grammars, dictionaries, and thesauri, such as Benjamin Hederich's *Lexicon Manuale Græcum Omnibus* and Paul Aler's *Gradus ad Parnassum,* described as "a sort of Roget's thesaurus" of synonyms, epithets, verse quotations, and phrases used in classical poetry.[73] Jefferson contributed to his friend's passionate study by sending him an edition of *Lud. Kusterus de Vero usu Verborum Mediorum eorumque Differentia a Verbis Activis & Passivis,* which Jefferson described as a treatise on "the use of the middle voice in Greek"; Jefferson wrote that "if it gives you half the pleasure it did me, mine will be doubled still."[74]

Wythe's affinity for Greek and Latin spilled over into other parts of his collection. For example, in his inventory of Wythe's library Jefferson recorded five Bibles or New Testaments—one Bible in English, one complete version of the Bible in Greek, and three Greek New Testaments. Wythe also owned Greek and Latin texts of the Psalms, Thomas Gale's edition of *Psaltērion Psalterium: Juxta Exemplar Alexandrinum,* George Buchanan's Latin paraphrase, *Poetarum fui Seculi Facilè Principis, Paraphrasis Psalmorum Davidis Poetica,* and Robert Lowth's Latin compilation of Hebrew poems, *De Sacra Poesi Hebræorum.* Wythe supplemented these with two versions of the Anglican liturgy, one in Latin and one in Greek. Twenty-seven other titles from Wythe's library were in one of the classical languages or a combination of the two. Some of these would have been available to Wythe only in Latin or Greek, such as Ralph de Hengham's *Registrum Brevium.* Others, like Sir Isaac Newton's mathematical work, Wythe purposefully acquired in Latin rather than the readily available English counterpart.

Classics permeated every area of Wythe's life. The chancellor made great use of his wide-ranging collection to support and inform his legal arguments and judicial decisions. As the Virginia legal historian W. Hamilton Bryson observed, "No judge or attorney seems to have resorted to the Roman law as often or as enthusiastically as George Wythe."[75] In an investigation of the use of classics in the courts, Richard J. Hoffman credited Wythe for using "many authors as a mine for illustrative anecdotes, institutions, historical events, myths, and *exempla* of various sorts." He furnished details: "While Wythe draws from 24 ancient authors, he is partial to literature in Latin or on Rome. His favorites are the *Corpus Iuris Civilis,* quoted or cited 21 times, Virgil, six times; and Cicero, seven times. Other authors from the Roman era include Caesar, Q. Curtius Rufus, Horace, Juvenal, Livy, Lucretius, Petronius, Plutarch, Quintilian, Suetonius, Tacitus, Terence, and Valerius Maximus. From the Greeks, Wythe utilizes Aeschylus, Demosthenes, Euclid, Herodotus, Homer, Sophocles, and Thucydides."[76] Another of Wythe's biographers wrote, "Very few men of that time and even fewer of our own can follow Wythe in some of his legal arguments, so involved, so filled with classical references, so complete with Anglo-Saxon precedents are they."[77] Still another twentieth-century historian described "the more unfamiliar Latin and Greek authors" as "quarries from which in concealed places [Wythe] dug out his allusions and quotations."[78]

In Hoffman's examination of Wythe's case reports, he identified eighty-five classical references in twenty-one cases. Nineteen are linked to no specific piece of literature, while the remainder derive from the works of twenty-four authors all known to have been in Wythe's library. According to Hoffman, "[T]he interplay of law and classics form [*sic*] an important part of his opinions." Wythe's allusions to such a wealth of classical sources may have served merely as a means to demonstrate the unquestionable superiority of his enormous erudition. "Even at his most pedantic," Hoffman admitted, "Wythe's use of classics is charged with meaning." Wythe "proposed that American judges—or at least Virginia judges—ought to follow a rational model of law and justice," and he sought to steer Virginia law away from some of the precedents of British common law toward the more logical approach he found in the ancient systems. To that end, Wythe used his collection of Greek and Roman classics. Hoffman concluded that Wythe's "classical references tended to heighten the break with Britain, and to connect the new Republic to something solid: in this case, the ancient past."[79]

More than once, Wythe turned to his knowledge of the classics, and specifically the classical reference works in his library, for artistic purposes in service to the Commonwealth of Virginia. In 1776 he was a member of the committee to create the official seal for Virginia; the design is frequently credited largely to him.[80] He and a colleague turned to Joseph Spence's 1744 *Polymetis: or, an Enquiry Concerning the Agreement Between the Works of the Roman Poets, and the Remains of the Antient Artists, Being an Attempt to Illustrate Them Mutually from One Another,* a large folio with drawings based on ancient artists for inspiration in the design that they proposed and that the Virginia Convention of 1776 adopted. It is still the official seal of Virginia.[81] Similarly, Wythe looked to the classics to create a seal for the chancellor's office after he became the judge in the new state's High Court of Chancery. In this instance, he derived the illustration from a passage in Herodotus in which the judgment seat of a Persian jurist was created from the flayed skin of his corrupt predecessor, a continual admonition for impartial justice.[82]

Wythe made one other great use of his library: for teaching and mentoring young men, law clerks, and law students. From the age of about thirty-five on, Wythe busied himself with teaching. His first identifiable student was Thomas Jefferson, beginning in 1762.[83] Wythe engaged Jefferson as his legal apprentice, yet multiple authors also credit Wythe with developing his student's nascent love of the classics.[84] What began as Jefferson's legal education developed into a lifelong friendship in which discussions of law, philosophy, science, and the classics all played a part. When Jefferson sent Wythe books from Europe, the majority of them were classics.[85]

Wythe no doubt shared the great legal texts of his library with his students and clerks. When Jefferson began to study law, Wythe directed him to Sir Edward Coke's *First Part of the Institutes on the Lawes of England,* more commonly known as *Coke upon Littleton,* the standard work on English property law for the previous two centuries.[86] By the time Wythe's other most famous student, John Marshall, enrolled in classes at William and Mary in 1780, Sir William Blackstone's *Commentaries on the Laws of England* had replaced *Coke upon Littleton* as the primary text for law students. It was this title, among a long list of other legal books, to which Wythe first directed his students.

Wythe viewed his teaching role as to prepare his students to be responsible republican citizens as well as practicing lawyers.[87] To that end, he encouraged his students to read widely beyond the law, including studying Greek and Latin classics to gain the wisdom and direction that Wythe had found in them. At least one of Wythe's students, Jefferson's nephew Peter Carr, lamented his teacher's emphasis on "the dead languages" and griped that his time could be better spent, but Carr also acknowledged "the attention which ought to be paid to his precepts."[88]

During his time at William and Mary and later, after he moved to Richmond, Wythe found one more use for his library of Greek and Roman literature. He augmented his legal teaching by tutoring young men in Greek and Latin. Littleton Waller Tazewell, a future governor and senator as well as respected attorney, was Wythe's first classics pupil. Tazewell started his lessons at the age of twelve and later in life provided this glimpse of his tutor's methods: "When I entered the room," Wythe "immediately took from his well-stored library some Greek book, to which any accidental circumstance first directed his attention. This was opened at random, and I was bid to recite the first passage that caught his eye.... Whenever in the course of our reading any reference was made to the ancient manners, customs, laws, superstitions or history of the Greeks, he asked me to explain the allusion, and when I failed to do so satisfactorily (as was often the case) he immediately gave full clear and complete account of the subject to which reference was so made."[89]

Wythe used this practice with many young men, including John Coalter, William Munford, and another Jefferson nephew, John Wayles Eppes. To Munford at least, Wythe imparted his great love of the classics, inspiring a man who later served in the General Assembly and reported cases from the Virginia Court of Appeals but who was better known for "his magnificent translation of the *Iliad*."[90]

It would be remiss to conclude without reiterating that Wythe's library was probably much larger than the lists that we can create today suggest. None of the bibliographies created to date can be considered definitive or exhaustive. Several circumstances may have contributed to the loss of volumes from his library. For example, neighbors and colleagues borrowed and lent books during the eighteenth century. In fact, Wythe advertised in the 1771 *Virginia Gazette* requesting the return of one such borrowed volume, a law book. "I miss a third volume of Burrow's Reports," his advertisement reads. "Whether it was lent out I forget.... Whoever will let me know where it is, I shall be obliged to him for the information."[91]

Another circumstance definitely affected our knowledge of Wythe's library. Shortly before Wythe died, his grandnephew sold "three trunks" of Wythe's "law books."[92] Obviously, the vague reference could mean anything, and it invites speculation as to precisely what George Wythe Sweeney (who by all accounts murdered his great uncle) may have stolen. How many titles and volumes did the three trunks contain, and if we could identify them, how would that change the composition of the collection as we understand it? Could the stolen books account for some of the uncharacteristic gaps in areas of law, or perhaps even the few missing classical authors? Sadly, we will probably never know.

What can be understood about Wythe from this exploration of his books? He clearly possessed an above-average law library that he used extensively in his various careers as lawyer, law professor, and judge. Wythe collected the major works in other areas typical for gentlemen of his age, but in most cases these sections of the library were not noteworthy. The great exception—and the thing that distinguishes Wythe from most of his contemporaries—was his collection of classics and the uses to which he put them. Beverley Tucker, son of one of Wythe's most accomplished law students, praised Wythe in comparison with other Virginia lawyers of the time, writing that "a learned lawyer was indeed a rara avis ... there was but one man in the state who had any claims to the character. I speak of the venerable Chancellor Wythe ... by nature and habit addicted to solitude, and his active mind found its only enjoyment in profound research. The languages of antiquity, the exact sciences, and the law ... to these he devoted himself, and he became a profound lawyer for the same reason that he was a profound Greek scholar, astronomer and mathematician."[93]

As we should expect, Wythe's library demonstrates its owner's dedication to the study and teaching of law. His books also reveal a man deeply devoted to the study of Greek and Roman classics, an avocation that enthralled and influenced the chancellor throughout his long life.

NOTES

1. Benjamin B. Minor, "Memoir of the Author," in *Decisions of Cases in Virginia by the High Court of Chancery: With Remarks Upon Decrees by the High Court of Appeals Reversing Some of Those Decisions,* by George Wythe, 2d ed. (Richmond, 1852), xxv.
2. Alonzo Thomas Dill, *George Wythe: Teacher of Liberty* (Williamsburg, 1979), 7.
3. Dice Robins Anderson, "The Teacher of Jefferson and Marshall," *South Atlantic Quarterly* 15 (1916): 335.
4. William DuVal to Thomas Jefferson, 12 July 1806, in Thomas Jefferson Papers, Library of Congress, available at http://hdl.loc.gov/loc.mss/mtj.mtjbib016305.
5. Endrina Tay and Jeremy Dibbell, "Reconstructing a Lost Library: George Wythe's 'Legacie' to President Thomas Jefferson, Tales from the Vault," *Common-Place* (Jan. 2010), an online journal available at http://www.common-place.org/vol-10/no-02/tales.
6. Mary R. M. Goodwin, *The George Wythe House: Its Furniture and Furnishings* (Williamsburg, 1958), available at http://research.history.org/DigitalLibrary/View/index.cfm?doc=ResearchReports/RR0216.xml.
7. Memorandum from Barbara C. Dean, Colonial Williamsburg Foundation, to Mrs. [Gregory] Stiverson, Colonial Williamsburg Foundation, 16 June 1975, copy on file at Wolf Law Library, College of William and Mary.
8. "Member: George Wythe," LibraryThing, http://www.librarything.com/profile/GeorgeWythe (last visited 1 Nov. 2013), click on link to "Your library" for listing of books.
9. Bennie Brown, "The Library of George Wythe of Williamsburg and Richmond," unpublished Microsoft Word file, May 2009, rev. May 2014. This bibliography has proven absolutely invaluable to my research on the contents of Wythe's library. Mr. Brown has kindly apprised me of all updates to his list as he has continued his research.
10. Bernard Schwartz, Barbara Wilcie Kern, and R. B. Bernstein, eds., *Thomas Jefferson and Bolling v. Bolling: Law and the Legal Profession in Pre-Revolutionary America* (San Marino, CA, 1997).
11. Several of the titles are proven items from Wythe's library because his copies still exist. More titles are identified in Jefferson's inventory (338 titles, 649 volumes, some of which overlap with Wythe's existing copies) because Wythe is known to have ordered

certain books or received them as gifts, because Wythe's students cited them in their commonplace books, or because Wythe cited them in his case reports or arguments as an attorney. The lists of books in the latter two categories are less definitive than the others, but for the purposes of understanding his use of books the books in those categories are treated as books that Wythe owned. For more information on the various bibliographies and the challenges of creating a catalog of Wythe's library, Linda K. Tesar, "Forensic Bibliography: Recreating the Library of George Wythe," *Law Library Journal* 105 (2013): 57–77.

12. Dill, *George Wythe: Teacher of Liberty*, 3.
13. Ibid., 7, 8.
14. Daniel Call, *Reports of Cases Argued and Adjudged in the Court of Appeals of Virginia*, 6 vols. (Richmond, 1801), 4:xi.
15. Robert Bevier Kirtland, "George Wythe: Lawyer, Revolutionary, Judge" (PhD diss., University of Michigan, 1983), 43; Dill, *George Wythe: Teacher of Liberty*, 10.
16. Thomas Hunter, "The Teaching of George Wythe," in *The History of Legal Education in the United States: Commentaries and Primary Sources*, ed. Steve Sheppard, 2 vols. (Pasadena, CA, 1999), 1:140.
17. Imogene E. Brown, *American Aristides: A Biography of George Wythe* (Rutherford, NJ, 1981), 244.
18. W. Hamilton Bryson, "Legal Education," in *Virginia Law Books: Essays and Bibliographies*, ed. Bryson (Philadelphia, 2000), 335.
19. Dill, *George Wythe: Teacher of Liberty*, 68.
20. George Wythe to John Norton, 15 May 1768, 18 Aug. 1768, 3 Aug. 1769, and 3 May 1770, in *John Norton & Sons, Merchants of London and Virginia: Being the Papers from their Counting House for the Years 1750 to 1795*, ed. Frances Norton Mason (Richmond, 1937), 52–53, 58–59, 101, 134.
21. Joseph Royle, *Virginia Gazette* Daybook, Albert J. and Shirley Small Library, University of Virginia.
22. Mason, *John Norton & Sons*, 54.
23. Wythe's inscribed copy of John Adams, *Thoughts on Government; Applicable to the Present State of the American Colonies*, reprint ed. (Boston, 1776), is in the John D. Rockefeller, Jr. Library, Colonial Williamsburg.
24. Wythe's copy of Hugh Blair, *Lectures on Rhetoric and Belles Lettres* (Philadelphia, 1784), is in the Earl Gregg Swem Library, College of William and Mary.
25. Wythe's copy of volume 1 of Call, *Reports of Cases Argued and Adjudged in the Court of Appeals of Virginia* (Richmond, 1801), is in the Library of Congress.
26. Jefferson to Wythe, 16 Sept. 1787, in *The Papers of Thomas Jefferson*, ed. Julian P. Boyd et al. (Princeton, NJ, 1950–), 12:129–30.
27. DuVal to Jefferson, 19 June 1806, Jefferson Papers, Library of Congress.
28. Alan McKinley Smith, "Virginia Lawyers, 1680–1776: The Birth of an American Profession" (PhD diss., Johns Hopkins University, 1967), 247, 248.
29. Ibid., 251; Goodwin, *George Wythe House*, 42.
30. Goodwin, *George Wythe House*, 43.
31. Tay and Dibbell, "Reconstructing a Lost Library."

32. W. Hamilton Bryson, *Census of Law Books in Colonial Virginia* (Charlottesville, 1978), vii, xi.
33. Schwartz, Kern, and Bernstein, *Thomas Jefferson and Bolling v. Bolling*, 303.
34. A treatise is "an extended, serious, and usu. exhaustive book on a particular subject." *Black's Law Dictionary*, 14th ed. (St. Paul, MN, 2014).
35. Bryson, *Census*, xv.
36. Ibid., xii. One of the excluded reporters, Atkyns, is probably represented by Bryson's entry no. 20 (p. 3).
37. Ibid.
38. John G. Marvin, *Legal Bibliography or a Thesaurus of American, English, Irish, and Scotch Law Books* (Philadelphia, 1847), 98, 311 (first quotation), 384 (second quotation).
39. Some of the titles counted as "owned" by Wythe derive from his students' commonplace books and citations Wythe made in his own case reports or in his arguments in *Bolling v. Bolling*. For these titles, there is no definitive proof that Wythe used his own copy rather than a borrowed copy.
40. *Black's Law Dictionary* defines law French as "[t]he corrupted form of the Norman French language that arose in England in the centuries after William the Conqueror invaded England in 1066 and that was used for several centuries as the primary language of the English legal system."
41. Herbert A. Johnson, *Imported Eighteenth-Century Law Treatises in American Libraries, 1700–1799* (Knoxville, 1978), xxxvi.
42. Bryson discovered *Every Man His Own Lawyer* in eight Virginia libraries, including those of John Mercer and "Councillor" Robert Carter. He found Webb's manual in the collections of Carter, Augustine Washington, John Minor, and seventeen others.
43. Schwartz, Kern, and Bernstein, *Thomas Jefferson and Bolling v. Bolling*, 147. For example, Wythe's first sentence in his argument for the plaintiff in *Bolling v. Bolling* includes three references to Henry Swinburne's *A Treatise of Testaments and Last Wills*, a citation to *The Reports of Sir Peyton Ventris*, and notations to four pages in Sir William Blackstone's *Commentaries on the Laws of England*.
44. *The Papers of John Marshall*, ed. Herbert A. Johnson et al., 12 vols. (Chapel Hill, NC, 1974–2006), 1:41–45. This count does not include titles from the unpublished portion of the law notes. For the purposes of this essay, I have assumed that Marshall cited books from Wythe's collection. While this cannot be conclusively proven for all of the titles, nearly half have been independently corroborated by other evidence, such as Jefferson's inventory, Wythe's case reports, and letters to merchants. Wythe's library would have been the most readily available to Marshall at the time. The College of William and Mary lacked an adequate legal collection during this period, and Marshall, an officer in the Continental Army, would have been unlikely to own the books himself.
45. George K. Smart, "Private Libraries in Colonial Virginia," *American Literature* 10 (1938): 25, 28.
46. Ibid., 33.

47. My thanks to Stephen N. Blaiklock at William and Mary's Wolf Law Library for helping me create this version of Smart's chart.
48. Smart, "Private Libraries in Colonial Virginia," 32–33.
49. Memorandum, Barbara C. Dean to Mrs. Stiverson, 16 June 1975, citing William Edwin Hemphill, "George Wythe: The Colonial Briton" (PhD diss., University of Virginia, 1937), 14–15.
50. Smart, "Private Libraries in Colonial Virginia," 32.
51. Ibid., 32, 33.
52. Ibid., 32–33.
53. Jan Golinski, *Science as Public Culture: Chemistry and Enlightenment in Britain, 1760–1820* (Cambridge, 1999), 111.
54. Smart, "Private Libraries in Colonial Virginia," 33.
55. Ibid., 38.
56. Dill, *George Wythe: Teacher of Liberty,* 19.
57. Federick B. Tolles, "Quaker Humanist: James Logan as a Classical Scholar," *Pennsylvania Magazine of History and Biography* 79 (1955): 419.
58. Charles F. Mullett, "Classical Influences on the American Revolution," *Classical Journal* 35 (1939): 92, 93.
59. Wythe's only copies of the writings of the jurists Ulpian and Gaius may have been the excerpts found in the *Corpus Juris Civilis.*
60. Wythe owned works by Aelian, Aeschylus, Anacreon, Antonius Liberalis, Appianus, Archimedes, Aristophanes, Bion of Smyrna, Callimachus, Clement of Alexandria, Colluthus, Demetrius, Diodorus Siculus, Dionysius of Halicarnassus, Euclid, Gellius, Hippocrates, Isocrates, Josephus, Justin, Longinus, Lycurgus, Lysias, Minicus Felix, Pausanius, Phaedrus, Phlegon of Tralles, Pindar, Plautus, Pliny the Elder, Polybius, Quintilian, Statius, Terence, Theocritus, Theophilus, Theophrastus, Tibullus, Tyrtaeus, Valerius Maximus, and Velleius Paterculus.
61. Meyer Reinhold, introduction to *The Classick Pages: Classical Reading of Eighteenth-Century Americans,* ed. Reinhold (University Park, PA, 1975), 8.
62. Smart, "Private Libraries in Colonial Virginia," 33.
63. Ibid. Carter owned nearly 200 classical titles; Lee, approximately 115.
64. Reinhold, introduction, 8–9.
65. Bernard Bailyn, *The Ideological Origins of the American Revolution,* enlarged ed. (Cambridge, MA, 1967), 26.
66. Trevor Colbourn, *The Lamp of Experience: Whig History and the Intellectual Origins of the American Revolution* (Indianapolis, 1974), 26.
67. Louis B. Wright, "The Classical Tradition in Colonial Virginia," *Bibliographic Society of America Papers* 33 (1939): 95.
68. Hemphill, "George Wythe: The Colonial Briton," 87–88.
69. Thomas Jefferson, "Notes for the Biography of George Wythe," 30 Aug. 1820, in Jefferson Papers, Library of Congress.
70. William Wirt, *Sketches of the Life and Character of Patrick Henry* (Philadelphia, 1817), 47.

71. William Wirt, *A Discourse on the Lives and Characters of Thomas Jefferson and John Adams Who Both Died on the Fourth of July, 1826* (Washington, DC, 1826), 27.
72. Minor, "Memoir of the Author," xxxiii.
73. Alastair Fowler, "Book Review: Classical Dictionaries: Past, Present and Future," *Translation and Literature* 21 (2012): 98.
74. Jefferson to Wythe, 23 Oct. 1794, in *Papers of Thomas Jefferson*, 28:181.
75. W. Hamilton Bryson, "The Use of Roman Law in Virginia Courts," *American Journal of Legal History* 28 (1984): 143.
76. Richard J. Hoffman, "Classics in the Courts of the United States, 1790–1800," ibid. 22 (1978): 59, 60.
77. William Clarkin, *Serene Patriot: A Life of George Wythe* (Albany, 1970), 43.
78. Anderson, "Teacher of Jefferson and Marshall," 335.
79. Hoffman, "Classics in the Courts," 57–59, 65, 73, 75.
80. Dill, *George Wythe: Teacher of Liberty*, 36.
81. John Page to Jefferson, 20 July 1776, in *Papers of Thomas Jefferson*, 1:468.
82. Brown, *American Aristides*, 257.
83. Hunter, "Teaching of George Wythe," 142.
84. Norbert Sand, "The Classics in Jefferson's Theory of Education," *Classical Journal* 40 (Nov. 1944): 92; Louis B. Wright, "Thomas Jefferson and the Classics," *Proceedings of the American Philosophical Society* 87 (1943): 224.
85. Jefferson to Wythe, 16 Sept. 1787, in *Papers of Thomas Jefferson*, 12:129, containing a list of "Contents of the box marked G. W. For Mr. Wythe. Polybius. Gr. Lat. 3. vols. 8vo.; Coluthi raptus Helenae. 8vo.; Fabulae Homericae de Ulixe. 8vo.; Guys. voiage literaire en Grece. 4. v. 8vo.; Savary sur l'Égypte. 3. vols. 8vo; Volney sur l'Égypte. 2. vols. 8vo.; Code de l'humanité. 13. vols. 4to."
86. John H. Baker, "English Law Books and Legal Publishing," in *The Cambridge History of the Book in Britain*, vol. 4, *1557–1696*, ed. John Barnard and D. F. McKenzie with the assistance of Maureen Bell (Cambridge, 1998), 483.
87. W. Edwin Hemphill, "George Wythe: America's First Law Professor and the Teacher of Jefferson, Marshall, and Clay" (master's thesis, Emory University, 1933), 52.
88. Peter Carr to Jefferson, 29 May 1789, in *Papers of Thomas Jefferson*, 15:156.
89. Littleton Waller Tazewell's untitled history of the Tazewell family (1823), 133, Swem Library, College of William and Mary.
90. Hunter, "Teaching of George Wythe," 158, 159 (quotation).
91. *Virginia Gazette* (Rind), 7 Feb. 1771.
92. Tay and Dibbell, "Reconstructing a Lost Library."
93. Beverly Tucker, *The Principles of Pleading* (Boston, 1846), 56.

THE LAW LIBRARY OF A WORKING ATTORNEY

THE EXAMPLE OF PATRICK HENRY

Kevin J. Hayes

Patrick Henry's copy of William Bohun's Declarations and Pleadings preserves a record of his purchase of it and also of later owners. William Bohun, Declarations and Pleadings in the Most Usual Actions Brought in the Several Courts of King's Bench and Common Pleas at Westminster (London, 1733). (Courtesy the Library of Virginia)

In 1757, after fire destroyed the house at Pine Slash, the modest plantation where Patrick Henry had first tried his hand as a farmer, he, his wife, Sarah, and their young children moved into Hanover Tavern. Though a good inn with a large hall and a covered portico ideal for spending the day chewing the fat, Hanover Tavern may not have been the best place to raise a family. Owned and operated by Sarah's father, John Shelton, it had been previously owned by Sarah's grandfather, the printer, publisher, and newspaper editor William Parks. Sarah's mother, Eleanor Parks Shelton, had inherited the establishment when William Parks died in 1750, and John Shelton had subsequently bought the tavern outright to save the place from being sold to pay his father-in-law's creditors. Like many taverns throughout Virginia, this one was erected across the road from the county courthouse, partly to accommodate the crowds that gathered there on court days and election days. Misfortune may have brought Patrick Henry to Hanover Tavern, but there he found a career ideally suited to his abilities. Hanover Courthouse first got him thinking about the legal profession.[1]

To provide for his family, Henry established a retail store nearby, and with the help of an overseer, he also maintained the farm at Pine Slash. Despite these strenuous activities, he had energy to spare. When business called John Shelton away, he left his son-in-law in charge. Henry welcomed guests and sometimes minded the taproom.[2] He felt comfortable there and enjoyed life at Hanover Tavern, especially when court was in session. Wide-eyed and open-minded, Henry relished the free flow of ideas that occurred as spirits loosened the tongues of the tavern's patrons.

As Patrick Henry's experience indicates, there was a close relationship between the county courthouses and the taverns that sprang up near them in colonial Virginia. On court days, people came from throughout the county to attend the legal proceedings and join in the fun. Defendants and plaintiffs, defense attorneys and prosecutors, justices and juries, onlookers and gawkers gathered in the courthouse by day and the tavern at night.[3]

The same personal qualities that won arguments before the bar enthralled listeners in the barroom. In both courtroom and tavern the eloquent held sway. Patrick Henry was quick to recognize the connection. Edmund Randolph, whose history of Virginia tells the story of many men he knew personally, linked Henry's social aplomb with his desire to become a lawyer. Describing the start of Henry's legal career, Randolph observed, "Having experienced his command in social discourse, he took refuge in the study and practice of the law."[4]

One crucial barrier separated Henry from shooting the breeze in the barroom and arguing cases in the courtroom. There were no qualifying exams for the former (would that there were), but he had to pass the bar before he could do the latter. He began studying for his bar exam but decided not to abandon his retail store, at least not yet. For the welfare of Sarah and the children, it would be safer to keep the store going until he passed the bar and established himself as a lawyer.

Early in April 1760 Henry reached Williamsburg, seeking admission to the bar. The precise date remains a mystery; 1 April is the best guess.[5] Thomas Jefferson, who had come to Williamsburg the previous month to begin his first year at the College of William and Mary, was surprised to see Henry in town and even more surprised to learn why. When they first met the previous Christmas, Jefferson had no idea Henry was studying for the bar.[6] Perhaps Henry had not begun reading law until after Christmas. Perhaps he had not even decided to become a lawyer then. Henry much later told Judge John Tyler that he had read law for only one month prior to sitting for his bar exam, restricting himself to the laws of Virginia and *Coke upon Littleton,* that is, Edward Coke's *First Part of the Institutes of the Laws of England: or, A Commentarie upon Littleton.*[7]

This nonchalant claim may be an instance of Henry's characteristic habit of downplaying his learning in the face of a more erudite acquaintance. One month seems far too short a time to read law before taking the bar. John Quincy Adams, who called *Coke upon Littleton* "one of those unlucky folios, which appear so formidable to many students in the profession," allowed himself three months just for that one book when he was reading law.[8] People who knew Henry assumed that his legal studies must have taken longer than a month, but estimates vary widely. Judge Edmund Winston, for one, said that Henry spent six weeks "reading of such Books as he could borrow, *without other* Assistance."[9]

Samuel Meredith, alternatively, believed that Henry spent "not more than six or eight months engaged in the study of the Law, during which time he secluded himself from the world, availing himself of the use of a few Law books owned by his father."[10] According to Meredith, Henry *was* reading law when he and Jefferson first met. If he remained tight lipped about his studies, he did so for the same reason that he kept his store going: he hesitated to make his future plans known until they were more certain.

Henry's assertion that he studied for the bar solely by reading the laws of Virginia and *Coke upon Littleton* reflects a fairly common approach among law students in colonial Virginia. The following decade, a contributor to the *Virginia Gazette* who signed himself "A Country Justice" argued that the College of William and Mary should establish a chair in law. To make his argument, this self-styled country justice described the present state of legal education in the colony. His description of the average Virginia lawyer's training sounds quite similar to what Henry told Judge Tyler. He observed, "When a young gentleman has resolved to study the law, he applies to some attorney for his advice, assists him in copying a few declarations, reads the first book of Coke upon Lyttleton, and the Virginia laws, and then applies for a license, and begins to practice a profession, the grounds and first principles of which he is perhaps utterly unacquainted with."[11]

The general state of legal education in Virginia did not change until after Thomas Jefferson's election to the governorship in 1779. As governor, Jefferson became a member of the William and Mary Board of Visitors and therefore was able to reform the curriculum and establish a professorship in law. He hired his former teacher George Wythe as the first chair in law at William and Mary. In this capacity Wythe profoundly influenced the rising generation of Virginia lawyers.[12]

It is not hard to guess where Henry found a copy of the Virginia laws. William Parks had been in the process of printing a new edition of the laws of Virginia at the time of his death. Though he died before completing the work, his will stipulated that his son-in-law John Shelton take responsibility for seeing it through the press. William Hunter took over the print shop upon Parks's death, and Shelton made sure he completed the new edition.[13]

The Acts of Assembly, Now in Force in the Colony of Virginia appeared in 1752 and attracted readers throughout colonial America, including Benjamin Franklin.[14] Since Eleanor Parks Shelton received the bulk of her father's estate, copies of other imprints from Parks's press—George Webb's practical manual *The Office and Authority of a Justice of Peace*, for instance—may have remained in the family. Furthermore, Henry could have read John Mercer's abridged version of the laws of Virginia, *An Exact Abridgment of All the Public Acts of Assembly, of Virginia, in Force and Use*, which Parks had published in 1737.

If Henry studied for the bar primarily by reading *Coke upon Littleton*, then even Jefferson could not quibble with his choice of textbook. Sir Edward Coke's multipart *Institutes* deserves its status as the premier textbook of modern English law. Familiarly known as *Coke upon Littleton*, the first part of Coke's *Institutes* presents the text of Sir Thomas Littleton's *Tenures* in law French, the Anglo-Norman language that had remained the language of court and Parliament into the sixteenth century. Coke's detailed commentary explicates and elaborates Littleton's original text.

At times, Coke's commentary becomes so detailed that it practically usurps the text it annotates. In terms of both form and content, *Coke upon Littleton* was a difficult and demanding work yet an essential one. Jefferson, whose collected writings contain much firsthand information regarding the study of law in colonial Virginia, observed that *Coke upon Littleton* "is executed with so much learning and judgment that I do not recollect that a single position in it has ever been judicially denied. And altho' the work loses much of its value by its chaotic form, it may still be considered as the fundamental code of English law." Elsewhere Jefferson spoke of the "deep and rich mines of Coke Littleton" and cautioned that Coke's opinion "is ever dangerous to neglect."[15]

To the young men who read law under him, Jefferson recommended *Coke upon Littleton* as the first book to read as they began their legal studies. Aware of its reputation as a tedious and intimidating work, Jefferson gently prepared his students for it, assuring them that after *Coke upon Littleton,* "what remains of law reading will be mere amusement." Of course, the process of reading this particular work typically involved rereading it. When his nephew Peter Carr began to read law, Jefferson advised him to read *Coke upon Littleton* "twice at least."[16]

Jefferson's advice calls to mind an anecdote that Lord Chancellor Campbell (John Campbell, 1st Baron Campbell) used to tell. Campbell had great respect for Coke's legal commentary: "He is certainly immethodical, but he is singularly perspicuous, he fixes the attention, his quaintness is often most amusing, and he excites our admiration by the inexhaustible stores of erudition, which, without any effort, he seems spontaneously to put forth." Campbell told a story about a young law student who had difficulty with *Coke upon Littleton.* He had read it twice but still did not fully understand it. When he asked his teacher what to do next, the teacher replied, "Read it three times!"[17]

Abridgments of English law also helped guide those studying for their bar exams in colonial America. In the eighteenth century, they filled the place now filled by digests. Abridgments remained useful to practicing lawyers as well. There is no evidence that Henry read any abridgments before he passed the bar, but once he began practicing law he obtained several. His library would contain such general abridgments as Matthew Bacon's *New Abridgment of the Law;* Knightley D'Anvers's *General Abridgment of the Common Law,* which continued a seventeenth-century work begun by Henry Rolle; and William Nelson's abridgment of cases, *Abridgment of the Common Law.*[18]

Copies of D'Anvers and Nelson could be found elsewhere in colonial Virginia. Reuben Skelton, who served in the House of Burgesses for Hanover County, had a copy of D'Anvers's *General Abridgment* in his library. Peyton Randolph, Speaker of the House of Burgesses and first president of the Continental Congress, had Nelson's *Abridgment* in his library. And Robert Carter had both D'Anvers and Nelson in his library at Nomini Hall.[19]

More recent than D'Anvers or Nelson, Bacon became the standard general abridgment with the publication of its initial volume in the 1730s. Many early American law students read Bacon. When William Franklin decided to study law, for instance, his father ordered a few basic texts to start. Besides *Coke upon*

Littleton, Benjamin Franklin asked his London bookseller to send his son Bacon's *New Abridgment.* John Quincy Adams described the work as "a book many instructors recommend to be read through in course." George Wythe, to take one prominent instructor as an example, had his students at William and Mary read Bacon.[20]

When Andrew Jackson was starting his career as a lawyer, he relied heavily on Bacon's *New Abridgment,* though the book once got him into trouble. Hearing Jackson cite Bacon's *New Abridgment* numerous times during a single trial, Waightstill Avery, the opposing counsel, taunted him for relying on Bacon too heavily. Avery obviously implied that his opponent knew little law beyond Bacon. Offended, Jackson replied that he knew the law well enough not to take illegal fees, referring to an incidental mistake Avery had made recently. The dispute reached a fevered pitch and led to a duel between the two, which ended harmlessly. After the duel, according to one version of this oft-repeated anecdote, Jackson gave Avery a rasher of bacon cut into the shape and size of a law book.[21]

The organization of Bacon's work made it more appealing than earlier abridgments. Instead of being organized as notes on cases and statutes arranged under alphabetical headings, as previous abridgments had been, it was a collection of authoritative essays on all aspects of the law. It was less an abridgment than a legal encyclopedia. As such, it greatly facilitated the study of English law. Not all appreciated the alphabetical organization. Though Jefferson found Bacon's alphabetical arrangements "better than Coke's jumble," he still preferred a more systematic organization, that is, a division into general subject areas that were subdivided into specific subjects. "The arrangement is under very general and leading heads," Jefferson said of Bacon's *New Abridgment,* "and these indeed, with very little difficulty, might be systematically, instead of alphabetically arranged and read."[22]

Theophilus Parsons, chief justice of the Supreme Judicial Court of Massachusetts, went further than Jefferson in his critique of Bacon's *New Abridgment.* Those who learned the law from Bacon would be nothing more than matter-of-fact lawyers, Parsons believed. They would remain unaware of the true principles on which the law was based or the necessary reasoning by which it was supported. Furthermore, Parsons continued, they would be incapable of applying legal principles to new cases or different circumstances.[23]

Henry realized that Bacon's *New Abridgment* did not supplant earlier abridgments or theoretical treatises. Good lawyers, like good scholars, understand that newer reference works may supplement earlier ones but never completely supersede them. Similar works can be read together to achieve consensus. St. George Tucker, who also read law under Wythe and later took over the chair of law at William and Mary, had copies of Bacon, D'Anvers, and Nelson in his library. So did Jefferson.[24] And, to repeat, so did Patrick Henry.

Law students typically kept commonplace books as they studied, using them to record important legal information gleaned from their reading.[25] George Wythe had his students keep commonplace books. John Marshall, who studied under Wythe at William and Mary, kept one. Marshall's surviving commonplace book shows how carefully he studied Bacon's *New Abridgment*.[26] There is no evidence that Henry kept a commonplace book before he sat for his bar exam, but while preparing for the British debts case many years later, he found it useful to commonplace the legal treatises he was reading. His extensive preparation for the British debts case suggests that Henry was reverting to a methodology he had learned earlier. Perhaps he kept a rudimentary commonplace book while studying for his bar exam that disappeared along with many of his other private papers.

Because the contents of Henry's library are known primarily by an inventory taken after his death, it is sometimes impossible to say precisely when he added any particular book to his collection. Some of the legal treatises may have been part of his personal collection of books as early as his Hanover Tavern days. Two of the most useful treatises in his law library were William Hawkins's *Treatise of the Pleas of the Crown* and Giles Duncombe's *Trials per Pais; or, The Law Concerning Juries by Nisi-Prius*.[27] Duncombe's *Trials per Pais* contains guidance for conducting a trial before a jury or a judge in the court with first jurisdiction, or nisi prius.

Hawkins, who offered readers a detailed discussion of laws relating to crime and punishment, divided his work into two parts, the first describing the nature of criminal offenses, the second explaining the manner of bringing offenders to justice. Hawkins's thoroughness and clear organization made his work superior to earlier treatises on the subject, despite the profound erudition of their authors.[28] Jefferson recommended Hawkins's treatise as one of the first books a law student should read. John Adams agreed. What made *Treatise of the Pleas of the Crown* an outstanding work was the way it set forth what John Adams called the "Divisions and Distributions" of the law. And understanding the organization of the law, Adams observed, was "the first Thing a student ought to aim at."[29]

Duncombe's *Trials per Pais* was the most widely read treatise in colonial America concerning evidence and courtroom procedure. Not only beneficial for lawyers and judges, it could also help those eligible for jury duty. The Library Company of Philadelphia had a copy in its holdings. After listing Duncombe's *Trials per Pais* in his catalog of the Library Company, Franklin noted the book's practical significance: "Very necessary for all to read that practice in Courts, or are likely to be Jury-men."[30] In his preface, Duncombe asked a question modern-day forensic scientists continue to ask: "Without Victory at the Trial, to what Purpose is the Science of the Law?"[31] This question offers a clue to Duncombe's approach in *Trials per Pais*. He stressed the practical, giving lawyers useful advice for defending their clients. As a kind of legal vade mecum Duncombe's work made a good circuit companion. It could be tucked into a saddlebag and toted around from one county courthouse to the next.

Reading Duncombe's book was almost like being in his company. His fascination with the law is infectious, and his personal writing style reveals both charm and devotion to the subject. His writing possesses an epigrammatic quality that lends itself to quotation. "If any Man be delighted in History," he observed, "let him read the Books of Law, which are nothing else but Annals and Chronicles of Things done and acted upon from year to year, in which each Case presents you with a petit history; and if Variety of Matter doth most delight the reader, doubtless, the reading of those Cases, (which differ like Men's Faces), tho like the Stars in Number, is the most pleasant reading in the World."[32] This passage seems to be speaking directly to Patrick Henry. Those who knew Henry testified that history was his favorite subject.[33] Giles Duncombe let him channel his love of history into the study of law.

Besides general works on English law, Henry would obtain a number of specialized treatises. In 1772 or after, he acquired a copy of Sir Francis Buller's *Introduction to the Law Relative to Trials at Nisi Prius*.[34] For Buller, drafting this guide for conducting jury trials was a labor of love. Buller's "idea of heaven," it has been said, was "to sit at nisi prius all day, and play whist all night."[35] Buller's *Introduction* helped Henry through many jury trials. Indeed, Henry excelled at nisi prius practice.

Henry's library contained two works treating decedent estates, which may have been part of his collection since the start of his legal career: Henry Swinburne's *Treatise of Testaments and Last Wills* and John Godolphin's *The Orphan's Legacy*.[36] Swinburne's treatise, the first work of ecclesiastical law published in English instead of in Latin, became the standard text in the field when it appeared in 1591. Aware that conservative readers might dislike his linguistic innovation, Swinburne admitted that some of the "natural Beauty and Grace" of the law might get lost in translation, but he clearly recognized the direction legal study was taking and told readers to accept law written in the vernacular.[37] Even in English, Swinburne could still display his vast knowledge of civil and canon law. Yet he did not make his erudition a barrier to study. As a recent commentator has observed, Swinburne wrote "with an eye to the needs of students." His work is "well-organized and lucid, with touches of homely wisdom."[38] Godolphin's work, written nearly a century later, gave Patrick Henry much additional information on last wills and testaments. *The Orphan's Legacy* is especially useful because of the cases Godolphin used to illustrate the work, cases that were both poignant and pertinent.

Patrick Henry knew his reading had not been as thorough as that of other contemporaries who had read law, but he did not let his lack of preparation shake his confidence. He reached Williamsburg in the spring of 1760 convinced that he had the stuff to be a good lawyer, even though he faced an examining board made up of the most distinguished attorneys in Virginia: Robert Carter Nicholas, John Randolph and his brother Peyton Randolph, and George Wythe. Happily, Henry did not have to face them en masse; he could approach each individually. Furthermore, he did not need to obtain signatures from all four men. Two signatures would suffice. George Wythe passed him first, though history is silent about the interview.

Wythe often peppered his conversation with sententiae from the literature of ancient Greece and Rome. Though Henry lacked the profound classical knowledge of his examiner, Wythe apparently recognized the young man's genius. Perhaps he saw a little of himself in Henry. Wythe knew from personal experience that learning could be achieved without a formal education. The traveler Andrew Burnaby, who met Wythe during his sojourn in Virginia, singled him out among all Virginians and praised his "perfect knowledge of the Greek language, which was taught him by his mother in the back woods."[39]

After obtaining Wythe's signature, Henry approached John Randolph. The biographer William Wirt told a detailed story of Henry's interview with Randolph, which he had heard from Judge Tyler, who had it from Henry himself. While such thirdhand stories must be read with caution, the story coincides with what other acquaintances had to say about Henry's bar exam.[40] It bears retelling.

Taking offense at Henry's ungainly appearance, Randolph initially refused to examine him at all, but on hearing that Henry had already obtained two signatures, he reluctantly agreed. Randolph had heard wrong. Henry so far had obtained only one signature. Randolph "continued the examination for several hours: interrogating the candidate, not on the principles of municipal law, in which he no doubt soon discovered his deficiency, but on the laws of nature and of nations, on the policy of the feudal system, and on general history, which last he found to be his stronghold."[41] Partway through the examination, it began to seem less like a test and more like a legal debate, with Randolph on the offensive and Henry defending his ideas and matching wits with his examiner.

"You defend your opinions well, sir," Randolph said after considerable discussion, "but now to the law and to the testimony."

Randolph escorted Henry to his law library, where they could look up the argument Henry was making.

"Behold the face of natural reason," Randolph said to Henry, checking his law books for precedents. "You have never seen these books, nor this principle of the law; yet you are right and I am wrong; and from the lesson which you have given me (you must excuse me for saying it) I will never trust to appearances again. Mr. Henry, if your industry be only half equal to your genius, I augur that you will do well, and become an ornament and an honour to your profession."

On Tuesday, 15 April 1760, Patrick Henry appeared at Goochland County Courthouse with a license to practice in the county and inferior courts bearing the signatures of George Wythe and John Randolph. After taking the necessary oaths, he was admitted to the local bar.[42] The detailed meteorological records that Lieutenant Governor Francis Fauquier kept make it possible to reconstruct local weather conditions that Tuesday.[43] It was hot for mid-April. The temperature reached eighty degrees at two o'clock that afternoon. Coming from the southwest, the wind blew in an afternoon thunderstorm. It is strangely appropriate that a thunderstorm should usher in the legal profession of Patrick Henry, the man whom his friend Roger Atkinson later called a "son of Thunder."[44]

Having promised his examiners that he would continue his studies, Henry did not disappoint them. Three days after being admitted to the bar, in fact, he augmented his law library with a copy of William Bohun's *Declarations and Pleadings,* a manual for practicing law in the common-law courts. Bohun's work continued the trajectory that Swinburne and others had begun in the sixteenth century, that is, to get legal erudition out of Latin and into the vernacular. Though Henry lacked a detailed knowledge of the classics, he entered the legal profession when it was becoming increasingly unnecessary to know Latin in order to practice law—much to the chagrin of purists like Jefferson and Wythe.

Bohun's work was especially useful at the start of Henry's legal career. It showed lawyers how to write declarations and pleadings for many different situations, including debt actions and cases of slander. In fact, several of Henry's early cases were debt actions, and late in the summer that year he was hired in a case of slander.[45] Henry internalized what Bohun had to say to such an extent that soon he no longer needed the book and apparently gave it to another young lawyer at the start of his career.

Henry's copy of Bohun's *Declarations and Pleadings* survives at the Library of Virginia. Few pieces of evidence better indicate his attitude toward books than this volume. Inscriptions in his hand confirm that he received the book on 18 April 1760 as a present from his kinsman Peter Fontaine. Other inscriptions on the last page of the table of contents show that before the decade was out it changed hands twice more. James Conedon acquired it before 20 August 1768, when he presented it to Michael Bowyer. It was passed around the Bowyer family—who were also related to Henry—for the next several decades until Bowyer Caldwell presented it to William Wirt Henry, the grandson of Patrick Henry who was named after his biographer.[46]

As a gift from a kinsman presented at the start of Patrick Henry's career, this copy of Bohun's *Declarations and Pleadings* might seem like a handsome keepsake worth retaining, but unlike other Virginia bookmen—William Byrd of Westover comes to mind—Henry had no desire to assemble a great library. After acquiring a book, as this volume and other surviving evidence suggests, he held onto it as long as it remained useful to him. It stopped being useful after Henry had internalized the book's contents. When he no longer needed it, he let someone else have the book. Patrick Henry shared his law books as readily as he shared his knowledge of the law.

Henry acquired another basic law book, *The Compleat Chancery-Practiser,* the year after he was admitted to the bar.[47] The standard manual of equity pleading and procedure, it was the work of Giles Jacob, a miscellaneous Grub Street writer who also wrote geographies, literary biographies, satirical verse, and even a hunting and fishing manual. But law was Jacob's forte. The "blunderbuss of Law," Alexander Pope liked to call him.[48]

The Compleat Chancery-Practiser begins like many other how-to manuals coming out of Grub Street. Jacob explains that he is presenting his matter in a plain and easy yet perfectly new method that will remedy the omissions and defects of all previous works on the subject. Henry's acquisition of Jacob's *Compleat Chancery-Practiser* after passing the bar suggests that he was still learning the basics of his profession.

Through his diligence, Henry was able to establish a thriving legal business in the next few years, but he had not come across the one case that would let him fully demonstrate his keen oratorical abilities. This situation changed late in 1763, when the well-known Parson's Cause came to a head. The Parson's Cause stemmed from a 1758 act passed by the Virginia General Assembly that had as one of its possibly unintended consequences a significant reduction in the salaries of the Anglican clergymen in the colony. Known as the Two-Penny Act, the law temporarily allowed vestries to pay parsons' salaries in money at a rate of approximately two pence for each pound of the legally established wage of sixteen thousand pounds of tobacco annually. At a time of a tobacco crop failure that significantly raised the price of tobacco, the law's stipulation effectively reduced their salary by two-thirds. The parsons appealed to the king, who repealed the act. With the repeal, they could sue for the balances of their salaries.

The case of John Maury, the rector of Fredericksville Parish, became a test case. Maury brought suit in Hanover County against the vestry of his parish. He hired Peter Lyons as his attorney, and John Lewis represented the vestrymen. Lyons won the case, and the court voted for the plaintiff. With the decision in Maury's favor, all that remained was for a special jury to award damages. Having lost the case, John Lewis was out as defense attorney. Instead, the defendants hired Patrick Henry, who completely transformed the situation. The proceedings to determine damages, which might have been a mere formality, emerged as one of the defining moments on the path toward American freedom.

Henry started slowly. His father, John Henry, who served as presiding judge, was embarrassed by his son's awkward beginning. Viewed in retrospect, Henry's awkwardness may have been a careful rhetorical strategy. The deliberately measured beginning became a hallmark of his mature oratorical style. The longer Patrick Henry spoke in defense of the rights and responsibilities of colonial Virginians on this occasion, the more he warmed to his subject, and the prouder his father became. For an hour Henry mesmerized the jurors, who took less than five minutes to reach a verdict: they awarded Maury damages of one penny! This occasion represents the first time Patrick Henry spoke out publicly against the power of the king to disallow acts passed by the colonial legislature. Fundamentally, his argument was based on the idea of natural rights: a king cannot act tyrannically toward the people.

The Parson's Cause solidified Henry's reputation as an orator, initiated his reputation as an American patriot, and revitalized his interest in the study of the law. After this case, he became more and more fascinated with the idea of natural law and natural rights. The following year he acquired one of the most well known and well respected legal treatises on the subject, Freiherr Samuel von Pufendorf's *Of the Law of Nature and Nations*. He also obtained another important treatise on natural and international law, Hugo Grotius's *Of the Rights of War and Peace*. With his forward-thinking ideas, Grotius helped free morality from religion. He argued that law—law based on reason and on man's natural responsibilities toward his fellow man—had existed prior to any political organization. Grotius deserves credit as the founder of the study of the law of nature and nations.

The presence of both Pufendorf and Grotius in Henry's library presents a more complex picture of his intellectual life than many people assume. The impressions of Thomas Jefferson have done much to affect the historical understanding of Patrick Henry.[49] In his correspondence with William Wirt, who incorporated his ideas in *Sketches of the Life and Character of Patrick Henry*, Jefferson portrayed Henry as a child of nature, someone whose knowledge and insight came not from books but from natural intuition. The contents of Henry's library, on the other hand, suggest that he learned about natural law by reading some of the same treatises on the subject that Jefferson read.

Thinking about Grotius, John Adams observed, "A Lawyer through his whole Life ought to have some Book on Ethicks or the Law of Nations always on his Table."[50] When Patrick Henry returned to the bar in the last decade of his life, he renewed his familiarity with natural law and the law of nations. The most important case he confronted during the final phase of his legal career was the British debts case. Involving the rights of British citizens to recover debts Americans had contracted prior to the Revolutionary War, the case demanded considerable research on Henry's part. His copy of Grotius served him well, but he found himself in need of a crucial work, Emmerich de Vattel's *Law of Nations*. Remembering that a friend who lived about sixty miles distant had a copy of Vattel, Henry dispatched his grandson Patrick Henry Fontaine to fetch it.[51]

When George Washington wanted to consult Vattel's *Law of Nations* during his first year as president, he borrowed the book from the New York Society Library.[52] In borrowing a friend's copy of Vattel, Henry reflected the more informal system of lending and borrowing books that existed in rural Virginia through the eighteenth century. Henry's personal library tells only part of the story of his intellectual life. Henry's network of friends and neighbors gave him access to many more books than he personally owned. When visiting others, he would look at their libraries and make mental notes of specific titles that caught his eye. As he needed to read other books, he would recall what his friends owned. When necessary, as the Vattel episode suggests, he would borrow books from others.

Henry excerpted numerous quotations from Grotius and Vattel, commonplacing them under various subject headings. By the time he finished preparing for the trial, he had filled a little bound manuscript volume more than an inch thick. Faced with a complex legal situation, this supposedly unsystematic man had suddenly developed a system. Even Jefferson had to admit that when it came to the British debts case, Henry "distinguished himself ... and not only seemed, but had made himself really learned on the subject."[53] For easy reference Henry kept this small yet thick notebook in his pocket. Before he went to Richmond to argue the case, he spent much time walking in his garden, frequently removing the notebook from his pocket, reading from it, and gesturing as he read.[54]

The evidence for Henry's acquisition of Pufendorf comes from the daybooks, or ledgers, of the *Virginia Gazette* office, which survive for the years 1764 and 1765. Though these daybooks have greatly aided the reconstruction of colonial Virginia book culture, they are less helpful for understanding Patrick Henry's intellectual predilections. Henry's acquisition of Pufendorf's *Of the Law of Nature and Nations* is Henry's only purchase that is recorded in the daybooks.[55] The absence of other titles does not necessarily mean that Pufendorf was the sole book Henry purchased from the *Virginia Gazette* office during the short period 1764–65. The daybooks list only items bought on credit, not those paid for in cash. Unlike many of his fellow Virginians, Henry avoided going into debt and much preferred paying cash for his acquisitions. For example, he most likely purchased his copy of *The Colonel Dismounted*, Richard Bland's political pamphlet, at the *Virginia Gazette* office. The daybooks show that his half-brother, John Syme, bought a copy of the work on credit there. Since the pamphlet was fairly inexpensive, many other customers simply paid cash for it, so their purchases, like Henry's, have escaped written record.[56]

Patrick Henry reached the pinnacle of the Virginia legal profession in 1769, when he qualified to practice before the General Court in Williamsburg. Only a small number of the most able and learned attorneys were admitted to practice in the colony's highest court. The following year, Henry acquired a copy of Timothy Cunningham's *Reports of Cases Argued and Adjudged in the Court of King's Bench,* one of many collections of law reports listed in his library catalog. Henry also owned a volume of Coke's *Reports,* the greatest collection of reports from the formative years of English law.[57] One authority considered Coke's *Reports* "so profound and fundamental, that whosoever is versed in them can do no less than make a sound lawyer." Had it not been for Coke's *Reports,* said Francis Bacon, "the law in that age would have been almost like a ship without ballast."[58]

Another set of legal reports in Henry's library, Harbottle Grimston's English translation from the law French of *The Reports of Sir George Croke,* covers the period from Queen Elizabeth's time to 1640. A model of law reporting, Croke's three-volume work records the arguments, the names of those who made them, and the decisions concisely, elegantly, and insightfully. George Wythe's heavily annotated copy of Croke's *Reports,* which survives at the Library of Congress, indicates how thoroughly he studied the work.[59] Henry's copy of Croke's *Reports* gives a similar impression. The volume of Croke from Henry's library that survived into the twentieth century was thickly annotated with marginalia in his hand.[60] Henry's impressive collection of law reports also included William Salkeld's *Reports of Cases Adjudged in the Court of King's Bench*—the standard work covering the period from the reign of William and Mary through the reign of Queen Anne—and William Peere Williams's *Reports of Cases Argued and Adjudged in the High Court of Chancery,* which is considered a classic of equity jurisprudence.[61]

Henry also obtained copies of the most comprehensive and fundamental works on English law. In 1768 he acquired Thomas Wood's *Institute of Laws of England.*[62] The leading eighteenth-century work on British law before Sir William Blackstone's *Commentaries,* Wood's *Institute,* written mainly for students, might seem too basic for someone who had passed the bar eight years earlier. But Henry's acquisition of Wood's *Institute* is consistent with other books in his library. Like some of the scientific books Henry owned, Wood's *Institute* is a digest, a work that condenses and systematizes the law.

Not content solely with Wood's *Institute,* Henry later obtained a copy of the Dublin edition of Blackstone's *Commentaries on the Laws of England.* Blackstone successfully synthesized the English tradition of jurisprudence as it had evolved since *Coke upon Littleton.* The first volume of Henry's copy of

Blackstone survives at the Lilly Library, Indiana University. Henry quickly recognized the work's tremendous practical value. On the first page of the table of contents two sections are marked in the margin. Henry's copy changed hands several times after his death, so it is impossible to say for sure whether the marks are Henry's, but they do reflect his interests. The first marked part is the second section of the introduction, "Of the Nature of Laws in General." The second marked part is the first chapter of book 1, "Of the Absolute Rights of Individuals."[63]

Henry also recommended Blackstone to others. When the Philadelphia publisher Robert Bell issued an edition of Blackstone the following year, its subscribers included Lew Bowyer, a brother-in-law who had read law with Henry.[64] Blackstone's *Commentaries* served Henry well for years to come, not only in the courtroom but also in the halls of legislation. Like many of his contemporaries who made their livings and their reputations in the legal and political world, Henry saw Blackstone's *Commentaries* as the finest and most comprehensive expression of British constitutional thought available.[65]

The records of the debates in the Virginia convention called to consider ratification of the proposed Constitution of the United States contain additional evidence to demonstrate the importance Henry attributed to Blackstone. One of the most vocal opponents of the Constitution as it was framed by the Constitutional Convention, Henry cited Blackstone multiple times during the state ratification convention. Blackstone's *Commentaries* proved useful for illustrating the drawbacks of the Constitution as Henry perceived them. Finding inadequate provisions in the Constitution for jury trials, he offered a rousing defense of trial by jury, which in his view was a hallmark of modern democracy. Henry observed:

> To hear Gentlemen of such penetration make use of such arguments, to persuade us to part with that trial by jury, is very astonishing. We are told, that we are to part with that trial by jury which our ancestors secured their lives and property with, and we are to build castles in the air, and substitute visionary modes of decision to that noble palladium. I hope we shall never be induced by such arguments, to part with that excellent mode of trial. No appeal can now be made as to fact in common-law suits.—The unanimous verdict of twelve impartial men, cannot be reversed. I shall take the liberty of reading to the Committee the sentiments of the learned Judge Blackstone, so often quoted, on the subject.[66]

After reading aloud Blackstone's famous paean to trial by jury, Henry continued: "The opinion of this learned writer is more forcible and cogent than any thing I could say. Notwithstanding the transcendent excellency of this trial, its essentiality to the preservation of liberty, and the extreme danger of substituting any other mode, yet we are now about to alienate it."[67]

Overall, Patrick Henry had many of the same legal works in his library as could be found in the great American law libraries of the eighteenth century. He had the same general abridgment of law as John Adams; the same manual of practice as Theophilus Parsons; the same treatise on uses and trusts as Thomas Jefferson; the same treatise on procedure and evidence as Benjamin Chew, chief justice of Pennsylvania; the same treatise on decedent estates as John Jay, the first chief justice of the United States; the same treatise on criminal law as Robert Treat Paine, attorney general of Massachusetts; and the same treatise on family law as Jasper Yeates, associate justice of the Supreme Court of Pennsylvania.[68] The list could go on.

Henry's acquisition of Pufendorf's *Of the Law of Nature and Nations* in 1764 suggests that he was eager to delve into the study of natural rights and natural law. He was not alone. As the events of the following year, the year of the Stamp Act, demonstrated, English law was becoming increasingly irrelevant to colonial rule. Colonists throughout North America were starting to formulate ideas of law that transcended national boundaries. Patrick Henry may have been somewhat ill-prepared when he passed the bar in 1760, but as the Revolutionary events in the ensuing decade began to unfold, he found himself well qualified to argue the case for the natural rights of the American people.

NOTES

1. Mark Couvillon, *Patrick Henry's Virginia: A Guide to the Homes and Sites in the Life of an American Patriot* (Brookneal, VA, 2001), 31–32; François Jean, marquis de Chastellux, *Travels in North America in the Years 1780, 1781, and 1782,* trans. and ed. Howard C. Rice Jr., 2 vols. (Chapel Hill, NC, 1963), 2:380.
2. Couvillon, *Patrick Henry's Virginia,* 31.
3. Rhys Isaac, *The Transformation of Virginia, 1740–90* (1982; reprint, New York, 1988), 88–94.
4. Edmund Randolph, *History of Virginia,* ed. Arthur H. Schaffer (Charlottesville, 1970), 168.
5. Robert Douthat Meade, *Patrick Henry: Patriot in the Making* (Philadelphia, 1957), 93.
6. Kevin J. Hayes, *The Road to Monticello: The Life and Mind of Thomas Jefferson* (New York, 2008), 43.
7. William Wirt, *Sketches of the Life and Character of Patrick Henry* (1817; reprint, New York, 1857), 34.
8. David Grayson Allen et al., eds., *Diary of John Quincy Adams* (Cambridge, MA, 1981–), 2:331.
9. Robert Douthat Meade, ed., "Judge Edmund Winston's Memoir of Patrick Henry," *Virginia Magazine of History and Biography* 69 (1961): 37.
10. Samuel Meredith, "Colonel Samuel Meredith's Statement," in *The True Patrick Henry,* ed. George Morgan (Philadelphia, 1907), 433.
11. "To Mrs. Rind," *Virginia Gazette* (Rind), 30 Dec. 1773.

12. E. Lee Shepard, "George Wythe," in *Legal Education in Virginia, 1779–1979: A Biographical Approach*, ed. W. Hamilton Bryson (Charlottesville, 1982), 749–55.
13. Lawrence C. Wroth, *William Parks: Printer and Journalist of England and Colonial America* (Richmond, 1926), 26–27.
14. Edwin Wolf 2d and Kevin J. Hayes, *The Library of Benjamin Franklin* (Philadelphia, 2006), no. 3524.
15. Thomas Jefferson to Thomas Cooper, 16 Jan. 1814, in *The Papers of Thomas Jefferson: Retirement Series*, ed. J. Jefferson Looney et al. (Princeton, NJ, 2004–), 7:126; Jefferson to John Tyler, 17 June 1812, ibid., 5:136; Thomas Jefferson, "Revisal of the Laws," in *The Papers of Thomas Jefferson*, ed. Julian P. Boyd et al. (Princeton, NJ, 1950–), 2:495.
16. Jefferson to St. George Tucker, 22 Dec. 1793, in *Papers of Thomas Jefferson*, 27:609; Jefferson to Peter Carr, 28 Mar. 1790, ibid., 16:277.
17. John, Lord Campbell, *The Lives of the Lord Chancellors and Keepers of the Great Seal of England, from the Earliest Times Till the Reign of King George IV*, 8 vols. (London, 1845–69), 7:38.
18. Kevin J. Hayes, *The Mind of a Patriot: Patrick Henry and the World of Ideas* (Charlottesville, 2008), nos. 44, 3, 136.
19. E. Millicent Sowerby, *Catalogue of the Library of Thomas Jefferson*, 5 vols. (Washington, DC, 1952–59), nos. 1790, 1789; W. Hamilton Bryson, *Census of Law Books in Colonial Virginia* (Charlottesville, 1978), nos. 331, 488.
20. Benjamin Franklin to William Strahan, 6 December 1750, in *The Papers of Benjamin Franklin*, ed. Leonard W. Labaree et al. (New Haven, CT, 1959–), 4:77; Clement Eaton, "A Mirror of the Southern Colonial Lawyer: The Fee Books of Patrick Henry, Thomas Jefferson and Waightstill Avery," *William and Mary Quarterly*, 2d ser., 8 (1951): 522.
21. Paul F. Boller Jr., ed., *Presidential Anecdotes*, rev. ed. (New York, 1996), 74–75.
22. Jefferson to Dabney Terrell, 26 Feb. 1821, in Thomas Jefferson Papers, Library of Congress.
23. *Diary of John Quincy Adams*, 2:394.
24. Herbert A. Johnson, *Imported Law Treatises in American Libraries, 1700–1799* (Knoxville, 1978), nos. 4, 56, 146.
25. W. Hamilton Bryson, "Legal Education," in *Virginia Law Books: Essays and Bibliographies*, ed. Bryson (Philadelphia, 2000), 320.
26. Bryson, *Census of Law Books*, no. 320; *The Papers of John Marshall*, ed. Herbert A. Johnson et al., 12 vols. (Chapel Hill, NC, 1974–2006), 1:38–39.
27. Hayes, *Mind of a Patriot*, nos. 94, 53.
28. Ibid., p. 38.
29. Thomas Jefferson to John Garland Jefferson, 11 June 1790, in *Papers of Thomas Jefferson*, 16:481; *Diary and Autobiography of John Adams*, ed. L. H. Butterfield, 4 vols. (Cambridge, MA, 1961), 1:56–57.
30. Benjamin Franklin, *A Catalogue of Books Belonging to the Library Company of Philadelphia* (Philadelphia, 1741), 27–28.
31. Giles Duncombe, *Trial per Pais: or, The Law of England Concerning Juries by Nisi*

Prius, 5th ed. ([London], 1718), sig. A3v; see also Terence F. Kiely, *Forensic Evidence: Science and the Criminal Law* (Boca Raton, FL, 2000), iii.
32. Quoted in Kiely, *Forensic Evidence,* iii.
33. Hayes, *Mind of a Patriot,* nos. 25–26.
34. Ibid., no. 23.
35. "Our Books," *Albany Law Journal,* 23 Dec. 1871, 343.
36. Hayes, *Mind of a Patriot,* nos. 163, 165.
37. Henry Swinburne, *A Treatise of Testaments and Last Wills,* 5th ed. (London, 1728), sig. A2v.
38. Sheila Doyle, "Swinburne, Henry," in *Oxford Dictionary of National Biography,* ed. H. C. G. Matthew and Brian Harrison, 60 vols. (New York, 2004), 53:492–93.
39. Andrew Burnaby, *Burnaby's Travels through North America,* ed. Rufus Rockwell Wilson (New York, 1904), 53.
40. Meade, *Patrick Henry,* 96–97.
41. Wirt, *Sketches of the Life,* 35.
42. Meade, *Patrick Henry,* 96.
43. Ibid., 93; Francis Fauquier, "Diary of the Weather," in *Travels through the Middle Settlements in North-America, in the Years 1759 and 1760,* by Andrew Burnaby (Ithaca, NY, 1968), 122.
44. Roger Atkinson to Samuel Pleasants, 1 Oct. 1774, in "Letters of Roger Atkinson, 1769–1776," ed. A. J. Morrison, *Virginia Magazine of History and Biography* 15 (1908): 356.
45. For the best survey of Henry's first year as a lawyer, see Meade, *Patrick Henry,* 99–113.
46. Hayes, *Mind of a Patriot,* no. 17.
47. Ibid., no. 110.
48. Alexander Pope, "The Dunciad," in *Poetry and Prose of Alexander Pope,* ed. Aubrey Williams (Boston, 1969), bk. 3, line 150.
49. Hayes, *Mind of a Patriot,* 1–15.
50. *Diary and Autobiography of John Adams,* 3:272.
51. Edward Fontaine, *Patrick Henry: Corrections of Biographical Mistakes, and Popular Errors in Regard to His Character,* ed. Mark Couvillon (Brookneal, VA, 1996), 10.
52. Rich Shapiro, "Read It and Weep, by George: Prez Racks Up 300G Late Fee for Two Books," *New York Daily News,* 17 Apr. 2010, 10.
53. Spencer Roane, "Judge Spencer Roane's Memorandum," in Morgan, *True Patrick Henry,* 441.
54. Couvillon, *Patrick Henry's Virginia,* 85.
55. Hayes, *Mind of a Patriot,* no. 147.
56. Gregory A. Stiverson and Cynthia Z. Stiverson, *Books Both Useful and Entertaining: A Study of Book Purchasing by Virginians in the Mid-Eighteenth Century* (1976; reprint, Williamsburg, 1984), 100.
57. Hayes, *Mind of a Patriot,* nos. 78, 83.
58. Quoted in "Characters of Reports," *American Jurist and Law Magazine* 8 (1832): 260–75, quotations on 262, 263.

59. Thomas Jefferson subsequently obtained Wythe's copy of Croke with the rest of Wythe's library. Sowerby, *Catalogue of the Library of Thomas Jefferson,* no. 2052, notes that the annotations in the volume are not in Jefferson's hand. Presumably, they are Wythe's.
60. Christopher W. Brooks, "Croke, Sir George," in Matthew and Harrison, *Oxford Dictionary of National Biography,* 14:262–63; Stan V. Henkels, *The Patrick Henry Papers and Relics and Other Important Historical Letters and Documents* (Philadelphia, 1910), lot 4221.
61. Hayes, *Mind of a Patriot,* nos. 77, 70; W. P. Williams, "Salkeld, William," rev. Anne Pimlott Baker, in Matthew and Harrison, *Oxford Dictionary of National Biography,* 48:720; D. E. C. Yale, "Williams, William Peere," ibid., 59:335–36.
62. Hayes, *Mind of a Patriot,* no. 186.
63. Ibid., no. 13; Jack P. Greene, *The Intellectual Heritage of the Constitutional Era: The Delegates' Library* (Philadelphia, 1986), 22; William Blackstone, *Commentaries on the Laws of England,* 4th ed., 4 vols. (Dublin, 1771), 1:v.
64. "Subscribers in Virginia to Blackstone's Commentaries on the Laws of England, Philadelphia, 1771–1772," *William and Mary Quarterly,* 2d ser., 1 (1921): 183.
65. Greene, *Intellectual Heritage,* 22.
66. Merrill Jensen et al., eds., *The Documentary History of the Ratification of the Constitution* (Madison, WI, 1976–), 10:1423.
67. Ibid.
68. Hayes, *Mind of a Patriot,* nos. 3, 23, 63, 108, 165, 94; Johnson, *Imported Law Treatises,* nos. 4, 29, 82, 106, 188, 98.

A VIRGINIA ORIGINAL

GEORGE WEBB'S
OFFICE AND
AUTHORITY OF A
JUSTICE OF PEACE

Warren M. Billings

THE
Office and Authority
OF A
Justice of Peace.

AND ALSO

The Duty of Sheriffs, Coroners, Church-wardens, Surveiors of Highways, Constables, and Officers of Militia.

Together with

Precedents of Warrants, Judgments, Executions, and other legal Process, issuable by Magistrates within their respective Jurisdictions, in Cases Civil or Criminal.

AND

The Method of Judicial Proceedings, before Justices of Peace, in Matters within their Cognisance out of Sessions.

Collected from the Common and Statute Laws of *England*, and Acts of Assembly, now in Force; And adapted to the Constitution and Practice of *Virginia*.

By GEORGE WEBB, Gent. One of His Majesty's Justices of Peace of the County of New-Kent.

WILLIAMSBURG:
Printed by WILLIAM PARKS. M,DCC,XXXVI.

George Webb's 1736 Office and Authority of a Justice of Peace was the first legal reference work of its kind compiled and printed in Virginia. George Webb, The Office and Authority of a Justice of Peace (Williamsburg, 1736). (Courtesy the Library of Virginia)

GEORGE WEBB'S *OFFICE AND AU-thority of a Justice of Peace and also the Duty of Sheriffs . . . Adapted to the Constitution and Practice of Virginia* is unique in the annals of American legal literature. Published in 1736 by the Williamsburg printer William Parks, it was the first law book of its kind ever composed by a Virginian. It remained authoritative until it was cast aside at the end of the eighteenth century in favor of more up-to-date manuals, whereupon it turned into an antique. Surviving copies eventually wound up in private collections or in research libraries, where they tend to be prized more for their rarity than for the knowledge they impart, and they remain little-known, seldom-examined relics from a distant past.

The book and its author deserve better.[1] Both invite and to some extent answer questions about legal literacy in eighteenth-century Virginia. Who was George Webb? What was his relationship with William Parks? What suited him to his task? Why did Webb write the book? Where did he turn for inspiration? Who were his intended readers? As for Parks, how did he design the book? How long did it take to produce it, and what was his probable press run? How did Parks market the book and at what price? When did the *Virginia Justice* fall into disuse, and what difference did it make? Answers to such queries reveal the significance of early law books and yield clues that may be found nowhere else about the spread of legal knowledge and the making of law in the Old Dominion.

George Webb lived in a county that lost all but mere fragments of its colonial records during the American Civil War. Meager goods—snippets here, strands there—cloak Webb more in shadow than in sunshine, and that makes him an elusive figure to reveal. About all that is known is this: A son of the London merchant Conrade Webb, he settled in New Kent County early in the 1700s. Quite possibly he emigrated to tend to family business in the area, though it is just as probable that he was a younger son who left home in search of betterment that he could not find in England. Evidently gifted with a sharp eye for lucrative opportunities that fell his way, he rapidly amassed substantial holdings in slaves and land. He even kept a ferry at one of his plantations that fronted the Pamunkey River, which linked him commercially to the opposite shore in King William County and yielded a reliable income from tolls. In one respect, Webb differed not a whit from other aspiring middling immigrants to Virginia. Like them, he regarded a strategic marriage as the swiftest, surest way to elevate his stature. He found just such a match when he wed a well-fixed widow, Lucy Foster Jones. There are no details about her dead husband, but the Fosters were early settlers in New Kent, and in Lucy's day they were among the more prominent residents of the county. Lucy's father had been a burgess in the General Assembly of 1702/3–1705 and a long-serving justice of the peace who died sometime in the mid-1710s. Her brother, also a member of the House of Burgesses and a magistrate, seems to have brought the couple together, because they wed at his plantation in 1728.[2]

After his marriage, Webb walked down a well-worn route to political preferment. He became a vestryman and warden of St. Peter's Parish in New Kent County. A stint as sheriff followed, as did a seat on the New Kent County Court, which he kept until his death. He never stood for the House of Burgesses, but that did not mean that his public career stopped at the New Kent County line. Quite the opposite: he fashioned connections with members of the General Assembly, with Lieutenant Governor William Gooch, and with William Parks, which dealt him a hand in shaping the law and public policy throughout the 1730s and 1740s.

The first sign of those links comes to light in the legislative journals of the Council of State. In June 1732 Gooch and the councillors concurred in a House resolution that Webb be paid two hundred pounds for "his Trouble and pains in preparing a Copy of the Laws of this Colony for the Press and composing a Table thereto."[3] That terse minute is illuminating on two counts. It establishes the earliest identifiable bond between Webb and Parks, and it reveals Webb's penchant for legal scholarship, which culminated in the *Virginia Justice*.

Webb's "Trouble and pains" eased the way for publication of a project that Parks had undertaken for the General Assembly half a decade earlier but had not completed.[4] In February 1727 a select committee headed by Speaker of the House of Burgesses John Holloway contracted with Parks to prepare an up-to-date edition of the Virginia statutes in force.[5] At the time Parks was heavily engaged as the public printer of Maryland and the editor of the *Maryland Gazette* even as he was in the process of moving his business from Annapolis to Williamsburg, where he founded the *Virginia Gazette* and became the colony's first public printer. The statutes project languished until Webb finished it by compiling, editing, and indexing *A Collection of all the Acts of Assembly, Now in Force in the Colony of Virginia,* which Parks finally issued in 1733.

Throughout the 1730s and 1740s Webb's name turns up in the journals of the House of Burgesses. It usually appears in references to his work as clerk to one of the House committees.[6] Those were not inconsequential appointments given that committee clerks wielded considerably more behind-the-scenes influence than one might expect. Aside from the requisite secretarial skills and the ability to remain discrete, clerks became clerks because of their detailed knowledge of matters that came before their committees and because of their adeptness at assisting the members in expediting the business of legislating.

More notably, they drafted the bills that went to the floor of the House for debate and passage into law. Committee clerks routinely coordinated with the clerk of the House and the Speaker, who had a hand in their selection. Then too, they often acted as go-betweens and negotiated the compromises with the Council that determined whether a bill became law and in what form. Webb's most important clerkships were those of the standing committee on courts of justice and the select committee on law revision, which drew up the 1749 recodification of the statutes at large.[7]

Speaker John Robinson also appointed Webb clerk of the treasury after Robinson succeeded John Holloway as treasurer of the colony. In that capacity Webb worked closely with the treasurer as Robinson tried to cleanse a financial mess that Holloway had left when he unexpectedly died of a fit. Ironically, Robinson's own fiddling with an issue of wartime currency, which came to light after his death in 1766, caused an even more serious fiscal and political crisis. That scandal left no marks on Webb, who did not live long enough to be tainted by it.[8]

Unraveling the ties between Webb and Gooch presents a rather more challenging problem because there is little overt evidence of a personal relationship between the two men. Appointed in 1727, Gooch (1681–1751) governed Virginia longer than anyone save Sir William Berkeley, whose style of rule he imitated, whether deliberately or not. Like Berkeley, he was graced with a personal charm that drew others to him, and he was always popular with the colonists. Like Berkeley, he came to his office well schooled in the arts of statecraft, and like Sir William, he appreciated the value of stagecraft to the tasks of governing. Again like Berkeley, he was quick to make common cause with the gentry and usually deferred to the councillors and burgesses, which endeared him to them and stood in marked contrast to the behavior of some of his recent predecessors.[9]

Webb probably first caught Gooch's eye while he was helping Parks with *A Collection of all the Acts of Assembly*. His appointment to the New Kent bench happened about that time, though it did not necessarily imply a special closeness to Gooch. It may have merely vouchsafed the recommendations of the senior county officials, which testifies to Webb's local standing. Webb dedicated the *Virginia Justice* to Gooch. That dedication suggests a degree of nearer proximity, but it too may signify nothing beyond a pro forma bow to a popular chief executive who had urged Webb on. Most compelling is Webb's vigorous brief in the *Virginia Justice* for the Tobacco Inspection Act of 1730.[10]

Highly controversial when Gooch pushed it through the General Assembly, the inspection law continued to be a source of contention even to the point of provoking riots in 1732. Gooch quickly quelled the violence with his signature firmness and fairness, although the disaffection continued to simmer. His anonymous pamphlet *A Dialogue Between Thomas Sweet-*

Scented, William Oronoco, Planters, both Men of Good Understanding, and Justice Love-Country, Who Can Speak for Himself (1732), tamped down the disaffection a bit more. Grumbles could be heard for years afterwards, and it is therefore easy to imagine Gooch encouraging Webb to defend the act in the *Virginia Justice* as yet another way of cooling the discontent. If that was Gooch's intent, then he saw in Webb an appropriate person for the job. Webb was a respected local magistrate and recognized legal scholar. In the House of Burgesses but not of it, he did not project a high political profile akin to that of the lieutenant governor or the leading assemblymen, who had whipped the votes necessary to win the bill's passage and continued vigorously to support the legislation. And unlike Gooch, Webb had no verifiable part in suppressing the riots, which all happened outside New Kent. Instead, Webb's public face, to the degree he had one, was that of a learned judge whose defense of the inspection act offered a seemingly low-key, nonpartisan personal commentary on a contentious statute, one about which Gooch cared deeply.[11]

Whether Webb and Parks were acquaintances before they collaborated on the *Collection of all the Acts of Assembly* is unverifiable. Certain it is, though, that the idea for the *Virginia Justice* came from Webb, not Parks. Entrepreneur that Parks was, he saw the book as a significant addition to his developing line of Virginia legal offerings. Another attraction was, in Webb's words, "THE *voluntary Subscriptions which were universally offer'd upon my Publishing Proposals for Printing this Book,*" which spared Parks the chore of rounding up the capital that underwrote the *Virginia Justice.* Although Webb called the contributors *"Persons of all Ranks,"* he mentioned none of them by name, nor did Parks disclose them in any of his advertisements, and their identity has never come to light. Conceivably, Webb invested some of his own money as well.[12]

Whereas the destruction of the New Kent records effectively hides whatever details they might have divulged about the nature of Webb's legal knowledge, the *Virginia Justice* bears vivid testimony to an unusual breadth of learning that prepared him for his task. Apparently without formal training, Webb first learned his law by the book, which is to say that well before his appointment as a justice of the peace he had already mastered the English legal writings that had informed untutored colonial magistrates since Virginia's earliest days.[13] At the top of his reading list would have been such standards as John Cowell's *A Law Dictionary: Or the Interpreter of Words and Terms;* Michael Dalton's *Countrey Justice: Or the Office of Justices of Peace out of their Sessions;* Dalton's *Office and Authority of Sheriffs;* William Lambarde's *Eirenarcha; or the Office of the Justices of Peace;* John Rastell's *Termes de la Ley;* Henry Swinburne's *Treatise of Testaments and Last Wills;* and William West's *Symboleographie: Which May be Termed the Art, or Description, of Instruments and Precedents.* Webb would also have acquainted himself with some of the literature that moved litigation through the royal courts at Westminster, as these were books that had drawn English and colonial practice closer together since the beginning of the eighteenth century. His own experience as a sitting justice of the peace and as editor of *A Collection of all the Acts of Assembly* broadened his learning even further. So as he began the *Virginia Justice,* his mastery equaled or perhaps even surpassed that of some of his more renowned contemporaries.[14]

The books to which Webb turned as he wrote the *Virginia Justice* amply demonstrated the weight of his erudition. He cited fifty-seven works, whose authors ranged from the familiar to the obscure, then and now. The library embraced a generous spread of topics that included case reports of decisions in the Crown courts at Westminster, statutory compilations in full text or in abridged versions, how-to manuals, treatises, commentaries, dictionaries, histories, and books of forms. Most were written in English. Fifteen were cast in Latin or law French, a bastard written variant of Norman French that was still used in English legal proceedings, as it had been since 1066. Their inclusion reveals Webb's facility with both languages, which was a rather uncommon skill for a Virginia magistrate of his generation. Fifty-one titles were published before the end of the seventeenth century. Many of those volumes were long out of print by the 1730s, which left Webb to rely on whichever impression was handy.[15]

Did Webb own all of the titles? Probably not. A private law library of that size would have been fairly unusual, as well as expensive, and because so many of its items were no longer in print, collecting serviceable copies would have been difficult. He probably purchased his own copies of Dalton, Swinburne, and Cowell as well as some of the other titles, but how many is anybody's guess. Whenever he needed books that he did not own, he would have borrowed them from neighbors, which was a common habit among eighteenth-century Virginians, no matter what they read, and so friends or acquaintances would have provided an avenue to an indeterminate number of the fifty-seven.

Then too, any time he was in Williamsburg, Webb could consult the library of the Council of State. The oldest law library in Virginia, the council library originated in the 1620s. It owed its existence to Councillor George Thorpe, who started it after he begged Sir Edwin Sandys, then treasurer of the Virginia Company of London, "to send us the newe booke of the abrigement of Statutes and Stamford's please of the Crowne and mr west presidents and what other Lawe books you shall see fit."[16] By the 1730s the collection had grown into one of the best libraries of its kind anywhere in the Old Dominion. Webb probably depended on its holdings for some of the scarce, old, or out-of-print books he used. Given these alternatives, owning all fifty-seven volumes was not a necessity, and not owning most of them was no impediment.

Webb explained his underlying rationale for the *Virginia Justice* quite succinctly. An "Increase of our People" occasioned a "new and greater Variety of Cases, Civil and Criminal, as well in Courts of Justice, as before Magistrates out of Session," and that growth magnified the necessity for a "work of this Nature." That demand resulted in his being frequently entreated "for Advice in Judicial Proceedings before Justices of Peace." The *Virginia Justice* responded to such pleas.[17]

Although he never said as much, Webb may also have envisioned a more radical purpose—replacing the English instructional manuals that had been normal fare for colonial magistrates ever since the days of George Thorpe. Cherished how-to manuals such as Lambarde's *Eirenarcha,* Dalton's *Countrey Justice,* and Swinburne's *Treatise of Testaments and Last Wills* were instrumental in the transit of English local law to Virginia, as he understood better than most, but Webb surely would have known that they were no longer as determinant as they once had been. First published in 1581, the *Eirenarcha* went out of print in 1619, and there were few copies still to be had in Virginia. Dalton's *Countrey Justice* appeared in 1619 and went through numerous reprintings, the most recent being a 1727 reissue. The final edition of Swinburne's *Treatise* came out in 1728. The wear and tear of constant use had taken their toll on the available manuals too, and as a result serviceable copies had grown increasingly scarce, especially in the newer counties. Scarcity created problems for justices in those jurisdictions because a 1666 act of assembly that required county courts to purchase Dalton and Swinburne was still good law, and justices were hard put to honor its mandate.[18]

The substance of the manuals was a drawback too. When Swinburne, Lambarde, and Dalton described English local courts and judicial processes, they spoke to homebound Britons. Whatever the edition or the impression, their discussions talked about practices and precedents from a remote past in a distant place. The tendency of writers who prepared later editions of these works was merely to update the original statutory and case citations instead of completely overhauling the texts themselves. They had less and less to say about the practical differences between English legal proceedings and their hybrid counterparts in Webb's Virginia. Then too, much of their content challenged colonial justices intellectually, because it incorporated long passages in Latin and law French, together with plentiful dollops of Greek or Hebrew thrown in for good measure, all of which were beyond the ken of many or most Virginia magistrates.[19]

Webb aimed his book at four specific sets of potential readers. The "Unlearned Reader," wrote he, will find "a plain and clear Explanation of every difficult Word, or Term in Law, wherever such occur; to which I have added under such Heads as are most material, diverse Historical Abstracts, which I conceiv'd might prove entertaining as instructive."[20] Next he courted experienced magistrates. For them, as for him, the *Virginia Justice* would be *the* ready modern reference work, to which they could turn individually or severally whenever a need presented itself.

Newly made justices of the peace made up a third set. They may well have been the readers Webb most earnestly desired to engage, because many of them came to their offices with little or no prior schooling in the law. As he remarked in his preface, "To the Reader," Virginia was in the midst of an explosive period of growth that swelled the population and extended the area of settlement from the Tidewater to the Piedmont to the Blue Ridge Mountains and beyond.[21] More people meant more litigation, which increased the burdens on existing local courts and raised pressures for the creation of new ones. Carving out additional county courts meant identifying men to stock each of the benches with eight or more justices.[22] Demand outpaced supply and created opportunities for recent arrivals or local men of less elevated standing than the members of the great planter families who made up the ruling elite. For such appointees the book would become their vade mecum.

County-court lawyers were the fourth group. In contrast to the Virginia of the 1600s, in which the colonists resolutely shunned trained barristers, the Virginia of Webb's day was an inviting place for lawyers to practice. Clients abounded, and as a contemporary observer noted, "Lawyers have an excellent Time here, and if a Man is a clever Fellow, that Way, 'tis a sure way to an Estate."[23] Although lawyering already bore the earmarks of a learned profession fit for the sons of elite planters and polished immigrants alike, the quality of legal representation left ample leeway for improvement. The better-educated lawyers congregated around Williamsburg and practiced in the General Court, whereas the more numerous lesser-skilled attorneys advocated in the county courts. Responding to complaints about the inadequacies of the latter, the General Assembly enacted legislation in 1732 that required would-be county-court lawyers to submit to an examination by a "person or persons, learned in the law." Those who passed the test received their licenses, but they could practice only in the local courts. The value of the *Virginia Justice* for those licensees lay in its handy compilation of laws and other information that were material to the representation of their clients.[24]

Webb cut the design for the *Virginia Justice* broadly to a pattern that he borrowed from an English prototype perfected at the beginning of the sixteenth century, Sir Anthony Fitzherbert's *The New Booke of Justices of Peace* (1543), which was an updated version of an anonymously authored work called the *Boke of Justices of Peace*, published in 1508 or perhaps earlier.[25] In keeping with the structural elements of his model, the book includes an imprimatur, a dedication, prefatory remarks, the text, and an index. The text comprises 299 subjects, or "Titles," arranged alphabetically, beginning with "Accessories" and ending with "Wreck'd Ships, Goods, &c." They vary in length from a few lines to as many as fifteen pages. Some also incorporate sample warrants, recognizances, mittimuses, and other procedural instruments—"precedents," as such documents were called—that one or more justices could issue to keep the peace. These were standard features of such manuals, but Webb excluded others that an English reader of, say, Lambarde or Dalton would normally have expected to find. For instance, the *Virginia Justice* does not begin with a discussion of the origins of the office of justice of the peace or the legal concept "peace." Missing too are tables of cases, lists of statutes bearing on the office of justice, appendices, or anything else Webb deemed irrelevant to his purpose.[26] Anticipating that he would be sharply criticized for such omissions, he confronted his likely censors head on. "My Design and Method being new," he wrote, "I make not Doubts but Critics will be Carping at the Performance: tho' 'twere better, they'd be less ill-natured: My advice to these Gentlemen, is, That they mend it by some of their own ingenious Compositions, their Work will be the easier, now I have found and clear'd a Road; if they do not, the World will have Room to suspect their Ability."[27]

Webb's remark draws a reader's eye to the two most visible differences between the *Virginia Justice* and its English model: the language and the subject entries. Save for the Latin names of certain writs and a few other terms, Webb wrote entirely in the vernacular. His pithy prose is akin to Dalton's, though it lacks the sauciness that Dalton was often capable of. That very plainness was a gift that made Webb's explanations of terminology much easier for his readers—then and now—to comprehend. Take as an example his definition of *murder*, which he paraphrases from a passage in Sir Matthew Hale's *Historia Placitorum Coronae: The History of the Pleas of the Crown*. "Murder is," he says, "the Killing any Person, within the Realm upon Malice forethought, the Death ensuing within a Year and a Day after the Stroke given."[28]

Among the book's more instructive features are Webb's identification of legal terminology and various aspects of English civil and criminal procedure that Virginians had appropriated extensively. In each of those instances, Webb drew on his reference works and cast the titles into concise definitions and explanations that encapsulated the essence of their subject matter. Taken together these sections of the *Virginia Justice* are remarkably evocative of the many English precedents that were engrafted wholesale, and without modification, onto colonial local law by 1736.[29]

Equally suggestive are two other types of entries, those illustrating which English precedents the Virginians took and then modified to fit colonial necessities and those addressing subjects that were unprecedented in English law. Webb's commentary on courts, juries, constables, justices, and sheriffs stand out as notable examples of this crossbreeding, which increasingly distinguished Virginia's law and legal institutions from England's.[30] Similarly, his discussions of Indian affairs, the militia, county formation, and labor relations point to legal arrangements the colonists cut from whole cloth.[31]

The titles "Blasphemy," "Churchwardens," "Clergy," and "Divine Service" are among those that Webb included to explicate ecclesiastical habits of governance in Virginia that were distinct from those in England.[32] Collectively, they afford modern readers a detailed statement of the laws and customs that governed Virginia's religious polity on the eve of the Great Awakening. They bespoke a stable institutional church controlled by the laity and dependent on secular authorities to enforce its doctrines and discipline. Furthermore, as Webb remarked, "Among the Inhabitants of this Colony we have not any known or reputed Popish Recusants, but are happy hitherto in a professed Conformity ... to the Church of *England;* We have no Separatists, or Nonconformists, except *Quakers,* and these enjoy a legal Toleration."[33] The "legal Toleration" of which Webb spoke came to pass when the General Assembly of 1699 first codified the English Act of Toleration.[34]

In a significant departure from English manuals, Webb also included a rather long entry about the General Assembly. Introducing the subject, he was quick to say that "nothing under this Head is within the Jurisdiction of a Justice of Peace," but he justified its inclusion with the observation that because the assembly was "one of the main Fundamentals of our Constitution, and the chief Support of the Liberty and Property of the Subject, some Knowledge of the Law in this Matter may be useful, or necessary to every Freeholder within this Dominion." A General Assembly was a meeting of governor, councillors, and burgesses for the purpose of "debating Matters touching the Common-Wealth; and especially, the making, amending, or repealing of Laws," and it was "of all other Courts, the Highest, and of greatest Authority." He continued with an explanation of who qualified as burgesses, who elected them, who they represented, their privileges, and how elections were supposed to work. His discussion is one of the clearest contemporary descriptions of early eighteenth-century election practices that modern scholars are likely to find anywhere.[35]

Elsewhere Webb broaches the tetchy issue of the relationship of colonial statutes to acts of Parliament. On the one hand, he acknowledges that "Acts of Parliament made in *England,* expressly declaring, That they shall extend to *Virginia,* or to his Majesty's *American* Plantations, are of full force in this Dominion, tho' not Enacted here," and he notes that the General Assembly appropriated "Divers other Statutes." On the other hand, he implies a certain equality between English and colonial legislation. Not unique to Webb, that implication enjoyed considerable currency in the colony. It had first been given a Virginia voice as early as 1647, when the General Assembly passed a statute declaring that "noe lawe should be established within the kingdome of England concerning us, without the consent of a grand Assemblye here." The assemblymen of 1647 found what they deemed a good precedent in a clause of the Virginia Company of London charter of 1606 that guaranteed to the original planters and their progeny "all liberties Franchises and Immunities within anie of our domynions to all intents and purposes as yf they had been abiding and borne within this our Realme of Englande or anie other of our saide Domynions." The matter was clearly unsettled in 1736, but Webb's understanding reflected the belief that "law" in the Old Dominion embraced English and Virginia customs, certain parliamentary statutes, *and* acts of the General Assembly, all of which were on a more or less equal footing. That was a rendering the Crown was never quite willing to accept, and while royal officials nibbled around the edges, they refrained from facing down the Virginians before the middle of the eighteenth century.[36]

"Tobacco" is the longest entry in the book, and it is there that Webb mounts his defense of the Tobacco Inspection Act of 1730. He begins by reminding his readers, "Since the first Settlement of this Colony, this Plant has been, and at this Day continues to be the Chief Staple of our Export: A Commodity of universal Consumption and Demand Abroad, but valuable more or less, according to its Quality and Quantity."[37] Then he recounts how for more than a century the General Assembly tried to stabilize the value of the weed via a bevy of statutes that aimed at assuring quality control. None achieved the long-desired result, though the ones that remained on the books laid the foundations for Gooch's inspection act, which he summarized in considerable detail.[38]

At that juncture Webb moved to combat opponents of the statute. To those who questioned the need for such an act, he argued that it served a sound public purpose. "The Intent and Policy of this Law" was threefold—to improve quality; to eliminate the export of trash tobacco, which "clogs the market, and depreciates the Value"; and to prevent the frauds that "are of pernicious Consequence to Trade." In Webb's estimation the inspection law met those ends almost as soon as it came into force. To prove his point, he adduced a series of statistics that demonstrated how the volume and the value of exports rose after the law went into effect, and he predicted that both would continue trending upward for time to come. He went on to argue that the real source of complaints against the act lay elsewhere. The stoutest objection seemed to be "the Charge of executing" the inspection procedures. "Thoroughly and impartially consider'd," those complaints amounted to naught, and he took some pains to prove how "frivolous and absurd" they were in fact. Nevertheless, he conceded that he was not "insensible in a Matter where so many different Interests are concerned it's impossible to reconcile Parties," but he expressed the hope that "whoever considers the true Interest of the Tobacco Trade" in conjunction with his defense of the act "will be convinced that the present Law is founded upon solid and substantial reasons." Webb closed the entry on a defiant note. "I have been the more particular upon this Subject," he wrote, "because it's a Matter of great Weight; and I have consider'd it with Candour and Impartiality, without other View but the Public Benefit only, I hope my plainness and Sincerity will not be misrepresented: Where every Man's Interest is concerned, every one has a Right to judge for himself; and in this Case the Reader is at Liberty to follow his own Opinion, if he is displeas'd with mine."[39]

Because Webb's notes and drafts disappeared centuries ago, pinning down when he began writing and when he handed the completed manuscript to William Parks is a matter of guesswork. Even so, he dropped an inadvertent clue that permits an approximation of how he could have proceeded. The hint is this: Webb strategically placed an abundant number of model precedents—sample writs, bonds, mittimuses, warrants, and similar documents—throughout the manuscript, and in each of them he usually entered an exact day, month, and year either in the opening or in the closing dateline. The first example of this contrivance appears in a sample recognizance that appears on page 8 of the book. It begins as follows: "Memorand. On this Second day of June Anno Dom 1733, personally came before me . . ." An additional twenty-two precedents, all dated between 2 June and 10 October 1733, appear between pages 9 and 101. Webb supplemented those examples with a cluster that he dated in the interval from 3 June to 20 December 1735. Those items are scattered throughout the pages that fall between 109 and 311. The final samples are on pages that lie between 331 and 362. They are dated 16 March, 25 March, and 26 April 1736.[40]

There is no obvious explanation for Webb's exactitude. His precision served no discernible legal or educational purpose. Webb was not trying to emulate Dalton, Swinburne, or Lambarde, who followed the long-standing English habit of leaving the datelines in precedents empty because they expected users to fill in the blanks when needed.[41] Whatever his reasons, however, his being so precise leads to a plausible reckoning of how much time it took to write the *Virginia Justice,* and that calculation sustains the following conclusion. Webb began crafting the manuscript no later than June 1733, and by that fall he had written the first portion. He was done with the second part in December 1735. All that remained was a final section, which he completed by April 1736.

Three years would not have been an excessively long time for Webb to put his manuscript together. If anything, he proceeded rather speedily considering that he could never have devoted his every waking hour to the project. Instead, he researched, drafted, revised, and edited piecemeal whenever he was not attending to his family responsibilities, his plantations, his judicial duties, or his committee work in the House of Burgesses.

After receiving the manuscript, Parks turned it into an octavo volume. On the whole the book is of an undistinguished yet serviceable design that is graced with a few decorative embellishments. Done on stark white paper, the leaves measure 7⅞ by 4¾ inches and run to 378 printed pages, counting front and back matter.[42] The font is an imported Dutch pica that Parks commonly used in his publications at the time. It shows more than a few signs of wear, though its impressions are legible throughout. Free leaves precede the title page, on whose verso is the imprimatur that reads, "The Abstracts and Precedents contained in this Book, have been composed with much Industry; and I conceive the Publishing them will be for the common Benefit of this Colony of Virginia. John Clayton, Attorn. Gen." Webb's dedication to Gooch and the prefatory "To the Reader" constitute the remaining front matter. The book also has an unpaginated four-page index. Glosses in the margins of the text guide readers to particular portions of the subject matter or to statutory references. The compositor set all of the precedents, cross references, and source citations in italics, which makes them easy to locate at a glance.

How long was the book in press? A brief explanation of the demands on Parks and how the shop went about its tasks points to a likely answer. The year 1736 was an unusually busy one for Parks. Including the *Virginia Justice,* his output totaled ten publications, the others being an almanac, a book of poetry, a volume of session laws, another of legislative journals, a broadsheet gubernatorial speech, an essay on pleurisy, a book on folk medicine, a theological treatise, and a book containing the charter and statutes of the College of William and Mary. The *Virginia Justice* was the longest of the lot. In terms of page count it surpassed the combined total of the others, meaning that it required more labor to produce than the rest. Setting the type and printing it and the other works was not the only demand on the shop, however. Parks also founded the *Virginia Gazette* in 1736. Publication commenced on a Friday that August and continued weekly thereafter, its preparation diverting his workers from their other tasks for as long as it took them to set, proof, and print each issue of the paper.[43]

These constraints on the shop's equipment and manpower would have compelled Parks to tackle the *Virginia Justice* in parts and to run out a requisite number of copies of each lot as it was completed, whereupon it was laid aside until the whole was done. Proceeding in that fashion, Parks's print shop probably finished the last batch by the end of the year or early in 1737. At that stage the various pieces were gathered into individual books that were eventually bound and covered according to the wishes of their owners. Just how many of those books made up the entire press output is debatable. For certain, Parks would have provided one or more copies to each of the subscribers. If Webb's patrons were nearly as numerous as those who underwrote *A Collection of all the Acts of Assembly* then Parks would have had to print more than two hundred just for them. Then he would have produced as many additional copies as he calculated the market might bear, which may have brought the total to upwards of five hundred or more impressions.[44]

John Mercer was among the first lawyers to own Webb's book, and he used it when he compiled *An Exact Abridgment of all the Public Acts of Assembly of Virginia, In Force and Use,* which Parks issued in 1737.[45] Apart from Mercer and the subscribers, who else actually bought copies is anybody's guess although a modern census suggests that it was the third most popular title in colonial law libraries.[46] Parks probably expected the General Assembly to require the county courts to buy the book, but that hope never happened, and when the initial burst of purchases diminished he was left with a stock of slow-moving books that gathered dust on his shelves. Three years after the book came out he began advertising it in the *Virginia Gazette* and in another of his serials, the *Virginia Almanac,* for the set price of ten shillings a volume.[47] Those advertisements yielded results because the new courts in Orange, Frederick, and Augusta Counties all acquired copies in the mid-1740s.[48] They may have accounted for sales in North Carolina and Maryland as well.[49] William Hunter, Parks's journeyman, who took over the shop and became the public printer after Parks died, ran the last of those ads in 1750, which suggests that the supply of unsold stock was finally depleted.[50]

By 1750, the *Virginia Justice* was ripe for revision, given the many changes in law and practice that had come to pass since its publication fourteen years earlier. So far as anyone knows, Hunter showed no inclination to produce an updated edition. Neither did Webb, especially after his experience of clerking for the committee of the General Assembly that undertook a top-to-bottom revision of the laws in force in 1745.[51] Four decades had passed since the previous overhaul. The lapse of that much time entailed on the committee a daunting chore that proved much more arduous and time-consuming than anyone expected. Their job wore on until 1749, and when they finished, the assembly adopted the whole revision without the sanction of the Crown. Webb worked closely with the committee, but there are hints that the relationship between them slowly soured.[52] In April 1749, pleading that he had been at "a Considerable Expense in attending the said Committee," furnishing it with books, paper, pens, ink, and other supplies, he petitioned the House for recompense, only to be denied summarily.[53] Thereafter, he never again served another House committee, although he did retain his clerkship in the treasury office until his death.[54]

There were two other probable reasons for Webb's lack of enthusiasm. He appears to have developed no noticeable ties to Gooch's successor, Robert Dinwiddie, so he got no prodding to take up his pen anew. A controversy between the General Assembly and the Board of Trade raised a second disincentive. Created in 1696, the Board of Trade received authority to review acts of colonial legislatures and to advise the Crown which laws should stand and which should be disallowed whereupon royal orders-in-council confirmed their recommendations. For decades, the board exercised its power rather casually, and in the eyes of Virginia legislators its unconcern was seen as tantamount to its consent to their enactments. However, the board's indifference abruptly ceased after George Montagu Dunk, 2d Earl of Halifax, assumed the presidency of the Board of Trade late in 1748 and began carefully scrutinizing colonial legislation with an eye to tightening the Crown's control of the assemblies.[55] As a result of that shift in policy, after the board received the revisal, it withheld its approval for two years. The General Assembly protested, but to no avail. Finally, on the board's advice the Crown disallowed a number of the revised laws and forced changes in others, which led to the momentary resurrection of the old statutes.[56] Under those circumstances Webb had little desire to undertake a new edition. And so the unrevised *Virginia Justice* remained in play for another quarter century.

It was replaced at the behest of a pair of William Parks's successors, Alexander Purdie and John Dixon. They recruited Williamsburg attorney Richard Starke to compile an entirely new manual in 1769, but he died before he finished the assignment.[57] Not wishing to squander their investment, Purdie and Dixon prevailed on several "Gentlemen of the Law" to complete the manuscript, which they published in 1774 over Starke's name as *The Office and Authority of a Justice of Peace Explained and Digested, Under Proper Titles*. Rife with errors, shoddy typesetting, and inept proof reading, all of which indicate great haste in finishing the book, Starke's *Justice* lacks the originality, careful scholarship, and crisp composition that are Webb's hallmarks. Although rendered entirely in the vernacular, it is however much closer in form and content to a traditional English magistrate's manual. Gone is any discussion about the nature of the General Assembly and church polity or any commentary on the subject matters that set Webb's work apart.

Whatever its shortcomings, and however much it departed from Webb's model, the book aimed to address a long-felt need. That need arose, as Starke observed in the Preface, because there was nothing *"on this Subject in Being, properly adapted to our Laws and Constitution, Except Mr. George Webb's Justice, which was published in the Year 1736, and must necessarily be deficient in many Instances, on Account of the Repeal of a great Number of our Acts of Assembly, and the Addition of others since that Time."* Furthermore, he wrote, Webb's volume was *"chargeable, too, with some dangerous Errours; and is besides, so very scarce, that, if it was a proper Guide, few could receive any Benefit from it."*[58] Starke turned to many of the same older English authorities on whom Webb had relied, but he also used newer works that did not exist in Webb's day, such as Matthew Bacon's *New Abridgement of the Law* (1736–59), Richard Burn's *Justice of the Peace and Parish Officer* (1755), or Sir William Blackstone's *Commentaries on the Laws of England* (1765–69). And like Webb he too would have had recourse to the holdings in the library of the Council of State in the Capitol in addition to whatever law books he owned himself.

Notwithstanding its flaws, Starke's *Justice* fulfilled its intended purpose. However, gauging who read it and its influence on those readers are difficult weights to measure. Rarely, if ever, do copies show up in modern censuses of law libraries of the time. That scarcity suggests the book never circulated widely, which seems probable given when Purdie and Dixon marketed the book. They put it up for sale only months before the revolutionaries declared Virginia's independence. Therefore, its useful life was quite short because, as William Waller Hening wrote in *The New Virginia Justice: Comprising the Office and Authority of a Justice of the Peace, in the Commonwealth of Virginia*, it circulated in the last days of "our subjection to a regal government, and before our laws had acquired any degree of stability."[59]

Hening brought out the *New Virginia Justice* in 1795, and he purposely designed it to instruct republican magistrates in the reach of their authority and the discharge of their duties. As such, the *New Virginia Justice* is especially telling of how the Revolution changed the office of justice and the county courts, and it remained in print through a series of new editions until the 1820s. As an author, Hening is closer to Webb than to Starke in the sense that he exhibited a scholarly bent and learnedness equal to Webb's. Even so, Starke and he added to the string of Virginia-specific law books that stretches from Webb's day to this.

NOTES

1. Copies are readily available in digital formats or as on-demand reprints. The source text I employed for this essay was a digitized facsimile of an inscribed original that once belonged to Benjamin Harrison (1726–1791) and now belongs to the New York Public Library.
2. "The Webb Family of New Kent County," *Virginia Magazine of History and Biography* 25 (1917): 99; Malcolm Hart Harris, *Old New Kent County: Some Account of the Planters, Plantations, and Places in New Kent County* (West Point, VA, 1977), 196.
3. H. R. McIlwaine, ed., *Legislative Journals of the Council of Colonial Virginia*, 2d ed., 3 vols. in 1 (Richmond, 1979), 2:80. Webb's petition for reimbursement appears in John Pendleton Kennedy and H. R. McIlwaine, eds., *Journals of the House of Burgesses of Virginia, 1619–1776*, 13 unnumbered vols. (Richmond, 1905–15), *1727–1740*, 141.
4. On Parks, see Lawrence C. Wroth, *William Parks: Printer & Journalist of England & Colonial American* (Richmond, 1926); J. A. Leo LeMay, *Men of Letters in Colonial Maryland* (Knoxville, 1972), 111–26; Calhoun Winton, "The Southern Book Trade in the Eighteenth Century," in *The Colonial Book in the Atlantic World*, ed. Hugh Amory and David D. Hall (New York, 2000), 224–32; and A. Franklin Parks, *William Parks: The Colonial Printer in the Transatlantic World of the Eighteenth Century* (College Park, PA, 2012).
5. Kennedy and McIlwaine, *Journals of the House of Burgesses, 1727–1740*, 25. The other members of the committee were burgesses John Clayton and Archibald Blair, in ad-

dition to John Randolph and William Robertson who were, respectively, clerk of the House and the Council of State.

6. Ibid., 174, 394; ibid., *1742–1749*, 354, 394.

7. William Hakewill, *The Manner How Statutes are Enacted in Parliament by Passing of Bills* (London, 1659), 131–34; Stanley M. Pargellis, "The Procedure of the Virginia House of Burgesses," *William and Mary Quarterly*, 2d ser., 7 (1927): 143–46.

8. "Sir John Randolph's Breviate Book," *Virginia Historical Register and Literary Companion* 1–2 (Richmond, 1848): 121–22; Jon Kukla, *Speakers and Clerks of the Virginia House of Burgesses, 1643–1776* (Richmond, 1981), 115–18; John E. Selby, "John Robinson," in *American National Biography*, ed. John A. Garraty and Mark C. Carnes, 24 vols. (New York, 1999), 18:662–64.

9. Paul David Nelson, "Sir William Gooch (1681–1751)," in *Oxford Dictionary of National Biography*, ed. H. C. G. Matthew and Brian Harrison, 60 vols. (Oxford, 2004), 22:740–42; Warren M. Billings, *Sir William Berkeley and the Forging of Colonial Virginia* (Baton Rouge, 2004), 51–57, 90.

10. "An Act for Repealing the Act for the better and more Effectual Improving the Staple of Tobacco: And for the better Execution of the Laws now in Force against Tending Seconds. And for the further Prevention thereof," in Parks, comp., *A Collection of all the Acts of Assembly, Now in Force in the Colony of Virginia* (Williamsburg, 1732), 417–36.

11. Webb, *Virginia Justice*, 337–42.

12. George Webb, "To the Reader," in ibid., vii–viii. Some of Webb's subscribers may also have underwritten *A Collection of all the Acts of Assembly*, because among them were assorted attorneys and magistrates, who would have seen value in Webb's book. The subscribers to *A Collection of all the Acts of Assembly* are identified in a list that Parks bound in some of the volumes. One such is in the holdings of the Virginia Historical Society. John Mercer noted in his *Exact Abridgment of all the Public Acts of Assembly, of Virginia in Force and Use* (Williamsburg, 1737), which Parks issued, that he and Webb shared "a great Number" of the same subscribers (iii). Unfortunately, he did not name them, nor did Parks list them in the front matter of the *Exact Abridgment*.

13. It occurred to me that Webb perhaps had formal legal training before he left England, but a search of matriculation records of the Inns of Court yielded negative results. I am indebted to my friend Catherine McArdle, deputy librarian at Lincoln's Inn, for her assistance via a series of e-mails we exchanged in January and February 2013.

14. Warren M. Billings, "'Send us . . . what other Lawe books you shall thinke fitt': Books That Shaped the Law in Virginia, 1600–1860," *Virginia Magazine of History and Biography* 120 (2013): 315–20.

15. Because most of the books went through more than one impression, it became necessary to determine the printings Webb actually used, which involved a three-step method of identifying the correct impressions. Webb abbreviated all of his source references, as in "*Dalt.* 200." Thus, the first step required turning every page of the *Virginia Justice* and recording each abbreviation and its accompanying page citation. Translating those abbreviations into a list of authors and titles was the next step. Some abbreviations were readily recognizable, such as *Dalt.* for Michael Dalton's *Countrey*

Justice or *H.P.C.* for Sir Mathew Hale's *History of the Pleas of the Crown*, but others were not. I gleaned the latter from three reference works—John Worrall's *Biblotheca Legum: Or, A Catalogue of the Common and Statute Law Books of this Realm, And some others relating thereto; From their First Publication to Easter Term, 1777* (London, 1777); John William Wallace's *The Reporters, Chronologically Arranged: With Additional Remarks Upon their Respective Merits* (Philadelphia, 1855); and Donald Raistrick's *Index to Legal Citations and Abbreviations* (London, 1981). After I established the authors and titles, the final step was merely a matter of trolling the Early English Books Online and Eighteenth Century Collections Online databases and matching page citations with the correct impressions.

16. George Thorpe and John Pory to Sir Edwin Sandys, 15 and 16 May 1621, in *Records of the Virginia Company of London*, ed. Susan Myra Kingsbury, 4 vols. (Washington, DC, 1906–35), 3:447. The titles he mentioned specifically were William Rastell, *A Collection, in English, of the Statutes now in Force . . .* (London, 1615); Sir William Staunford, *Les Plees del Coron Divises in Plusiours Titles and Common Lieux . . .* (London, 1583); and William West's *Symboleographie* (1590).

17. Webb, "To the Reader," vii.

18. "An Act Commanding Law-Books to be provided for each County," in Parks, *Collection of all the Acts of Assembly*, 43.

19. Billings, "Books That Shaped the Law in Virginia," 318.

20. Webb, "To the Reader," viii.

21. Warren M. Billings, John E. Selby, and Thad W. Tate, *Colonial Virginia: A History* (White Plains, NY, 1984), 208–53.

22. "An Act for Establishing County Courts, and for Regulating and Settling the Proceedings therein," in Parks, *Collection of all the Acts of Assembly*, 248–56.

23. "Itinerant Observations in America," *London Magazine, or, Gentleman's Monthly Chronologer*, July 1746, 323.

24. Alan McKinley Smith, "Virginia Lawyers, 1680–1776: The Birth of An American Profession" (PhD diss., Johns Hopkins University, 1967); A. G. Roeber, *Faithful Magistrates and Republican Lawyers: Creators of Virginia Legal Culture, 1680–1810* (Chapel Hill, NC, 1981), chap. 2; "An Act to prevent frivolous and vexatious Suits; and to Regulate Attorneys practicing in the County Courts," in Parks, *Collection of all the Acts of Assembly*, 494–97.

25. On how Fitzherbert came to prepare his version, see J. H. Baker, "Sir Anthony Fitzherbert," in Matthew and Harrison, *Oxford Dictionary of National Biography*, 19:873–74.

26. See, e.g., William Lambarde, *Eirenarcha, Or the Office of Justices of Peace, in Foure Bookes* (London, 1614), esp. 3–10.

27. Webb, *Virginia Justice*, x.

28. Ibid., 231.

29. See, e.g., the titles "Coroner," "Forcible Entry, and Forcible Detainer," "Indictment," and "Felonies," ibid., 97–104, 154–62, 186–88, 144–51.

30. Ibid., 106–9, 192–200, 89–97, 200–208, 292–306.

31. Ibid., 183–85, 221–26, 106, 281–86, 288–92, 318–22.

32. Ibid., 61–62, 71–80, 80–83, 128–33.

33. Ibid., 268.
34. The codification appeared in "An Act for the more effectual suppressing of Blasphemy, Swearing, Cursing, Drunkenness, and Sabbath breaking," and it was reenacted in the revisal of 1705. See Parks, *Collection of All the Acts of Assembly*, III, 179–80.
35. Webb, *Virginia Justice*, 17–22.
36. Ibid., 18, 115, 324; acts of assembly, 5 Apr. 1647, in *The Papers of Sir William Berkeley, 1605–1677*, ed. Warren M. Billings (Richmond, 2007), 76; letters patent to Sir Thomas Gates and others, 10 Apr. 1606, in *The Jamestown Voyages Under the First Charter, 1606–1609*, ed. Philip L. Barbour, 2 vols. (Cambridge, 1969), 1:31–32. See also Jack P. Greene, "Law and the Origins of the American Revolution," in *The Cambridge History of Law in America*, ed. Michael Grossberg and Christopher Tomlins, 3 vols. (Cambridge, 2008), 1: 447–53.
37. Webb, *Virginia Justice*, 326.
38. Ibid., 327–29, 330–37; Billings, Selby, and Tate, *Colonial Virginia: A History*, 236–41; Stacy L. Lorenz, "'To Do Justice to His Majesty, the Merchant, and the Planter': Governor William Gooch and the Virginia Tobacco Inspection Act of 1730," *Virginia Magazine of History and Biography* 108 (2000): 345–92.
39. Webb, *Virginia Justice*, 337–42.
40. Ibid., 8–361 passim.
41. Compare Lambarde's sample of an arrest warrant for a barretor in *Eirenarcha*, precedents, s.v., "Against a common Barretour," with Webb's sample in *Virginia Justice*, 39–40.
42. Wroth, *William Parks*, 53.
43. Nine of those publications are enumerated and described in ibid., 51–53. The tenth, *Every Man his own Doctor: Or the Poor Planter's Physician*, which is attributed to John Tennent, apparently escaped Wroth's notice. A copy of it is reproduced in the online version of the Charles Evans's *Early American Imprints*, series 1, no. 4013. I am grateful to Peter Stinely for calling Tennent's book to my attention.
44. The foregoing discussion derives from a series of conversations and e-mail notes between 1 Feb. and Apr. 2013 that I exchanged with Peter Stinely, the master printer at Colonial Williamsburg. He and his colleagues at the Printing Office were most helpful in bringing me to an understanding of how Parks would have managed the production of the *Virginia Justice*, how long it took to do the book, and the probable size of the press run. As Stinely pointed out, the most skilled compositor working six ten-hour days a week would have needed about a month and a half just to render the entire manuscript into type. Then more time was required for proofreading, the actual printing, and distributing the type. Based on our conversations, it soon became clear to me that Parks lacked the ability to assign the production of the *Virginia Justice* to a single team of his workers. As to the size of the press run, Stinely was of the opinion that five hundred was the most likely number of impressions.
45. Mercer, *Exact Abridgment*, viii.
46. W. Hamilton Bryson, *Census of Law Books in Colonial Virginia* (Charlottesville, 1978), xvi–xvii.
47. *Virginia Gazette*, 16 Feb. 1739; *Warner's Almanack . . . for the Year of our Lord Christ*

1742 (Williamsburg, 1742), unpaginated; *Virginia Almanack, for the year 1747* (Williamsburg, 1747), unpaginated; *Virginia Almanack, for the year 1748* (Williamsburg, 1748), unpaginated; *Virginia Almanack, for the year 1749* (Williamsburg, 1749), unpaginated.

48. Inventory of John McDowell's estate, 20 Apr. 1743, Orange Co. Will Book 1, with Inventories and Accounts (1735–42), 271 (microfilm, Library of Virginia); Frederick Co. levy accounts, 12 Oct. 1744, Frederick Co. Order Book 1 (1743–44), 207 (microfilm, LVA); Frederick Co. levy accounts, 5 Nov. 1745, Frederick Co. Order Book 2 (1745–48), 1 (microfilm, LVA); order for purchase of law books, 16 July 1746, Augusta Co. Order Book 1:69–70 (microfilm, LVA). I am indebted to Professor N. Turk McCleskey, of the Virginia Military Institute, for bringing these references to my attention.
49. Richard Beale Davis, *Intellectual Life in the Colonial South, 1585–1763*, 3 vols. (Knoxville, TN, 1978), 2:602; 3:1593.
50. Wroth, *William Parks*, 27.
51. "An Act, for the revisal of the Laws," William Waller Hening, ed., *The Statutes as Large: Being a Collection of All the Laws of Virginia from the First Session of the Legislature in the Year 1619 . . .* , 13 vols. (Richmond, New York, and Philadelphia, 1809–23), 5:321–24.
52. Ibid., 5:409–558; 6:1–215.
53. Kennedy and McIlwaine, *Journals of the House of Burgesses, 1742–1749*, 354.
54. Webb died before 26 June 1758. See Churchill G. Chamberlayne, ed., *The Vestry Book and Register of St. Peter's Parish: New Kent and James City Counties, 1680–1786* (Richmond, 1937), 336.
55. W. A. Speck, "George Montagu Dunk, second earl of Halifax (1716–1771)," in Matthew and Harrison, *Oxford Dictionary of National Biography*, 17:303–5.
56. Billings, Selby, and Tate, *Colonial Virginia: A History*, 254–56.
57. I am indebted to Gary M. Williams, clerk of the Sussex Co. Circuit Court, for sharing with me his unpublished research about Starke.
58. Starke, *Virginia Justice*, iii. Starke neglected to specify the "dangerous Errours."
59. William Waller Hening, *The New Virginia Justice, Comprising the Office and Authority of a Justice of the Peace in the Commonwealth of Virginia*, 2d ed. (Richmond, 1810), v.

A HANDBOOK FOR ALL

WILLIAM WALLER HENING'S *THE NEW VIRGINIA JUSTICE*

R. Neil Hening

THE
NEW VIRGINIA JUSTICE,

COMPRISING THE

OFFICE AND AUTHORITY

OF A

JUSTICE OF THE PEACE,

IN THE

COMMONWEALTH of VIRGINIA.

TOGETHER

WITH A VARIETY OF USEFUL PRECEDENTS
ADOPTED TO THE LAWS NOW IN FORCE.

To which is added,

An APPENDIX containing all the moſt approved forms of
CONVEYANCING, commonly uſed in this country,
Such as Deeds, of Bargain and Sale, of
Leaſe and Releaſe, of Truſt, Mort-
gages, &c.—Alſo the duties of
a Juſtice of the Peace ariſ-
ing under the laws of
the United States.

BY WILLIAM WALLER HENING,
ATTORNEY AT LAW.

RICHMOND: PRINTED BY T. NICOLSON, 1795.

William Waller Hening's 1795 New Virginia Justice superseded outdated English and Virginia reference works. William Waller Hening, The New Virginia Justice (Richmond, 1795). (Courtesy the Library of Virginia)

THE TWO THOUSAND OR MORE justices of the peace who served on the county courts of Virginia at any one time late in the eighteenth century needed up-to-date manuals and practical how-to legal guides in their daily work. Their own personal business affairs gave some of them familiarity with legal principles and various kinds of legal documents, but very few justices of the peace were learned in the law, and their roles as judges and local magistrates exposed them to novel situations that required them to issue or review legal instruments with which they may have been unfamiliar. The two existing published guides for Virginia justices of the peace were both badly out of date by then as a consequence of the many changes in Virginia law and practice following the American Revolution. William Waller Hening, a prolific author, scholar, and law compiler, was one of the Virginia legal writers who produced a homegrown line of law books that replaced older English texts. He began in 1795 with the first edition of *The New Virginia Justice, Comprising the Office and Authority of a Justice of the Peace in the Commonwealth of Virginia*.[1]

Hening was born in 1767, the son of a prominent Culpeper County landowner, and became the most eminent of four brothers, all of whom had a close association with the law.[2] His brother Samuel was a justice of the peace in Culpeper and later in Louisville, Kentucky. George moved to Franklin County, Georgia, after serving in the Revolutionary War and was a justice of the peace and sheriff in that county. Robert was the commonwealth's attorney in Stafford County and later clerk of the district court of Fredericksburg. There is no collection of William Waller Hening papers, and the records of his tenures as deputy adjutant general of Virginia and clerk of the Superior Court of Chancery for the Richmond District were destroyed in Richmond's evacuation fire of 1865. Therefore his biography has been assembled, with some difficulty, from other surviving government records, legislative journals, his publications, newspaper accounts, personal papers, Masonic archives, and small groups of his letters scattered in many different institutions.

After qualifying at the bar in Fredericksburg and practicing there for four years, Hening moved his practice to Charlottesville in 1793. Within four years his practice covered all of the counties included in the district courts of Fredericksburg and Charlottesville plus six other county courts and the High Court of Chancery in Richmond. The bulk of his practice involved trying to collect money from insolvent debtors. He remarked that while practicing in Charlottesville he had "been consulted as counsel in every case of bankruptcy which has been prosecuted in this part of the state."[3] By age twenty-six he was already quite successful.

From Charlottesville, Hening launched the political and publishing careers in which he engaged for thirty-three years. Before beginning his political career he participated in many local affairs in Albemarle County. He helped with the restoration of court records that the British had destroyed during the Revolution, was a trustee for the town of Milton and for Albemarle Academy, and represented local investors at annual meetings of the Mutual Assurance Society of Virginia. He also became a protégé of Albemarle County's most distinguished citizen, Thomas Jefferson, who in 1802 appointed him a federal commissioner of bankruptcy for Virginia.

In Hening's day, good family connections enabled young men to move ahead politically. He was fortunate to have been born with some helpful family relationships. His mother was a Waller whose near relatives included Benjamin Waller, of Williamsburg, who had been a judge of the Virginia Court of Admiralty during and after the American Revolution, and Littleton Waller Tazewell, who served in the US Senate and as governor of Virginia. Hening forged important new family alliances that facilitated his political and professional ambitions when he married Agatha Banks, the only daughter of Gerard Banks, sheriff of Stafford County. One of her brothers represented Culpeper County in the House of Delegates and another, the wealthy Henry Banks, had represented Greenbrier County. Through these kinships and others, Hening fulfilled the all-important family-relations tests necessary for a career in Virginia politics.

In 1804 Hening won election to the House of Delegates for the first of two consecutive one-year terms. Service in the General Assembly introduced him to dozens of men who were equally well or even better connected in their regions of the state. The attorneys and justices of the peace in the assembly would have known his name, even if they did not know him personally, by then because of his reputation as a lawyer and his valuable publication *The New Virginia Justice*. Hening's political star rose quickly in the legislature. In 1806, during his second term, it elected him to the eight-member Privy Council, or Council of State, which served both as an advisory council to the governor and as the assembly's watchdog over the governor. Hening served on the council for four and a half years, during which he spent much of his time in the capital city of Richmond and met most of the state's leading attorneys and judges.

Given his passion for the law and the functions of the judiciary, it is not surprising that Hening twice sought elevation to the bench. In 1806 he tried for the office of judge of the Court of Chancery to succeed the late George Wythe, but the General Assembly elected Creed Taylor. In 1808, after the assembly abolished the district courts and replaced them with superior courts of law and enlarged the number of courts, Hening sought appointment to one of three new vacancies. The result was the same. In neither instance could he muster the necessary political support in the assembly.

In August 1810, though, Taylor appointed Hening clerk of the Court of Chancery for the Richmond District. No doubt Hening actively sought the appointment. By that time he had published two editions of his manual for justices of the peace; two volumes of early Virginia laws, entitled *The Statutes at Large;* three volumes of court reports; and a pamphlet containing Virginia's militia laws. Hening and Taylor had known each other professionally for years, had served together in the legislature, and were both members of the board of trustees for the Richmond Female Academy. Taylor was also one of the three men the assembly appointed to authenticate the texts in the early volumes of the *Statutes at Large*.

With his appointment to the clerkship Hening got the recognition for his legal talents that he deserved and had worked hard to earn. What was more important, it was a position that provided a reliable income stream. As clerk he was entitled to a percentage of the fees the court collected. From then on, his livelihood was no longer tied to the minor salary he received as a member of the council and the often unreliable payments from his clients. Hening's steady income permitted him to devote the necessary time to his considerable publishing career. He also held one additional public office concurrent with his clerkship. He was deputy adjutant general of Virginia from 1811 to 1814. The normally undemanding job increased significantly in importance and in the amount of work it required of him during the War of 1812.

Hening is best known now for compiling and editing the thirteen volumes of the *Statutes at Large,* which included all of the then-known laws of Virginia up to 1792. The General Assembly provided for authenticating the texts in order that Virginians could for the first time have access to early statutes that had never been published or existed only in scarce volumes or in rare abridgments. It immediately became, and remains, an essential source for all researchers working on colonial and Revolutionary Virginia history.[4] During his lifetime, though, Hening was better known for researching, writing, and publishing a large number of eminently practical legal works. Between 1794 and 1826 he published four editions of his manual for justices of the peace (including a second printing of the first edition); a two-volume American pleader's guide; American editions of three English works on legal maxims and precedents; four volumes of court reports, including the first advance sheet system in Virginia and a revised edition of volume one of the court reports; two pamphlets; and the thirteen-volume set of Virginia's early laws, four volumes of which required second editions. In addition, on three occasions (1803, 1808, and 1819) he assisted with the preparation, certification, or revision of the Virginia code. Hening was the most prolific legal author in Virginia, perhaps in the nation, at that time. During a thirty-year period he published on average one scholarly or legal reference volume per year.

The work that launched Hening's publishing career, reached more hands, and probably had more influence than any other during his lifetime was *The New Virginia Justice*. It is not entirely clear why he undertook the work. He may have realized that a new guide was needed as early as when he first qualified for the bar in 1789 and the justices of the peace could not find an authority to verify whether the colonial statute requiring attorneys to post a fifteen-pound bond was still in force.[5] Other, more senior men with longer careers at the bar, such as St. George Tucker and George Wythe, were eminently or even better qualified, but Hening may have staked out the territory early on when no one else wanted to spend the time and energy, much less expend the capital and assume the financial risk of paying for the printing.

The lack of competition could be deemed a nod to Hening's abilities and reputation. No one else stepped forward, his friends assured him that he was well qualified for the task, and several gentlemen of the bar promoted his publication.[6] Hening wrote in the preface to *The New Virginia Justice* in 1795 that he had long realized the need for updating the early manuals and had been collecting material for some time. He might have published it sooner had the General Assembly's revision of the state's laws adopted in 1792 been printed at that time rather than two years later, in 1794. Hening may have begun his work from the 1792 copy he owned of the printed *Draughts of Such Bills as Have Been Prepared by the Committee Appointed under the Act, Intituled, An Act to Amend an Act Intituled An Act Concerning a New Edition of the Laws of this Commonwealth*.

Hening's *New Virginia Justice* superseded a large number of manuals then in use. Nineteen titles of English manuals for justices of the peace have been documented in the libraries of colonial Virginians, and many attorneys and justices of the peace owned one or both of the two that were native to Virginia, George Webb's *The Office and Authority of a Justice of Peace* (1736), commonly referred to as Webb's *Justice*, and Richard Starke's *The Office and Authority of a Justice of Peace* (1774), commonly referred to as Starke's *Justice*, both published in Williamsburg. Webb's *Justice* was the third most common title found in colonial Virginia law libraries.[7] By the time Hening came to the bar, Webb's was old and in many parts obsolete, and neither it nor Starke's defective edition was of much real use because of the many changes made to Virginia laws and court practices during and after the American Revolution.

The timing of its publication is always critical to the success of a book. The publication of the new edition of the code in 1794 made a new manual for justices of the peace even more necessary and therefore likely to sell. Hening's timing was excellent, better than it would have been had he completed his work earlier as intended. *The New Virginia Justice* appeared within a year after the publication of the revisal, not unlike Webb's *Justice,* which had been published in 1736, three years after publication of the first compilation of Virginia laws printed in Virginia. The title of a book is also important for its commercial success. Hening gave his almost the same familiar title as Webb's and Starke's books but added the important word *New.* And like them, it too was commonly referred to by its abbreviated title, Hening's *Justice.*

Hening made many changes to the form and substance of the existing manuals to correct what he characterized as faults in the systems or arrangement of information; in his view, almost every section in the old manuals contained "some dangerous defect." Moreover, the General Assembly had enacted "innumerable statutes more suitable to its genius" as a state in the Union than as a royal colony, and the laws had acquired a better "degree of stability." Hening's new manual therefore required "a greater variety of precedents, besides several additional titles" to bring it up to date and meet all the needs of justices of the peace, attorneys, and people engaged in commerce.[8] In addition to justices of the peace and attorneys, Hening intended his book to be useful for merchants and members of the landed gentry who needed to know their powers and duties in their roles as customs officers, tax collectors, sheriffs, or estate administrators in the new legal environment. Hening's *Justice* filled an important void.

While working on *The New Virginia Justice,* Hening certainly had access to or owned a copy of Webb's *Justice,* and he definitely owned a copy of Starke's. For his later editions, Hening had an additional advantage comparable to Webb's service as clerk to the committee appointed to compile the statutes that were published three years before he issued his manual. Hening personally worked on or certified the updates to the code of 1792 that Samuel Pleasants published in 1803 and 1808, and later he worked with Benjamin Watkins Leigh and William Munford on the revised code of 1819.

The work immediately preceding Hening's was Starke's *Justice.* Not only was it out of date, it was badly flawed. The author had died before completing it, and his printer had to rely on "some benevolent Gentlemen of the Law to continue the work." Surprisingly, they worked without communicating with one another, and the printer candidly admitted that the volume contained "some few Errours."[9] This hastily compiled and disjointed book was the product of too many hands and too little coordination, leading to a text "rife with errors that are compounded by sloppy typesetting and careless proof reading."[10] This is a sad legacy considering that Starke, like Webb, was an insider in the legal community of Williamsburg. He clerked for three committees of the House of Burgesses and held the advocate's role in the Virginia Court of Vice-Admiralty. Hening gave Starke's *Justice* a backhanded compliment by writing in his own preface that it had "long afforded considerable assistance to our magistrates."[11] Two decades after its publication, however, it was hard to come by and "cannot be bought for less than twenty shillings Virginia currency."[12] All of which suggests that Starke's work, even with its faults, was still in use and of some value.

The revisions of Virginia's legal code during and after the American Revolution and some modifications in the jurisdictions of courts required Hening to revise or completely rewrite some of the entries Webb and Starke had included in their guides. One of the most important reforms of the Revolution led Hening to eliminate several entries relating to the Church of England. The disestablishment of the church in January 1786 stripped clergymen, vestrymen, and churchwardens of their public responsibilities. It also changed the relationship between parishes and ministers, which the law had formerly regulated, into a private contractual relationship. Those changes in turn modified the legal duties of judges of the county courts with respect to church officials. Following the disestablishment of the church, justices of the peace no longer shared with vestries responsibilities for the poor and orphans, which new county boards of overseers of the poor or the county courts assumed; and vestrymen no longer shared with justices of the peace responsibility for presenting the court with evidences of adultery, fornication, blaspheming, willful absence from church services, drunkenness, and swearing or cursing. Hening eliminated most of Starke's long entries governing the obsolete interrelated responsibilities of justices of the peace with vestrymen, churchwardens, and ministers as well as sections relating to recusants (people who refused to adhere to the tenets of the Church of England) and prohibiting Catholics from holding public office. Hening retained the title of the entry on blasphemy, alphabetically the first of the topics relating to the church, but rather than treat what had formerly been a crime, he praised the disestablishment of the church and celebrated the concept of religious liberty, which made it unnecessary to have a substantive entry on blasphemy in *The New Virginia Justice*.

In this new republican climate, which required an updated and current legal handbook, it is easy to ask what Hening believed or whether he was simply pandering to an audience. Hening was no sycophant. On the issue of religious tolerance, for example, two samples serve to affirm his belief in the new system. In 1792 he asserted that "in America no man is compelled to contribute to the support of a religious institution which does not accord with his own sentiments," and "in America, a man may be promoted to any office in the state provided his merit will entitle him to it, be his religious opinions what they may."[13] Likewise, in his *Statutes at Large* he inserted a footnote to Virginia's 1699 law, which in general terms accepted the 1689 English Act of Toleration. There Hening took the opportunity to take a firm swipe at the law's attempt to promote religious tolerance. In the footnote he states, "It is surely an abuse of terms to call a law a *toleration act,* which imposes a religious test, on the conscience, in order to avoid the penalties of another law, equally violating every principle of religious freedom."[14]

Hening compiled a thirty-two-page appendix with twenty-two topics describing the duties of the state's justices of the peace under the US laws imposing some new responsibilities on the local magistrates. One of the most important concerned fugitives. The US Constitutions contained explicit provisions on fugitives from justice and fugitives from labor that justices of the peace needed to understand. Hening therefore carefully distinguished fugitives from justice and fugitives from labor, chiefly comprehending people who escaped from slavery. So important was this appendix that in some instances it can be found disbound from the original book as a separate book of reference.

Hening used the common subscription method for financing his new work, requiring a down payment prior to publication. He offered purchasers a copy for three dollars if they paid one dollar in advance. That gave him the capital he needed to put the book through the press. In May 1794 Hening sent out a printed circular letter asking men to help with the solicitation and enclosed a subscription paper for prospective purchasers to complete and return. He promised that his work would not be "the hasty production of an itinerant scribler, calculated merely to supply the wants of the present moment; but the offspring of immense labour and study" and without any of the defects found in Starke's *Justice*. No list exists of the people Hening called on to solicit subscriptions, but it may have been a long one. When he employed the same process for his volume of court reports twelve years later, he sent copies to more than 200 people in ninety-eight locations. In February 1795, when he announced the close of his subscription campaign for *The New Virginia Justice*,[15] Hening had signed up 1,611 subscribers for 1,902 copies of the book.

As authors often did, Hening flattered his subscribers and gave his work additional credibility by printing their names in the front of the book. The subscribers included distinguished attorneys, judges, statesmen, and businessmen, among them George Wythe, John Marshall, Thomas Jefferson, James Madison, Robert Gamble, John Hook, and William F. Ast. Legislators and county officials from almost every county and town in the state, such as Jacob Rinker, surveyor of Shenandoah County, and James Breckinridge, deputy clerk of Botetourt County, subscribed to the volume, as did men from Baltimore, Philadelphia, Washington, DC, and the states of Kentucky and Georgia. Given the extent of the subscriber list, it is fair to presume that the attorneys and justices of the peace fully expected the book to serve the uses and purposes of a wide-ranging readership.

Hening predicted that his work would fill at least 600 pages, but when completed it contained 512 pages, 160 more than Starke's *Justice* and 148 more than Webb's *Justice*. As Hening had promised, it was printed on good-quality paper and handsomely bound and lettered in one large octavo volume. Copies that exist today demonstrate that the book held up well, even though many are found with the nineteen-page list of subscribers detached from the book.

The absence of the subscriber list is a clear indication that the list served other purposes, such as giving owners of the book names of attorneys and prominent men in distant jurisdictions.

While the subscription solicitation was still circulating, Hening expressed some apprehension about the project to his neighbor Thomas Jefferson. "I feel all that diffidence which is natural to an author, particularly one of my age," the twenty-seven-year-old wrote. Probably hoping to receive some positive word of endorsement from the prestigious Jefferson, Hening admitted that he was "sensible that no man can be a judge of his own performances" and that subscribers "have a right to expect some better assurance of the merit of the performance than the author himself is able to give." He asked Jefferson to revise some sheets and point out any defects in the plan and execution of the work.[16] Jefferson did not provide an endorsement, but he did advise Hening not to employ any of the Richmond printers, who, as he wrote later, often produced "wretched samples."[17] Much later, Jefferson praised *The New Virginia Justice* as "a work of great utility for the public generally."[18]

In December 1794 Hening asked the well-known Philadelphia printer and bookseller Mathew Carey to submit a proposal for printing two thousand copies of the book. He also inquired about the quality of available paper and about binding.[19] Carey's proposals do not survive, but they must have been unsuitable, because Hening commissioned the Richmond printer Thomas Nicholson to publish the book. Nicholson was for all practical purposes apolitical,[20] and the other leading printer in Richmond, Augustine Davis, was decidedly Federalist,[21] which may have dissuaded Hening from employing him and thereby alienating some potential purchasers.

Nicholson printed two thousand copies, probably four or five times the size of the printings of Webb's and Starke's earlier manuals. The large number of subscribers speaks loudly to the desire for the new work, and *The New Virginia Justice* was a financial success from the minute Nicholson published it in the summer of 1795. Hening sold nearly the entire press run within three years and planned a second printing in the summer of 1799. His brother-in-law Henry Banks provided the capital and anticipated sharing with the author a profit of as much as three thousand dollars. Augustine Davis produced the second printing. By then no longer the state's public printer, Davis had joined the ranks of Richmond's nonpartisan job printers and probably offered a better price than any of his competitors. The book's pagination differed from that of the first edition, and it sold for four dollars a copy. Printed in 1799, the book went on sale in the spring of the following year.

Hening's *Justice* filled an immediate and widespread need for a basic legal handbook for a wide-ranging readership. A self-contained work, it did not require its owners to have access to other expensive reference works. It thereby met the needs of both the legal and business communities. Although the book was specifically addressed to the work of justices of the peace, Hening correctly predicted that "private gentlemen, as well as the several officers of the court, will find in it much useful information."[22] Later, the printer of the revised, 1810 edition advertised the work in similar language. To justices of the peace "it is indispensable, to gentleman of the bar it will be found a most useful companion: many points of the law which daily occur in practice, being more fully discussed in it, than any other treatise."[23] In order to make it a handbook with appeal to these widest possible audiences, Hening danced on the line between professional and lay users. He avoided adding any new Latin words or phrases so that the work would not be too learned for ordinary gentlemen. Justices of the peace were probably familiar with some of the common Latin phrases necessary to perform their duties, but in a bow to his other subscribers and to simplify the work, he avoided Latin as much as possible but retained some of the Latin terms in common use. In that, he adopted and extended the democratization of the law that Webb had begun in 1736 and that Starke evidently wished to continue with his 1774 volume. Hening also included what is in essence a law dictionary explaining the meanings of fifty-eight legal phrases and abbreviations. It concludes with a note that other explanations or definitions "may generally be found in those parts of the book, in which the terms occur."[24]

Hening also provided the titles of all seventy-one references cited in the text. More than half of them are reports of court cases, but the list also includes four English manuals for justices of the peace, one of which does not appear in the census of law books in colonial Virginia. That manual is Richard Crompton's *Office and Authority of Justices of Peace,* first published in 1581. The other three are William Lambarde's *Eirenarcha; or, Of the Office of the Justices of Peace, in Foure Bookes,* first published in 1581; Michael Dalton's *The Countrey Justice,* first published in 1618; and Richard Burn's *Justice of the Peace and Parish Officer,* first published in 1755. Dalton's book was the one most frequently found in Virginia colonial law libraries.[25] Interestingly, a later inventory of Hening's personal law library did not include any of the four titles, but he did possess a copy of Michael Dalton's *Officium Vicecomitum; The Office and Authority of Sheriffs.*

Other titles Hening listed treating different branches of the law were by Matthew Bacon, Sir William Blackstone, Sir Edward Coke, Matthew Hale, and Thomas Wood, whose works Hening is known to have owned. A majority of the citations were to reports of cases. Hening probably did not anticipate that owners of his manual would also own or have access to many of the works in his bibliography or often check his citations. Providing the citations assured his subscribers that he had done is homework. Curiously, Hening cited neither Webb's nor Starke's manual, although some of Starke's references carry over into Hening's.

In addition to covering the legal ground necessary for justices of the peace to perform their duties, Hening provided valuable information for the legal and business communities and two informative appendices, one covering the duties of a justice of the peace under the laws of the United States, the other providing forms for conveyancing.[26] The appendix on conveyancing, a specialty of Hening's, was a collection of forms laymen could use without the aid of legal counsel, but he cautioned people that in matters of importance and difficulty "knowledge of the laws which regulate real property is indispensably necessary."[27] Interestingly, the Richmond printer John Dixon set and printed the two appendices, perhaps because Nicholson's press was fully engaged. Hening's or Nicholson's employment of Dixon as a secondary printer was logical, as he was the son of Nicholson's former printing partner.

Even after demand necessitated the reprinting of the first edition, Hening could hardly expect the continued success his *Justice* received. He prepared new editions in 1810, 1820, and 1825, the first after he certified the accuracy of Pleasants's revisions to the code issued in 1808 and the second after he completed work on the code of 1819. Each of the revised editions required him to do additional research, and each was longer than its predecessor, reflecting the increasing complexity and detail of Virginia's statutes. Hening never enjoyed the luxury of a government subsidy for *The New Virginia Justice* as he did for the *Statutes at Large*. The state declined to subsidize his 1820 edition as a companion to the code of 1819. Although the state provided a subvention for his 1825 edition to supply a copy to every magistrate and court clerk in the state, a fraudulent printer cheated him out of his contract, and back-room political maneuvering caused him a severe financial loss.

The New Virginia Justice was the bread-and-butter publication of Hening's career. Initially an eighteenth-century publication, it went through four editions and was the standard work of its kind in Virginia for the first half of the nineteenth century. In 1844, sixteen years after Hening's death, a person whose name is lost with the application forms filed for copyright on a new edition, but it was never printed.[28] Four years after that, eighty-seven men from nineteen cities and counties petitioned the General Assembly to authorize another edition, but the legislators declined, even though the men provided data to support their assertion that reprinting the book would generate a profit and provide income for the state's literary fund and even though a new revision of the code then in the works would have made it very desirable.[29]

What distinguishes Hening's work is its place in the evolution of Virginia law books, which replaced English texts with a homegrown line of reference works. It was among the earliest attempts to provide republican Virginians with republican law books.[30] Hening deliberately removed the regal tone that characterized the style of his predecessors and wrote in a style consistent with the nation's new legal and political systems. He provided justices of the peace a reliable manual for their work that was not too learned for magistrates who were unschooled in the law and that gave attorneys and others references to legal authorities for difficult or complex subjects. From the beginning, Hening's stated purpose had been to enable "every magistrate to procure a plain and easy guide in the duties of his office."[31] Magistrates could keep the peace, prevent quarrels between neighbors, and punish the guilty using common sense coupled with authoritative legal principles.[32]

The New Virginia Justice was also indispensable to fledging attorneys and could even serve as a modest textbook for junior members of the bar. There was no formal textbook in the modern sense, and Hening's instructive language in the simplified republican style could fill the bill for a young lawyer just establishing a practice. No doubt it found its way into many a saddlebag when lawyers rode their circuits. Unlike a junior magistrate, who could always consult a senior member of the court without fear of trespassing on the other's livelihood, young attorneys were not so fortunate. After gaining his license, each was pretty much on his own to build a reputation and a practice, which placed him in competition with all the others. Opportunities at the bar had never been greater than in post-Revolutionary Virginia, but there was plenty of competition, as the legal profession began to draw a large number of young men.[33]

Hening's *New Virginia Justice* had a secondary benefit in that it raised his professional profile. One year after his first edition appeared, he was admitted to practice in the Virginia Court of Appeals and, shortly thereafter, in the federal court for Virginia. His reputation continued to spread. By the time he was first elected to the General Assembly nine years after publishing his guide, a fellow legislator referred to him as "William W. Hening, author of the Virginia Justice."[34] *The New Virginia Justice* marked a clear turning point in the history of legal publications in Virginia and is distinctive for several reasons. In the words of the Virginia legal historian W. Hamilton Bryson, "It is an encompassing work that provided guidance and direction for the justices of the peace in criminal matters and also gave them direction in civil and administrative matters. This is a marked difference from the English texts. Justices in England had jurisdiction only over criminal cases, whereas the Virginia justices had both criminal and civil jurisdiction, as well as administrative duties."[35]

NOTES

1. Warren M. Billings, "'Send us ... what other Lawe books you shall thinke fitt': Books that Shaped the Law in Virginia, 1600–1860," *Virginia Magazine of History and Biography* 120 (2012): esp. 327, 331.

2. Events of Hening's life derived from the author's research for a biography.
3. William Waller Hening to James Madison, 3 Feb. 1803, James Madison Papers, Library of Congress.
4. William Waller Hening, ed., *The Statutes at Large of Virginia: Being a Collection of All the Laws of Virginia, from the First Session of the Legislature, in the Year 1619,* 13 vols. (Richmond, Philadelphia, and New York, 1809–23); see also Brent Tarter, "Long Before the NHPRC: Documentary Editing in Nineteenth-Century Virginia," *Documentary Editing* 30 (2008): 36–46, esp. 36–38, 44–45.
5. Alvin Thomas Embrey, *History of Fredericksburg, Virginia* (Richmond, 1937), 154–55.
6. William Waller Hening, *The New Virginia Justice, Comprising the Office and Authority of a Justice of the Peace in the Commonwealth of Virginia* (Richmond, 1795), ii.
7. W. Hamilton Bryson, *Census of Law Books in Colonial Virginia* (Charlottesville, 1978), xvii.
8. Printed circular letter, 1 May 1794, broadside 1794:3, and *Proposals for Printing by Subscription,* undated broadside, 1795:1, both by Hening, Virginia Historical Society, Richmond; Hening, *New Virginia Justice,* preface, unpaginated.
9. Preface to Richard Starke, *The Office and Authority of a Justice of Peace* (Williamsburg, 1774), unpaginated.
10. Billings, "Books That Shaped Colonial Virginia," 322.
11. Hening, *New Virginia Justice,* i.
12. Hening, *Proposals for Printing by Subscription.*
13. Hening to Mathew Carey, 3 Dec. 1792, Edward Carey Gardiner Collection, Historical Society of Pennsylvania, Philadelphia.
14. Hening, *Statutes at Large,* 3:171.
15. *Republican Journal & Dumfries Weekly Advertiser,* 19 June 1795.
16. Hening to Thomas Jefferson, 24 July 1794, in *The Papers of Thomas Jefferson,* ed. Julian P. Boyd et al. (Princeton, NJ, 1950–), 28:105.
17. Jefferson to Hening, 26 Feb. 1808, Thomas Jefferson Papers, Library of Congress.
18. Jefferson to Hening, 8 Apr. 1822, ibid.
19. Hening to Carey, 3 Dec. 1794, Gardiner Collection, Historical Society of Pennsylvania.
20. A. Paull Hubbard, *Notes on the Book Trade in Richmond, Va.: Fascicle II, Thomas Nicholson* (Richmond, 1989), 7.
21. W. Hamilton Bryson, *Virginia Law Books: Essays and Bibliographies* (Philadelphia, 2000), 533.
22. Hening, *New Virginia Justice,* iii.
23. *Virginia Patriot* (Richmond), 14 Aug. 1810.
24. Hening, *New Virginia Justice,* law dictionary, 4.
25. W. Hamilton Bryson, ed., *Virginia Law Books,* Memoirs of the American Philosophical Society, vol. 239 (Philadelphia, 2000), xvii.
26. Hening, *New Virginia Justice,* iii.
27. Ibid., preface to appendix 1, "Conveyancing."
28. Waverley K. Winfree, "Acts Not in Hening's *Statutes,* 1702–1732: With a Biographi-

cal Sketch of William Waller Hening" (master's thesis, College of William and Mary, 1957), 4.
29. Legislative Petitions, Prince George County, received 11 Dec. 1848, Record Group 78, Library of Virginia.
30. Billings, "Books that Shaped the Law in Virginia," 331.
31. Hening, *Proposals for Printing by Subscription*.
32. F. Thornton Miller, *Juries and Judges versus the Law: Virginia's Provincial Perspective, 1783–1828* (Charlottesville, 1994), 6.
33. E. Lee Shepard, "Lawyers Look at Themselves: Professional Consciousness and the Virginia Bar," *American Journal of Legal History* 25 (1981): 3.
34. William Munford to Sally Munford, 22 Feb. 1805, Munford-Ellis Papers, Perkins Library, Duke University.
35. Bryson, *Virginia Law Books*, 244.

ST. GEORGE TUCKER

JUDGE,
LEGAL SCHOLAR,
AND REFORMER
OF VIRGINIA LAW

Charles F. Hobson

BLACKSTONE'S COMMENTARIES:

WITH

NOTES OF REFERENCE

TO THE

CONSTITUTIONS, AND LAWS,

OF THE

FEDERAL GOVERNMENT

OF THE

UNITED STATES;

AND OF THE

COMMONWEALTH OF VIRGINIA.

With an APPENDIX to each volume, containing short tracts upon such subjects as appeared necessary to form a connected view of the LAWS of VIRGINIA as a MEMBER of the FEDERAL UNION.

BY S! GEORGE TUCKER, PROFESSOR OF LAW IN THE UNIVERSITY OF WILLIAM AND MARY, AND ONE OF THE JUDGES OF THE GENERAL COURT, IN VIRGINIA.

St. George Tucker's hand-lettered design for the title page of his five-volume 1803 edition of Blackstone's Commentaries: With Notes of Reference to the Constitutions and Laws, of the Federal Government of the United States; and of the Commonwealth of Virginia. *(Courtesy Earl Gregg Swem Library, College of William and Mary)*

Sт. george tucker (1752–1827) was a seminal player in the legal history of post-Revolutionary Virginia and of the United States, a key participant in the debates about the role of law and courts in the early republic. Politically, he was a loyal adherent of Thomas Jefferson, but he stood with Alexander Hamilton and John Marshall in recognizing the potential of judges and courts to make republican government more rational and just. Unlike Jefferson, Tucker admired the English jurists William Murray, Lord Mansfield, and Sir William Blackstone, compiler of the monumental four-volume *Commentaries on the Laws of England* (1765–69). Tucker had great faith in English common law and believed that properly adapted, it could work well in Virginia and the new nation. He had no reservations about using Blackstone to instruct American law students. In 1803 he published his five-volume *Blackstone's Commentaries*. This marked the culmination of nearly seventy years of law publishing by Virginians, which had begun with George Webb's *Office and Authority of a Justice of the Peace* (1736).

Blackstone's Commentaries was an outgrowth of Tucker's lectures at the College of William and Mary. With its detailed annotations and appended essays, Tucker's *Blackstone* was an ambitious attempt to adapt the great English commentator's work to an independent and republican America. Known principally as a scholar and commentator, Tucker has received less attention for a long judicial career in which he sat on Virginia's General Court from 1788 to 1803, the Court of Appeals from 1804 to 1811, and the US District Court for Virginia from 1813 to 1825. Thanks to his scrupulous record keeping, Judge Tucker's legal archive is unmatched among surviving collections of legal papers from the early national period. The heart of his collection is three dozen notebooks reporting about eleven hundred cases in Virginia's courts. These notebooks were published in three volumes in 2013 as *St. George Tucker's Law Reports and Selected Papers, 1782–1825*. Tucker the law professor and judge identified, disseminated, explained, and ultimately shaped Virginia law during an epochal period of transition when the former British colony became a republican commonwealth and member of a new American federal union.

A native of the island of Bermuda, Tucker was from an early age intended for the bar, though his ultimate decision to embrace the profession was not inevitable.[1] His father sent him to Williamsburg in 1771 to study law with George Wythe. First, however, Tucker spent a year taking the regular curriculum at the College of William and Mary. His college sojourn and law study ended about 1773. By 1775 he had qualified to practice law in both the county courts and the General Court, the colony's only superior court. With war and the closing of the courts looming, this was not an auspicious time to begin a career in law. Tucker went home to Bermuda, only to return to Virginia early in 1777 to manage the mainland side of his family's clandestine mercantile venture smuggling salt and munitions on behalf of the patriot cause.

Marriage in 1778 to Frances Bland Randolph, an attractive young widow with three young sons and three large estates, signified Tucker's intention to settle permanently in Virginia and also instantly placed him at the pinnacle of Virginia's plantation society. After several years "entirely domestic," in 1781, in response to the British invasion of the state, Tucker joined the local militia. He served with distinction in the southern campaign and participated in the siege at Yorktown.

After the war, Tucker settled contentedly into the role of gentleman planter, living with "Fanny" Tucker at Matoax, near Petersburg. Here he fashioned himself into a paragon of refinement, good taste, and cosmopolitanism. He was a devotee of science, a versifying man of letters who delighted in entertaining and instructing his close circle of family and friends. Yet he was quick to perceive that the future of Virginia's plantation economy was bleak. By the end of the 1780s he had made a striking change of course. He shed the life of a planter, sold off much of his land, and finally began to practice law in earnest. Fanny Tucker's death early in 1788 precipitated a move to the town of Williamsburg. Henceforth he based his financial security on income derived from law and investments in bank stock and in companies promoting internal improvements.

During a brief period at the bar Tucker demonstrated sufficient competence to secure election as a judge of the General Court. His commission also required him to hold courts in districts throughout the commonwealth. From 1789 to 1803 Tucker followed an arduous regimen of judicial traveling that took him from his Williamsburg home northwest as far as Morgantown (near the Pennsylvania border) and southwest as far as Sweet Springs (near the more well-known resort at White Sulphur Springs). Court business also took him frequently to Winchester, Staunton, Charlottesville, and Fredericksburg. His "home" circuit began at Northumberland Court House in the Northern Neck, continued to King and Queen County and Williamsburg, and ended at Accomack on the Eastern Shore.

To plot these circuits on a map is to gain a sense of the dedication and sacrifice of Tucker and his fellow itinerants in bringing justice to the citizens of an extensive commonwealth. He attended these circuits in the spring and fall of each year and then sat en banc with the other judges in June and November sessions of the General Court. During judicial vacations Tucker somehow managed to squeeze in his law lectures, write essays on commercial and political topics, and attend to the care and education of an extended family that included three Randolph stepsons, five children of his own by Fanny, and two more stepchildren after his 1791 marriage to Lelia Skipwith Carter.

In 1804 Tucker joined the Court of Appeals, filling the vacancy created by the death of Edmund Pendleton, the longtime president of that court. This relieved him of the drudgery of constant travel, except for the short trip to Richmond several times a year. His tenure on the court had its share of disappointment and unpleasantness. Tucker grew increasingly frustrated with a legislature that proved impervious to his urgent calls for judicial reform, particularly his proposals for reducing the enormous influx of appeals. A much greater source of distress was mounting dissension between him and Judge Spencer Roane, which after an open confrontation in the spring of 1809 became a permanent rupture. The antipathy between these two judges originated in a clash of personalities and particularly from Roane's perception of Tucker as a rival to succeed Pendleton as leader of the court. Discouraged by an unheeding and ungrateful legislature and increasingly uncomfortable sitting with a judge whom he despised, Tucker resigned from the Court of Appeals in April 1811.[2]

Two years later Tucker accepted President James Madison's appointment as judge of the US District Court for Virginia. On this court he heard admiralty and prize cases and cases arising from violations of the revenue laws. The court met twice a year, in Norfolk and in Richmond. In the capital he also sat with Chief Justice Marshall on the US Circuit Court, which was principally a trial court for common-law cases. In the chief justice, Tucker had a congenial colleague who also detested Spencer Roane. Unhappily, Tucker's years as a federal judge were marred by deteriorating health. During the next dozen years Tucker suffered a litany of fevers, aches, pains, and various other ailments. Through it all the judge persevered, dutifully attending court until June 1825, when "various infirmities," including an "almost total Loss of Hearing," compelled him to resign.[3] He endured another two years of afflicting pain before a paralytic stroke ended his life on 10 November 1827.

The foundation of Tucker's prodigious knowledge of English law and nascent Virginia law was an ample library whose law component, about 40 percent of the whole, eventually grew to several hundred volumes. History, government, and political theory made up a large portion of the remainder. Tucker's interests ranged well beyond this core, however, with volumes devoted to science, geography and travel, poetry, and classics. He also had a large collection of English and American periodicals.[4] Tucker acquired books not for ornamental display, to show off his gentlemanly tastes, but for information and knowledge that served him in his vocational and avocational pursuits. His was essentially a working library, many of whose titles are cited multiple times in his *Blackstone's Commentaries* and in his judicial opinions.

Tucker made a good start to his law collection in 1774, when he acquired sixty-five volumes of English law reports, his share of the library of his uncle John Slater, his first law teacher and attorney general of Bermuda. In subsequent years Tucker regularly purchased from booksellers and at estate sales. As early as 1786, when a budding practitioner asked permission "to occupy a corner" in his library, Tucker was known for possessing an excellent set of law volumes.[5] In addition to reports of cases in the Courts of King's Bench, Common Pleas, and Exchequer and the High Court of Chancery from the reign of Elizabeth I to his own time, Tucker owned many of the important treatises, abridgments, dictionaries, and handbooks of English law, as well as volumes of parliamentary statutes. The oldest volumes in his extant collection are William Staunford's *Les Plees del Coron* (1560) and Robert Brooke's *Graunde Abridgement* (1573). In time his library encompassed Virginia and US law, as well as the major works of the law of nations. His collection of Virginia laws was perhaps second only to Jefferson's and included all the printed compilations and abridgments of colonial laws, the General Assembly's session laws commencing in 1776, and the several codes of Virginia. These scattered editions of the laws were indispensable to lawyers until William W. Hening's *Statutes at Large* superseded them early in the nineteenth century.

In March 1790 Tucker was appointed professor of law and police at the College of William and Mary to succeed George Wythe, who had moved to Richmond as sole judge of the High Court of Chancery. Besides providing welcome supplemental income, this post appealed to Tucker's evident pedagogical impulses. He eagerly embraced the opportunity to educate the rising generation to be proficient lawyers and sound republicans. The curriculum and method Tucker adopted for his law course were born of necessity. Lacking time to prepare a full set of lectures, he turned to Blackstone's *Commentaries* as his basic reading text, which he supplemented with passages from other works (e.g., the first volume of Sir Edward Coke's *Institutes,* also referred to as *Coke upon Littleton*) to illustrate or elaborate on an important point. In subsequent years Tucker came to regard "police," understood in the broad sense of governmental policy and administration, as equal in importance to technical law in his curriculum. A list of readings drawn up in 1800 included, in addition to English law reports and treatises, works on political theory, political economy, and constitutional history. Among the authors in this syllabus were John Locke, Adam Smith, and Charles-Louis Secondat, Baron de La Brède et de Montesquieu.[6]

Tucker taught law as a "liberal science," an academic subject requiring intensive study. By all accounts his course was strict and demanding, in keeping with his broader mission to improve the quality of the legal profession, to train lawyers who would displace the pettifoggers who flourished in the county courts. He believed his academic approach would benefit the aspiring attorney in the long run, though he might have difficulty at first mastering the practical side of lawyering. The numerous applications from those seeking to study under his tutelage testified to a general opinion that his course offered an entry to the profession that was superior to reading law with a practicing lawyer. A former student offered a dissenting view, complaining that "Bacon, Selden, Rolle, Plowden, Coke & other fathers of nonsense & pedantry" were of little practical use to a Virginia practitioner.[7]

Although Tucker valued the *Commentaries* "as a model of methodical elegance and legal perspicuity" and venerated the author for his "classical purity and precision as a scholar, and his authority as a lawyer,"[8] he used this text guardedly. In general, he found the English commentator a safe and reliable guide to private law, though even here important changes to and departures from English common law had taken place in Virginia, such as the abolition of entailed estates and the right of primogeniture and the establishment of an entirely new system concerning the heritability of estates. In the area of public law Tucker recognized that the *Commentaries* had serious shortcomings as a text for American students. The Revolution had rendered much of Blackstone either irrelevant or inimical to the new republican order established in the United States. He accordingly found it necessary to prepare original lectures on subjects not covered in Blackstone, such as the Constitution of the United States, the Virginia constitution, and slavery.

Tucker at first taught his course during the winter and summer judicial vacations, lecturing three times a week. Because of low attendance, Tucker eventually dropped the shorter summer term, compensating with two additional weekly lectures during the winter. At some point, he began holding his classes at his home instead of in the college because of the inconvenience of transporting his books back and forth. These arrangements eventually ran afoul of college regulations directing that the law course be taught in both winter and summer terms and that all lectures be delivered in the college. Sensitive to criticism that he had willfully flouted the college's statutes, Professor Tucker wrote impassioned letters to the Board of Visitors noting that his original appointment had not specified particular duties and that he had assumed that it was up to him to decide how best to fulfill his commitment as professor of law and police. In the summer of 1803 the college adopted regulations requiring professors to submit their class rolls to the Board of Visitors and to make twice-weekly visits to the students' college rooms. An indignant Tucker recoiled at this affront to his honor and dignity as "a professor of a liberal science." To be a "superintendent of the little truants of a country village," to "perform the duties of a beadle, or at the utmost of the proctor of an University . . . must degrade the professor in the eyes of his pupils, and of the public, & the man in his own eyes." The professor accordingly resigned effective at the end of the winter term in March 1804, shortly before he took his seat on the Court of Appeals.[9]

Despite this unhappy parting, Tucker enjoyed a successful tenure as a professor and produced a tangible legacy, an annotated edition of Blackstone's *Commentaries,* which earned him an enduring reputation as a legal scholar and constitutional commentator. Although not published until 1803, this work had begun to take shape in the mid-1790s and was ready for publication as early as 1797. The final result directly reflected his method of using Blackstone as his teaching text and supplementing it with his own lectures. "My method at first," he wrote in 1801, "was to make marginal references in Blackstone's Commentaries . . . & to read the passages referred to, out of the Books themselves. In process of time I found leisure to transcribe many of the shorter passages referred to, which now constitute notes, in an interleaved Copy of the Commentaries." Tucker created his interleaved copy by cutting the pages from a copy of the eleventh edition, published in 1791, and pasting them in the leaves of a blank volume. He entered his notes in the ample space surrounding the page of the marked passage of the *Commentaries.* The aim of these notes, he explained, was "to adapt that inimitable work" to American circumstances "either because the law had been confirmed, or changed, or repealed, by some constitutional or legislative act of the Federal Government or of the Commonwealth of Virginia."[10] The interleaved notes ultimately became numbered footnotes in his own edition. Tucker transcribed his separate lectures on subjects outside the scope of the *Commentaries* on blank leaves that became the appendices to his edition.

The idea of publication apparently first occurred to Tucker early in 1795, perhaps implanted by his good friend John Page. Well into his career as a professor and judge, Tucker had not envisioned law as his pathway to reputation and fame. He confided to Page that he would be known to posterity only by his "telegraph" invention (a mechanical means of communicating over long distances using an upright post with moveable arms). "[B]ut surely, " replied Page, "your Poems, your political Essays, independent of your Law Lectures, which I seriously advise you to publish, will gain you more Credit with Posterity than the Invention of a Telegraph," adding that Tucker's "Character as a Soldier, & Statesman, & Judge cannot escape the biographer."[11]

From the initial conception, Tucker had ambitious plans to transform his law course at William and Mary into a publication that would make him a name beyond Virginia. No local printers were capable of executing such a project, so he turned to Philadelphia, then the seat of government and the center of publishing in the new nation. He had already published poems in Philadelphia newspapers and in the *American Museum,* a literary magazine put out by Mathew Carey, with whom he soon formed an association to publish political pamphlets and essays. By June 1796 Tucker had drawn up a "Plan of an American Edition of Blackstone's Commentaries." He apparently sent copies of his proposal to various Philadelphia booksellers and publishers.[12]

The "Plan" stated that the proposed edition would contain an "Introduction, or Preface" by the editor, along with the editor's notes showing where English law had been "adopted or confirmed; altered and amended; or wholly changed and repealed" by American law. Each volume would also have an appendix of longer notes and essays drawn from the editor's law lectures. The "Plan" contained a detailed list of the topics to be covered in the appendices, which included the federal and Virginia constitutions, slavery, and the authority of English common law in the United States. To accommodate so much additional matter, the American edition would divide Blackstone's first volume into two parts. The price for the full set of "five very large octavo volumes" was to be twenty dollars.[13]

In addition to his "Plan of an American Edition," Tucker wrote "The Editor's Preface," a twenty-page pamphlet that was printed under obscure circumstances.[14] It had no separate title page to indicate either the place or date of publication. The concluding page bore Tucker's signature and the date 8 February 1797.[15] A likely conjecture is that Tucker meant the preface to be read in conjunction with the "Plan" and circulate among persons connected with the Philadelphia book trade. In both documents he tried to make the best possible case for an annotated American edition of Blackstone. A multivolume work requiring intricate typesetting—for example, to distinguish Blackstone's notes, the notes of his English editor, and those of the American editor—was not an easy sell.

Tucker accordingly devoted "The Editor's Preface" to explaining why such an edition was needed. "When a work of established reputation is offered to the public in a new dress," he wrote, "it is to be expected that the Editor should assign such reasons for so doing, as may not only exempt him from the imputation of a rash presumption, but shew that some benefit may be reasonably expected to result from his labours."[16] His argument essentially was that the *Commentaries* continued to be an immensely popular law text even in America, relied on virtually to the exclusion of other sources of legal knowledge. For that very reason, he said, Blackstone had to be overlaid with a protective layer of annotation to make it a trustworthy compendium for educating American lawyers.

Tucker readily acknowledged Blackstone's great achievement, writing that "the laws of England, from a rude chaos, instantly assumed the semblance of a regular system." However, the *Commentaries* made English law so accessible and so easily understood that a student was lulled into believing that by reading it "three or four times over" he would become "a thorough proficient in the law" without having to labor through Coke's "rich mine of learning." The work's very success had the unhappy effect of producing "a great number" of fledgling lawyers "whose superficial knowledge of the law" was "almost as soon forgotten, as acquired." Insufficient by itself for educating lawyers in England, the *Commentaries* was still less adequate "to the formation of a lawyer" in the colonies. The "colonial student," wrote Tucker, was "wholly without a guide" to the important changes made by the local codes. Even after the massive changes wrought by the Revolution and independence, the English commentator's work continued to be the American law student's only text, leaving newly licensed professionals thoroughly lacking in knowledge of "the laws of *their own country*." By this time, Tucker warned, the *Commentaries* was not merely a defective but an unsafe guide, for in many important respects the constitutions and laws of the United States were contradictory to English law and principles of government. Blackstone's work was fit only for describing "the general outlines of law" in the new nation "or at most" for explaining "what the *law had been*."[17]

Taking into account the continuing popularity of the *Commentaries*, Tucker proposed to remedy its manifest deficiencies with an edition that would essentially reproduce the course he taught at William and Mary. As a professor and scholar, he had collected and digested the voluminous sources of an indigenous law: dispersed and incomplete collections of Virginia colonial and state statutes, convention and legislative journals, proceedings and ordinances of the Continental and Confederation Congresses, federal statutes, and debates and proceedings of the US Congress. He had embodied much of this material in short annotations inserted at appropriate places in his interleaved copy of Blackstone's text. But Tucker promised much more than an annotated American edition of Blackstone. He proposed in effect a "different work," one that would preserve the "incomparable" *Commentaries* while rendering it "a *safe*, as well as delightful guide" to budding American lawyers.[18]

Tucker presented himself not just as an editor but as a commentator in his own right, contributing scholarly essays on topics outside the scope of the *Commentaries* but essential to American law students. Foremost among these were his lectures on the US Constitution and the nature of the American federal system. He forthrightly acknowledged that his exposition of the American system of government would go beyond mere description to embrace the normative purpose of demonstrating the superiority of the new republican order of America to the discarded British constitution and monarchy. He particularly wished to register his "dissent" to the received maxim that sovereignty was indivisible and embodied in an omnipotent Parliament. That doctrine had been irretrievably overthrown, Tucker insisted, by American experience since 1776, which had provided empirical proof that sovereignty ultimately resided in the people (as Locke had argued) and could be divided among different levels of government.[19]

Much of Tucker's preface previewed the supplementary writings to be appended to the *Commentaries*. These included, besides his disquisition on the Constitution, a "full and candid discussion" of the Virginia constitution, whose authority had been brought into question by one of the country's "most enlightened politicians," an allusion to Thomas Jefferson. Another inquiry concerned the "authority and obligation" of English common law within the individual states and the United States collectively, a topic of much controversy at the time. The American editor also promised to treat the subject of domestic slavery, an institution seemingly incompatible with "the principles of a free republic," and consider whether the time was right "to wipe off that stigma from our nation and government."[20]

Tucker also previewed some tracts more narrowly focused to meet the needs of Virginians, including those on Virginia statutory law, court organization, and rules of inheritance. He would have preferred to incorporate the jurisprudence of all the states, but such a project was "too voluminous" to execute. He therefore had to be content with an edition that would be "particularly useful" to Virginia students and "generally so" to those outside Virginia who cared to learn about the principles of the US Constitution and laws. Tucker concluded his preface by urging the importance of a free republican citizenry's possessing a thorough knowledge and understanding of its constitutions and laws. "Man only requires to understand his rights to estimate them properly," he wrote, adding that "the ignorance of the people is the footstool of despotism." The case for his American edition of Blackstone thus ultimately rested on its value as a repository of knowledge "to preserve the blessings of freedom."[21]

To Tucker's disappointment, no Philadelphia publisher was willing to undertake his Blackstone project. Publishers balked at the risk of incurring large costs for a publication likely to have limited appeal outside Virginia. Some were willing to proceed with the more modest plan of publishing a selection of Tucker's lectures. In September 1796, for instance, Carey published the lectures on slavery as *A Dissertation on Slavery: With a Proposal for the Gradual Abolition of It, in the State of Virginia*. Tucker never abandoned the larger enterprise, however, stubbornly adhering to the scope and conditions set forth in his original proposal. Negotiations continued sporadically until the spring of 1802, when Tucker met the Philadelphia bookseller Abraham Small in Williamsburg. Eventually Tucker accepted an offer from Small and his partner, William Young Birch, to print the manuscript in return for the copyright, which Tucker sold for four thousand dollars. He then prudently had his manuscript transcribed for transmittal to the Philadelphia publishers.[22]

In September 1802 Birch and Small printed a two-page advertisement, *Proposals for Publishing an American Edition of Blackstone's Commentaries*, which circulated as a broadside and was also inserted in newspapers. The text, with slight alterations, was taken from Tucker's 1796 "Plan," with the addition of Birch and Small's "Address By the Publishers." The Philadelphia publishers urged potential purchasers to sign up as soon as possible, noting that the work could not be printed until there was a sufficient number of subscribers. As an inducement, anyone who procured nine subscribers would receive a free set. In addition to providing subscription papers to local postmasters, Birch and Small listed the names of booksellers and printers who would take subscriptions. Most of these were located in Virginia—Richmond, Petersburg, Norfolk, Williamsburg, Fredericksburg, Alexandria, Martinsburg, and Winchester. Other subscription agents were in Baltimore, Washington, DC, Raleigh, and Charleston. At twenty dollars for the five volumes, Tucker's *Blackstone,* so the publishers claimed, was "considerably the lowest priced law book" of such extent to have "appeared for many years either in America or Europe."[23]

Tucker and his friends actively solicited subscribers, including nearly all members of the Richmond bar, and at the end of November 1802 he reported that the efforts had secured nearly two hundred subscribers throughout Virginia. In time, subscriptions reached a high enough level to proceed to publication; the first volume was printed in May 1803, and in October a Richmond bookseller announced that the entire set was ready for delivery to subscribers. For the next several months sales were steady, including a gratifying fifty copies sold in Philadelphia. Although the great majority of purchasers resided south of Philadelphia, mostly in Virginia, booksellers advertised the edition as far north as New York and Boston.[24]

The edition of *Blackstone's Commentaries* published in 1803 was essentially the manuscript Tucker had completed seven years earlier. He changed the date of the "Editor's Preface" from 8 February 1797 to 10 July 1802. Having purchased a new edition of the *Commentaries* published in London with notes by Edward Christian, Tucker added a selection of Christian's notes "as appeared to him most likely to be of use to an American Student." He informed his readers of these additions by an "Advertisement" dated 12 May 1803, inserted in each of the volumes. The most extensive changes were new notes citing state and federal acts and legal decisions as late as 1803. For Virginia statutes enacted since the last edition of the laws, published in 1794, Tucker cited the "Sessions Acts," published annually after each session of the General Assembly. A new edition of Virginia laws appeared in 1803, while his own work was still in press. Tucker accordingly inserted a useful table in his first volume listing the chapter numbers of the "Sessions Acts" from 1795 through 1801 and the corresponding numbers in the 1803 edition of Virginia laws. He also took care to cite cases in recently published Virginia law reports and others recorded in his own manuscript legal casebook. In his "Summary View of the Laws Relative to Glebes and Churches," appended to the first volume, Tucker reproduced an extract of a law report printed in a newspaper late in September 1802. This extract and his additional commentary enlarged the original appendix by six printed pages.[25]

Blackstone's Commentaries in five volumes reproduced the English commentator's four volumes, supplemented by more than a thousand footnotes and eight hundred pages of appendices written by the Virginia editor. More than half of the content of the appendices appeared in the first volume, leaving just over a hundred pages to Blackstone himself. The centerpiece appendix of this volume was "View of the Constitution of the United States," a treatise of more than two hundred pages, which Tucker most counted on to elevate his edition above the level of a parochial law text. In this respect, in setting forth a Jeffersonian understanding of the nature of the Constitution as a compact in which federal powers were to be strictly construed and in which the states retained ample residual sovereignty, Tucker's "View" resonated with the recent Republican political triumph. So, too, did another long appendix, on the authority of English common law in the United States, which followed immediately after the treatise on the Constitution. This was a reprint of a pamphlet drawn from Tucker's law lectures and published in 1800, in which Tucker emphatically argued that the Constitution had not adopted the common law as the law of the United States collectively.[26]

Another of Tucker's essays that reached beyond the local Virginia context was "On the State of Slavery in Virginia," a reprint of his 1796 *Dissertation on Slavery*. Tucker had presented the *Dissertation* and its accompanying abolition plan to the Virginia General Assembly. Despite its proposal for an abolition so gradual as to be imperceptible (taking place over more than a century), requiring no sacrifice of slaveholders' property rights, and imposing harsh and punitive conditions on newly emancipated slaves in the hope that they would migrate beyond the state, the legislature had rudely dismissed Tucker's accommodating plan.[27] By reproducing the *Dissertation* in *Blackstone's Commentaries,* Tucker ensured greater permanence for its learned exposition of the law of slavery in Virginia. Perhaps he hoped as well that its ameliorative aspirations would eventually find a receptive audience.

In the decades following its publication, Tucker's *Blackstone* acquired a firm reputation as a monumental text and sourcebook of American law. Although addressed principally to the aspiring Virginia lawyer, the work was known throughout the land and circulated generally from Pennsylvania southward. Neither the editor nor the publisher appears to have contemplated a second printing or edition, but at some point Tucker began to enter marginal annotations in his own copy of *Blackstone's Commentaries,* keeping it up to date on the latest developments in state and federal law.

Early in 1818 a New England printer and publisher wrote to Tucker about reprinting four of the appendices to the first volume, including "View of the Constitution." Tucker referred him to Birch and Small, holders of the copyright. Shortly thereafter Abraham Small wrote to Tucker informing him of his intention to reprint the edition and asking for suggestions and alterations. Small had not then heard from the New England printer but doubted that he would be willing to secure the copyright on the terms they proposed. Three years later Small wrote again with the same request. Tucker answered "fully," but his reply has not been found.[28]

In the meantime, or perhaps even before his 1818 communications with Small, Tucker constructed a working copy of *Blackstone's Commentaries,* interleaving pages of the 1803 edition with pages in a blank notebook—the same procedure he had used in making the original. On this interleaved copy he made changes and additions, mostly citations of cases and acts after 1803. He entered notes in all four volumes, with no references later than 1821. In that year he wrote an addendum entitled "Supplement to Note H, On the State of Slavery in Virginia." It filled seven manuscript pages, which he directed to be inserted at page 79, near the end of the note.[29] In the preceding pages he had discussed the obstacles to internal colonization of free blacks, while noting the "immense unsettled" territory of Louisiana and territories belonging to Spain as offering a more favorable prospect. This vast area, extending from the Mississippi River to the Pacific Ocean, now belonged to the United States as a result of the 1819 treaty with Spain. Ratification of the treaty rekindled Tucker's hopes for the gradual abolition of slavery. His supplement sketched a plan to settle free blacks in the West in small communities, or "asylums," geographically separated and surrounded by white settlements.[30]

The supplementary note on slavery was the most substantive entry Tucker made in his interleaved copy of *Blackstone's Commentaries,* amounting to a short essay. The absence of further correspondence with Small after 1821 suggests that editor and publisher concluded that there was not enough new material to justify a second printing. Perhaps, too, years of deteriorating health had diminished Tucker's energy and enthusiasm for the task. Four years after Tucker died in 1827, his son Henry St. George Tucker published *Commentaries on the Laws of Virginia,* drawn from his own lectures at the Winchester Law School. This two-volume work brought students up to date on Virginia and federal law, but it was not (and not intended to be) a second edition of *Blackstone's Commentaries.* Like his father, Henry Tucker founded his course on Blackstone, but instead of leaving the English commentator's text intact, he eliminated the "obviously obsolete and irrelevant" parts. The result was a treatise more heavily concentrated on the municipal law of Virginia.[31]

If largely supplanted as a text for Virginia law students, the elder Tucker's *Blackstone's Commentaries* nevertheless retained a continuing vitality well into the nineteenth century. As the first major treatise on American law and the earliest commentary (after *The Federalist*) on the Constitution, Tucker's *Blackstone* was unsurpassed until the appearance of the monumental works of James Kent and Joseph Story in the 1820s and 1830s. As the only annotated American edition of Blackstone until the eve of the Civil War, it constituted an important part of a lawyer's library. Even today, Tucker's *Blackstone's Com-*

mentaries remains a valuable repository and reference, used by lawyers, judges, legal scholars, and historians. From the beginning, the Supreme Court has cited Tucker on numerous occasions, including a dozen landmark cases. Legal historians and scholars in particular rely on his *Blackstone* as a principal source for showing how a distinctive American law emerged from its foundation in English common law and how the founding generation understood the meaning of the Constitution and the Bill of Rights.[32] Reprints of *Blackstone's Commentaries* in 1969 and again in 1996, along with the separate publication of his most important appendices, testify to the growing reputation of the work and its author in recent years.[33]

At the time he published *Blackstone's Commentaries* in 1803, Tucker was also busily compiling a series of law notebooks. He had begun his lifelong practice of entering notes and memoranda of cases in small blank notebooks during his first appearance at the bar of the General Court in the spring of 1786. During the next quarter century he filled nearly three dozen notebooks of case reports in the higher courts of Virginia. He eventually had the notebooks bound together in three manuscript volumes entitled "Notes of Certain Cases in the General Court, District Courts, and Court of Appeals in Virginia, from the year 1786 to 1811." This is the principal document reproduced in *Law Reports and Selected Papers.*

As a notetaker, Tucker carried on a long tradition of Anglo-American law reporting dating from the thirteenth century. The practice originated in the need of students and practitioners to go beyond the bare record of a case (which stated only the court's formal judgment) to learn what lawyers and judges had said during the hearing. The earliest English reports were anonymous "year-books," referring to the mode of citation by regnal year. Reports began to proliferate during the Tudor period and came to be known by the name of the author or compiler, usually a lawyer or judge. These reports were often haphazardly produced and varied in their quality and authority. By the time of Lord Mansfield in the latter half of the eighteenth century, English reporting had become more standardized and authoritative with the emergence of professional reporters.[34]

Reporting of Virginia cases began during the first half of the eighteenth century, though the first publication of Virginia reports did not take place until the end of the century. Five sets of reports of cases in the General Court are known to have been compiled and to circulate in manuscript. Those of Sir John Randolph and Edward Barradall, covering cases from 1729 to 1741, were published early in the twentieth century. William Hopkins assembled at least two manuscript volumes of reports from the same period, but these were subsequently lost. Thomas Jefferson, who practiced law during the decade preceding independence, made a compilation that included extracts from the reports of Randolph and Barradall and his own reports of cases from 1768 to 1772. Jefferson's grandson and executor published the reports in 1829. The manuscript of John Randolph (son of Sir John and father of Edmund Randolph) also circulated and was cited, but it too was lost and never published.[35]

With independence and the establishment of new state superior courts, lawyers continued to cite manuscript reports of colonial cases. For current cases, Tucker and his contemporaries at the superior court bar had to be their own reporters, jotting down the facts of the case, summarizing the arguments of counsel, and most important, preserving a memorandum (or perhaps obtaining a copy) of the court's opinion. Bar and bench cooperated with each other in circulating their notes, memoranda, and opinions. Most of these manuscripts have long since been lost or destroyed. The notes of Bushrod Washington were the basis of the first published reports of cases in the Court of Appeals. His two volumes appeared in 1798 and 1799 and reported cases from October 1790 through October 1796. Washington informed users that his reports were simply an extension of the notes he kept for his own use, "without any view to a publication."[36]

Daniel Call assumed the task of reporting after Washington joined the US Supreme Court in 1798. He published three volumes of cases from the spring term of 1797 through the fall term of 1803.[37] Perhaps because of the expense and labor, Call suspended publishing after his third volume. In consequence, there was no contemporaneous publication of Court of Appeals cases decided between April 1804 and October 1806. Reporting resumed at the latter term under the direction of William Waller Hening and William Munford. The appearance of their first volume in 1808 marked a distinct advance toward professional reporting, with the reporters eschewing the "usual apology, 'that the notes were taken merely for their own private use'" but "professedly with a view to disseminate" the court's decisions "as early, and in as authentic a manner as possible."[38] Hening and Munford published four volumes, followed by six more by Munford alone. These volumes reported cases from October 1806 through April 1820. Reporting was solely a private enterprise until the latter year, when the General Assembly provided for the appointment of an official reporter, to receive partial compensation in public funds.[39]

Tucker, like Washington and other post-Revolutionary practitioners, commenced notetaking for his own professional use. He never indicated any intention to publish his notebooks, not even after he had them bound in 1811. By that time there was less incentive to publish, because much the greater portion of his manuscript covered the same period reported by Hening and Munford. Had he remained at the bar and developed a practice in the Court of Appeals during the 1790s, Tucker might have ventured into publishing reports before Washington and Call got into the act.

Tucker's "Notes of Cases" is one of the few extant manuscripts of Virginia law reports dating from the late eighteenth and early nineteenth centuries.

W. Hamilton Bryson collected and published these manuscripts, exclusive of Tucker's, in 1992. Bryson's slender volume includes the reports of Charles Lee, who practiced in the superior courts during the 1780s and 1790s, and John Brown, who was clerk of the Court of Appeals from 1785 to 1810.[40] In density and span of time covered, Tucker's notebooks are singular, without comparison among personal legal archives from this period that have escaped loss or destruction.

After his notebooks were bound in 1811, Tucker wrote in a prefatory note that they had been "preserved for my own use, & that of my own Family."[41] His family included sons Henry St. George and Nathaniel Beverley, both of whom achieved prominence as lawyers and professors of law. The notebooks were widely known outside the Tucker household as well and continued to have currency within Virginia's legal profession for years after Tucker's death in 1827. While teaching his law course at William and Mary in the 1790s, Tucker drew on his case notes to keep his students abreast of the most recent developments in Virginia law. While sitting on the Court of Appeals from 1804 to 1811, Tucker assisted Hening and Munford in preparing their reports by lending them his notebooks at the end of each term.[42] He also allowed members of the bar to consult his notes and answered inquiries concerning specific cases he had reported.[43]

Although Tucker's notebooks were never published, some of his reports made their way into print. In 1815 the General Court judges William Brockenbrough and Hugh Holmes published a volume of cases in that court. To their report of *Commonwealth v. Myers* (1811) the reporters appended Tucker's reports of *Thomas Sorrel's Case* (1786) and *John Bailey's Case* (1798). They noted that the former case "was reported in MS. by Saint George Tucker, Esq. whilst he was at the bar, and a copy of his report was shewn to the general court during Myers's trial."[44]

The most important professional use made of Tucker's notebooks was by Daniel Call. In the spring of 1825 Call wrote to Tucker about his plan to publish unreported Court of Appeals cases since that court's inception in 1779, principally those decided during the gap between Call's third volume and Hening and Munford's first volume. This gap coincided with Tucker's first two years on the court. Having used Tucker's notes when at the bar, Call had firsthand knowledge of their value. Tucker generously lent Call his entire three-volume manuscript, which he "put up in a small box, with my name on the top." He advised Call to place the volumes in the box when not using them "to prevent their being mislaid."[45] Tucker's manuscript served as the principal source for cases reported in Call's fourth, fifth, and sixth volumes, which were published as a set in 1833, six years after Tucker's death.[46]

Call was likely still in possession of the manuscript volumes at the time of Tucker's death. Whether he returned them to the Tucker family before his own death in 1840 is not known. Whatever the circumstances, the volumes passed out of the Tucker family at some point during the nineteenth century, only to be returned in 1880. Among those who held the volumes during that period were William T. Joynes (1817–1874), who served on the Virginia Supreme Court of Appeals from 1866 to 1869 and from 1870 to 1873, and William Green (1806–1880), a renowned appellate advocate and author of scholarly legal articles.[47] Green's brother turned them over to J. Randolph Tucker (1824–1897), St. George Tucker's grandson, in 1880. The volumes were among a group of papers and bound volumes that a Tucker descendant donated to the College of William and Mary in 1938. This gift became the nucleus of the Tucker-Coleman Papers in the Swem Library's Special Collections. For many years Tucker's volumes lay dormant in the library, uncataloged and virtually unknown to researchers until the 1960s, when they were in effect rediscovered thanks to the probing investigations of a young graduate student who was then writing a dissertation on Tucker.[48]

From the time he began riding circuit in the spring of 1789 until his last circuit in the fall of 1803, Tucker reported upwards of four hundred cases in the district courts and the General Court. These reports merit particular notice. Whereas reported cases are typically confined to the highest appellate court, Tucker was essentially a trial judge during these years. His notes reveal what was happening at the trial and intermediate appellate level, imparting a sense of the judicial system as it operated in the various districts both near and remote from the capital at Richmond. They constitute an unrivaled primary record for tracking the newly independent commonwealth's efforts to establish a system of state superior courts operating alongside the older county courts, dating from the colonial period. More broadly, they provide an invaluable source for studying the "republicanization" of the common law as it unfolded in the Commonwealth of Virginia.[49] They also afford a fascinating glimpse of Virginia's distinguished post-Revolutionary bar, which included a future chief justice and a future associate justice of the US Supreme Court (John Marshall and Bushrod Washington), two future attorneys general of the United States (Edmund Randolph and Charles Lee), and a future president (James Monroe).

The district courts were primarily trial courts. Much the greater portion of Tucker's civil cases concerned the recovery of a debt or a property dispute about land and slaves. Slavery permeated the legal system, with scarcely a case on the docket that did not involve enslaved persons held as property. Judge Tucker also heard criminal cases, for crimes including murder, manslaughter, mayhem, burglary, forgery, assault, horse stealing, and perjury. He was alert to new and interesting questions of law that arose even in the most mundane cases he heard on circuit. He took the initiative in shaping lawsuits to raise such issues and, if necessary, to get them finally settled by adjournment to the full bench of the General Court or by appeal to the Court of Appeals.

At King and Queen District Court in April 1795, for example, Tucker fashioned a case to raise the vexing question of whether a defendant in an action brought by a British creditor for a debt incurred before the War of Independence was entitled to discount interest during the war years. Although the plea of "British debt" no longer sufficed to deny or delay suits for such debts in Virginia courts, juries routinely subtracted eight years' interest in rendering their verdicts—over the loud protests of British plaintiffs. In the federal court juries deducted interest despite explicit instructions from the judge that interest must be regarded as part of the debt. Because this disallowance was part of a general verdict, the question could not be appealed. All that a judge could do was order a new trial—which produced the same result.[50] In the case in the King and Queen District Court, the defendant's lawyer moved to enter a plea of "British debt." Tucker said that the plea could "neither operate in Bar nor in Abatement," but as to the question of war interest intended to be raised by the plea, "he thought it high time the point should be settled." He then added: "The difficulty was in what shape to bring it on. If plaintiff were really absent during the War, & no Agent or Attorney within the State, this for ought he knew might be proper Evidence for the Consideration of a Jury; but he knew of no method of bringing on the Question by pleading." In order to have the question decided and justice "no longer delayed by Doubts on the subject," Tucker recommended that the defendant give the plaintiff written notice of his intention to move the court to offer evidence to prove that the plaintiff had been absent during the war and had no agent to whom the debt could be paid. At the ensuing trial, on the motion to introduce evidence Tucker said: "Without giving any Opinion whether the Evidence be proper or not, I agree that it may be offered to the Jury in order that this long contested point may be settled." The plaintiff's lawyer then tendered a bill of exceptions, making this ruling part of the record for a possible appeal. When the jury deducted eight years' interest, the plaintiff appealed. The Virginia Court of Appeals upheld Tucker's ruling and the jury's verdict in 1797.[51]

At Dumfries District Court in May 1793 Tucker refused to issue an injunction as directed by a recent act of the state legislature, thus precipitating—no doubt by design—the most important case heard in Virginia at this time. The judge believed the act unconstitutionally vested common-law judges with equity jurisdiction (equity was a separate system of law administered by courts of chancery). The case was adjourned for "novelty and difficulty" to the November 1793 term of the General Court in Richmond, where Tucker and the four other sitting judges unanimously ruled that the act was unconstitutional.[52]

Kamper v. Hawkins (as the case was styled) became a leading precedent for judicial review, the cornerstone doctrine of American constitutional law, proclaiming that judges are duty bound to regard constitutions as applicable law. Tucker by that time had been advocating the doctrine for more than a decade. As early as 1782 he had delivered an amicus brief in the notable "Case of the Prisoners," which presented the question whether a state law was in conflict with the state constitution. Setting forth arguments founded on the separation of powers, the judiciary's province to interpret the law, the inviolability of the constitution against legislative amendment, the distinction between the "constructive" British constitution and Virginia's "express" constitution, Tucker had emphatically affirmed the proposition that courts were bound to consider written constitutions as operative law and that judges were accordingly authorized to void statutes deemed to be in conflict with that law.[53]

Tucker from the outset held the view that judicial review was embodied in the very idea of a written constitution enacted by the people themselves. In his law course, he considered whether Virginia's constitution was an ordinary act of the legislature and therefore alterable and revocable by the legislature. Jefferson in his recently published *Notes on the State of Virginia* had censured the constitution as a mere legislative enactment, prompting Professor Tucker to enter a vigorous rebuttal. He contended that Virginia's Revolutionary conventions, including that of June 1776, which declared Virginia's independence and adopted a new constitution, were not legal or constitutional parts of an existing government but the "people themselves." Tucker made this argument early in the 1790s in a case that was unreported and apparently undecided, but he later reproduced it in his *Kamper* opinion. He also set it down in finished form in his *Blackstone*.[54]

Kamper v. Hawkins afforded Tucker his first opportunity as a judge to expound the Virginia constitution and to pronounce an act of the state legislature void as repugnant to the constitution. His opinion was his most definitive statement of the doctrine of judicial review as it came to be formulated in the early republic. He defined a constitution as fundamental and paramount law, to which government was a mere creature and from which government derived all its power and authority. It was, he said, "the *first law of the Land*, and as such must be resorted to on every occasion where it becomes necessary to expound *what the law is*. This Exposition it is the Duty and Office of the judiciary to make." He insisted that the constitution was "a rule to *all* the Departments of the Government, to the *Judiciary*, as well as to the Legislature." For good measure, Tucker quoted a long passage from Alexander Hamilton in *Federalist* No. 78 and commended "the reasoning of one of the most profound politicians in America" as "so full, so apposite, & so conclusive" that nothing more on the subject needed to be said.[55]

In his law lectures, writings, and judicial opinions, notably *Kamper v. Hawkins,* Tucker as much as anyone placed the doctrine of judicial review on a solid republican foundation that won acceptance across a broad political spectrum. Published reports do not disclose the names of the lawyers who argued *Kamper*. Thanks to Tucker's notes entered on the blank sheets of a docket book, we now know that one of those lawyers was John Marshall. Ten years later, in the celebrated case *Marbury v. Madison,* Chief Justice Marshall affirmed the doctrine in language strikingly similar to Tucker's.

Tucker made the most of his few judicial opportunities to decide broad public questions and promote his view that judges could determine whether legislative acts passed constitutional muster. More typically, he dealt with narrow though often intricate questions arising from the private law of debt, contract, and property. In these the judge and law professor often merged to produce learned disquisitions based on deep research in the vast repository of English law, confirming his reputation as "decidedly the most learned judge" of the General Court after Henry Tazewell was promoted to the Court of Appeals in 1793.[56] Tucker rarely met a pertinent case or authority that he did not want to quote or cite, often cramming additional citations in the margins. His legal inquiries sometimes had the aspect of an extended dialogue with such English luminaries as Coke, Mansfield, and Blackstone.

Tucker's years as a judge of the Virginia Court of Appeals, 1804 to 1811, fill the other twenty-odd notebooks of "Notes of Cases," which contain largely his opinions. Although most of his Court of Appeals opinions are included in the volumes of Call, Hening and Munford, and Munford, Tucker recorded much interesting matter not to be found in their reports, including his memoranda of court conferences and of his points of agreement and disagreement with the other judges. The reporters did not always include the full text of Tucker's opinion, omitting, for example, his statement of the case or passages dealing with points that did not enter into the court's decision. Tucker also wrote more than two dozen opinions that were never published because the cases were not reported, because he did not deliver his opinion in court, or because they were not finally decided until after his resignation. *Tucker's Law Reports* presents the full texts of all of Tucker's opinions, published and unpublished.

Tucker devoted the last two notebooks in "Notes on Cases" not to cases but to a detailed inquiry into the causes of the great upsurge of business in the Court of Appeals. He traced the principal cause to the deeply entrenched right of arbitrary appeal, which he contended had ceased to be an instrument to promote justice and instead had become a mechanism that debtors resourcefully exploited to delay indefinitely the day of reckoning and deprive creditors of their just claims. In consequence, the Court of Appeals, instead of being a tribunal to correct substantive errors of law, risked becoming "but a *single Court* for the Administration of Justice in this populous, and extensive State: for thither every litigious, or dishonest defendant would be sure to fly for sanctuary; and having arrived there, he might ever after rest in security."[57] An inveterate reformer, Tucker expended much effort to persuade the General Assembly to pass a bill he had drafted to regulate the right of appeal and remedy delays in the administration of justice. In this endeavor, however, he found only disappointment and frustration. Along with his acrimonious rupture with Judge Roane, Tucker's failure to secure enactment of what he believed to be sensible and necessary judicial reform undoubtedly hastened his decision to resign from the Court of Appeals in 1811.

Tucker's "Notes on Cases" enjoyed a long and widespread professional use in its unpublished state. No longer an important repository for law students and practitioners, these notebooks since their rediscovery have found a new use as a source for the scholarly study of Virginia and American law in the post-Revolutionary era. The publication of *Tucker's Law Reports* is belated recognition of the importance of this remarkable archive for historical inquiry and research. It ensures permanence and wide dissemination, its accessibility and usability enhanced by accompanying annotations and editorial apparatus. While providing a unique picture of a legal system operating at different levels and in different jurisdictions for an extended period of time, this edition offers abundant documentation of Tucker the judge, bringing to light a relatively neglected aspect of a productive and creative career in law. Judge Tucker's reports richly illustrate the practical working out of a process that formed the central theme of his *Blackstone:* the adaptation of English common law to the particular circumstances of republican America.

NOTES

1. This brief biographical sketch is drawn from a larger sketch in my general introduction to *St. George Tucker's Law Reports and Selected Papers, 1782–1825,* ed. Charles F. Hobson, 3 vols. (Chapel Hill, 2013), 1:3–19.
2. See Charles F. Hobson, "St George Tucker, Spencer Roane, and the Virginia Court of Appeals, 1804–11," *Virginia Magazine of History and Biography* 121 (2013): 3–43.
3. St. George Tucker to Henry Clay, 30 June 1825, in *Tucker's Law Reports,* 3:1738.
4. Jill M. Coghlan, "The Library of St. George Tucker" (master's thesis, College of William and Mary, 1973).
5. Daniel Call to Tucker, 4 May 1786, Tucker-Coleman Collection, Swem Library Special Collections, College of William and Mary (hereafter T-C).
6. Tucker to John Ambler, 16 Dec. 1801, Virginia Historical Society; copy of a letter to the rector of the Convocation of Visitors & Governors of William & Mary College, 9 Dec. 1803, T-C; "A System of reading on the Subjects of Politics & Law ... ," 1 Dec. 1800, in *St. George Tucker and Law in Virginia, 1772–1804,* by Charles T. Cullen (New York, 1987), 205–7. See also Davison M. Douglas, "The Jeffersonian Vision of Legal Education," *Journal of Legal Education* 51 (2001): 203–7.

7. Garritt Minor to Joseph C. Cabell, 20 May 1801, Cabell Family Papers, University of Virginia, quoted in Cullen, *St. George Tucker,* 134.
8. St. George Tucker, preface to *Blackstone's Commentaries: With Notes of Reference, to the Constitution and Laws, of the Federal Government of the United States; and of the Commonwealth of Virginia,* 5 vols. (Philadelphia, 1803), 1:vi.
9. Copy of a letter to the rector of the Convocation of Visitors & Governors of William & Mary College, 9 Dec. 1803.
10. Tucker to Ambler, 16 Dec. 1801; Tucker to Board of Visitors, 9 Dec. 1803, T-C; Tucker, preface to *Blackstone's Commentaries,* 1:vi.
11. John Page to Tucker, 6 Jan. 1795, T-C.
12. Zephaniah Swift wrote Tucker from Philadelphia on 1 June 1796 (copy in T-C) that he had seen his "plan for an edition of Blackstone."
13. "Plan of an American Edition," as quoted in Cullen, *St. George Tucker,* 225.
14. The pamphlet is confusingly catalogued under Tucker's name as *Proposals for Publishing an American Edition of Blackstone's Commentaries* (Philadelphia, [1797?]). This is the same title as a Philadelphia broadside printed in 1802 by Birch and Small as an advertisement for their publication of Tucker's edition. To add to the confusion, the 1802 broadside was evidently an updated version of the 1796 "Plan of an American Edition." There is a copy of the pamphlet version of the "Editor's Preface" at the Small Special Collections Library, University of Virginia.
15. This was the date Tucker affixed to the handwritten preface he entered in his interleaved Blackstone. On the interleaved copy he later struck out "1797" and inserted "1803." When the edition was eventually published in 1803, Tucker dated the preface 10 July 1802.
16. Tucker, preface to *Blackstone's Commentaries,* 1:iii.
17. Ibid., iii–v.
18. Ibid., vi.
19. Ibid., vi–viii. For an excellent brief assessment of Tucker's *Blackstone,* see the book review by Robert Cover in *Columbia Law Review* 70 (1970): 1475–94.
20. Tucker, preface *Blackstone's Commentaries,* 1:viii, xi–xii.
21. Ibid., xiv, xvi–xvii.
22. Cullen, *St. George Tucker,* 226–27.
23. *Judge Tucker's Blackstone: Proposals for Publishing an American Edition of Blackstone's Commentaries* (Philadelphia, 1802). This advertisement appeared in the Richmond *Virginia Argus,* 18 Sept. 1802, and on subsequent dates.
24. *Virginia Argus,* 5 Nov. 1803; Cullen, *St. George Tucker,* 228. Northern newspapers advertising the edition included the *Commercial Advertiser* (18 Oct. 1804) and the *Daily Advertiser* (22 Feb. 1805) in New York and the *Independent Chronicle* (14 May 1804) in Boston.
25. Tucker, *Blackstone's Commentaries,* appendix to vol. 1, note M, 104–18.
26. *Examination of the Question, "How Far the Common Law of England Is the Law of the Federal Government of the United States?"* (Richmond, [1800]), reprinted, with a postscript, in Tucker, *Blackstone' Commentaries,* appendix to vol. 1, note E, 378–439.

See Cullen, *St. George Tucker,* 154–55; David Thomas Konig, "St. George Tucker and the Limits of States' Rights Constitutionalism: Understanding the Federal Compact in the Early Republic," *William and Mary Law Review* 47 (2006): 1327–29; and Ellen Holmes Pearson, *Remaking Custom: Law and Identity in the Early American Republic* (Charlottesville, 2011), 27–29.

27. Tucker, *Blackstone's Commentaries,* appendix to vol. 1, pt. 2, note H, 31–85. See Cullen, *St. George Tucker,* 149–52; and Phillip Hamilton, *The Making and Unmaking of a Revolutionary Family: The Tuckers of Virginia, 1752–1830* (Charlottesville, 2003), 80–83.

28. Herman Mann to Tucker, 20 Jan. 1818; and Small to Tucker, 13 Feb. 1818 and 16 Mar. 1821, all T-C.

29. "Supplement to Note H, On the State of Slavery in Virginia," interleaved copy of Tucker, *Blackstone,* 1, pt. 2, appendix, note H, 79 and n.

30. Tucker's "Supplement" is noted in Phillip Hamilton, "Revolutionary Principles and Family Loyalties: Slavery's Transformation in the St. George Tucker Household of Early National Virginia," *William and Mary Quarterly,* 3d ser., 55 (1998): 555–56.

31. Henry St. George Tucker, *Commentaries on Virginia Law, Comprising the Substance of a Course of Lectures delivered to the Winchester Law School,* 2 vols. (Winchester, VA, 1831). On the younger Tucker, see Pearson, *Remaking Custom,* 187–89.

32. Paul Finkelman and David Cobin, introduction to the 1996 reprint edition of Tucker, *Blackstone's Commentaries: With Notes of Reference, to the Constitution and Laws, of the Federal Government of the United States; and of the Commonwealth of Virginia,* 5 vols. (Union, NJ), 1:i–ii, v–vi, xiii.

33. In this regard, see the "Institute of Bill of Rights Law Symposium: St. George Tucker and His Influence on American Law," *William and Mary Law Review* 47 (2006): 1111–25. Tucker's enhanced reputation also owes much to the online availability of his *Blackstone.*

34. John H. Baker, *An Introduction to English Legal History,* 3d ed. (London, 1990), 204–11.

35. W. Hamilton Bryson, ed., *Miscellaneous Virginia Law Reports, 1784–1809* (Dobbs Ferry, NY, 1992), xxix–xxxi.

36. Bushrod Washington, "To the Reader," in *Reports of Cases Argued and Determined in the Court of Appeals of Virginia,* 2 vols. (Richmond, 1798–1800), vol. 1. The earliest publication of Virginia cases was George Wythe's *Decisions of Cases in Virginia by the High Court of Chancery* (1795). Wythe's cases were not "reports" in the conventional sense but a vehicle for defending his decrees, many of which had been modified or overruled by the Court of Appeals. See E. Lee Shepard, "George Wythe," in *The Virginia Law Reporters Before 1880,* ed. W. Hamilton Bryson (Charlottesville, 1977), 90–95.

37. Call appended to his third volume a handful of John Marshall's reports, the manuscript of which has also been lost. *The Papers of John Marshall,* ed. Charles F. Hobson et al., 12 vols. (Chapel Hill, 1974–2006), 5:454–55, 473–74.

38. William Waller Hening and William Munford, preface to *Reports of Cases Argued and Determined in the Supreme Court of Appeals of Virginia . . . ,* 4 vols. (Philadelphia, 1808–11), vol. 1.

39. Samuel L. Walker Jr., "William Waller Hening," in Bryson, *Virginia Law Reporters*, 18–24; Pamela I. Gordon, "William Munford," in ibid., 25–32; *Acts Passed at a General Assembly of the Commonwealth of Virginia* (Richmond, 1820), 16.
40. Bryson, *Miscellaneous Virginia Law Reports.*
41. *Tucker's Law Reports*, 1:127.
42. William Waller Hening to Tucker, 10 Feb. 1808, 31 July 1809, T-C; William Munford to Tucker, 12 Sept. 1811, T-C; Tucker to Cabell, 19 Dec. 1808, 8 Jan. 1810, Bryan Family Papers, University of Virginia; Cabell to Tucker, 29 Jan. 1811, Cabell Family Papers.
43. Merit M. Robinson to John Robinson, 9 May 1811, 3 Sept. 1811, Robinson Family Papers, Swem Library Special Collections, College of William and Mary; Albert Allmand to Tucker, 11 Mar. 1819, T-C; Edmund J. Lee to Tucker, 22 Jan. 1822, T-C.
44. William Brockenbrough and Hugh Holmes, *A Collection of Cases Decided by the General Court of Virginia, Chiefly Relating to the Penal Laws of the Commonwealth*, vol. 1 (Philadelphia, 1815), 188, 252–62 (reporting *Commonwealth v. Myers* [Gen. Ct., 1811]). For *Thomas Sorrell's Case* and *John Bailey's Case*, see *Tucker's Law Reports*, 1:117–19, 442–45.
45. Tucker to Call, 25 May 1825, T-C.
46. Call evidently expected these volumes (or at least the fourth) to be published in 1827, as indicated by his preface to the fourth volume, dated 1 May 1827, to which he added a letter of the same date addressed to Tucker as a "public testimonial of my esteem for your virtue and talents." See Daniel Call, "The Reporter's Preface," in *Reports of Cases Argued and Adjudged in the Court of Appeals of Virginia*, ed. Call, 6 vols. (Richmond, 1830–33), vol. 4.
47. J. Randolph Tucker, "The Judges Tucker of the Court of Appeals of Virginia," *Virginia Law Register* 1 (1896): 792.
48. That student was Charles T. Cullen, whose dissertation, "St. George Tucker and Law in Virginia, 1772–1804" (University of Virginia, 1971), was subsequently published as *St. George Tucker and Law in Virginia, 1772–1804* (New York, 1987).
49. Ellen Holmes Pearson, "Revising Custom, Embracing Choice: Early American Legal Scholars and the Republicanization of the Common Law," in *Empire and Nation: The American Revolution in the Atlantic World*, ed. Eliga H. Gould and Peter S. Onuf (Baltimore, 2005), 93–111.
50. Charles F. Hobson, "The Recovery of British Debts in the Federal Circuit Court of Virginia, 1790 to 1797," *Virginia Magazine of History and Biography* 92 (1984): 193–95.
51. *McCall v. Turner*, 20 Apr. 1795, in *Tucker's Law Reports*, 1:335–36; Call, *Reports*, 1:133.
52. "Anonymous Case" (*Kamper v. Hawkins*), 23 May 1793, in *Tucker's Law Reports*, 1:264–66.
53. See argument in the "Case of the Prisoners" (*Commonwealth v. Caton*), Court of Appeals, [31 Oct. 1782], in *Tucker's Law Reports*, 3:1741–48.
54. *Kamper v. Hawkins*, in *Tucker's Law Reports*, 1:275–79, quotation on 277; Tucker, *Blackstone*, appendix to vol. 1, note C, 83–95.
55. *Kamper v. Hawkins*, in *Tucker's Law Reports*, 1:279–82, quotations on 280. In discussing the judiciary department in his *Blackstone*, Tucker quoted nearly the entirety of *Federalist* Nos. 78 and 79. Tucker, *Blackstone*, appendix to vol. 1, note C. 127–35.

56. Daniel Call, "Biographical Sketch of the Judges of the Court of Appeals," in *Reports,* 4:xxviii.
57. "Enquiry into the Causes of the Accumulation of Business in the Courts of Chancery and Court of Appeals" and "Sketch of a Bill for Regulating the Right of Appeal in Civil Cases," in *Tucker's Law Reports,* 3:1576–89 (quotations on 1577), 1590–1601.

CONTRIBUTORS

WARREN M. BILLINGS, PhD, is Distinguished Professor of History Emeritus at the University of New Orleans, the Bicentennial Historian of the Supreme Court of Louisiana, and the author of numerous publications about the history of law in early Virginia and Louisiana.

BENNIE BROWN is an independent scholar, cataloger, and bibliographer who lives in Williamsburg, Virginia, and studies early Virginia libraries and their owners.

W. HAMILTON BRYSON, JD, PhD, is the Blackstone Professor of Law at the University of Richmond, a member of the Virginia State Bar, and a fellow of the Royal Historical Society.

KEVIN J. HAYES, PhD, Professor of English Emeritus at the University of Central Oklahoma, now lives and writes in Ohio. He is the editor of *A History of Virginia Literature* and the author of *The Mind of a Patriot: Patrick Henry and the World of Ideas*, *The Road to Monticello: The Life and Mind of Thomas Jefferson*, and *The Library of William Byrd of Westover*, for which he received the Virginia Library History Award.

R. NEIL HENING is an independent scholar who specializes in the life and work of William Waller Hening. He is retired from careers in the Army Reserves and public service with Henrico County, Virginia. He is the son of a circuit-court judge who taught him early on to appreciate and explore Virginia's legal heritage.

CHARLES F. HOBSON, PhD, is the author of *The Great Chief Justice: John Marshall and the Rule of Law*, editor of the *Papers of John Marshall*, and editor of *St. George Tucker's Law Reports and Selected Papers, 1782–1825*.

JOHN RUSTON PAGAN, JD, DPhil, is University Professor and Professor of Law at the University of Richmond Law School. His writings on Virginia legal history include the prizewinning *Anne Orthwood's Bastard: Sex and Law in Early Virginia*.

BRENT TARTER is a founding editor of the Library of Virginia's *Dictionary of Virginia Biography* and editor of the seven-volume *Revolutionary Virginia, the Road to Independence*. Cofounder of the annual Virginia Forum, he is the author of *The Grandees of Government: The Origins and Persistence of Undemocratic Politics in Virginia* and numerous articles on Virginia history.

LINDA K. TESAR is Technical Services Librarian and Head of Special Collections at the Wolf Law Library, College of William and Mary.

INDEX

Italicized page numbers refer to illustrations.

Accomack County Court, 66–67, 70–71, 71–72
Adair, William, 44
Adams, John, 117, 120, 144, 149, 153
Adams, John Quincy, 140, 143
Addison, Joseph, 125
Albemarle Academy, 182
Albemarle County Court, 182
Aler, Paul, 128
Andrews, George, 120
Andros, Edmund, 75
Ast, William F., 187
Atkinson, Roger, 147
Atkyns, John Tracy, 46, 47
Augusta County Court, 171
Avery, Waightstill, 143

Bacon, Francis, 16, 21, 33, 50, 122, 151
Bacon, Matthew, 46, 105, 121, 142–43, 172, 189
Ballard, Thomas, 65
bankruptcy, 181–82
Banks, Gerard, 182
Banks, Henry, 182, 188
Barclay, Robert, 124
Barnardiston, Thomas, 120
Barradall, Edward, 100, 209
Barthélemy, Jean-Jacques, 128
Battaley, Moses, 105
Bayle, Pierre Bayle, 50
Bearer, John, 50
Beawes, Wyndham, 105
Bell, Robert, 152
Berkeley, Edmund, 122, 123
Berkeley, William, 62, 63, 79, 161

Beverley, Harry, 78–79, 106
Beverley, Robert, 48, 49, 75, 101, 106
Beverley, Robert, of Newlands, 106
Bible, the, 51, 103, 124, 128
Bilder, Mary Sarah, 59
Billinghurst, George, 26n46
Birch, William Young, 205
Blackstone, Henry, 119
Blackstone, William, 31, 68, 189, 197; *Commentaries on the Laws of England*, 33, 46, 47, 52, 130, 151–52, 172; *Tucker's Blackstone, 180,* 196, 202–9
Blair, Catherine Eustace, 50
Blair, James, 49, 75
Blair, John, 43
Bland, Richard, 107, 150
Bland, Theodorick, 65
Blount, Thomas, 25n27
Board of Trade, 171–72
Bohun, William, 105, *138,* 147–48
Bolling v. Bolling (1774), 116, 118, 121
Book of Common Prayer, 51, 124
Bowyer, Lew, 152
Bowyer, Michael, 147
Boyle, Robert, 50
Bracton, Henry de, 34, 119
Breckinridge, James, 187
Brent v. Dunne (1690), 87n97
Breton (Britton), John le, 34
Brock, Robert A., 44
Brockenbrough, William, 211
Brooke, Robert, 17, 31, 119, 200
Brown, Bennie, 116
Brown, John, 211
Brown, William, 119

Brownlow, Richard, 106, 107
Bryson, W. Hamilton, 118–19, 129, 191, 211
Buchanan, George, 50, 124, 128
Buller, Francis, 145
Bulstrode, Edward, 18
Bunbury, William, 31
Burghley, 1st Baron (William Cecil), 50
Burn, Richard, 32, 105, 172, 189
Burn, Robert, 32
Burnaby, Andrew, 146
Burnet, Gilbert, 49
Burnham, John, 72–74
Burrow, James, 46, 47
Burt, Edward, 109
Burwell, Lewis, 72–74
Byram v. Johnson (1685), 71
Byrd, William (c. 1652–1704), 42
Byrd, William (1674–1744), of Westover, 42; law books, 29, 34, 35, 40, 119, 121, 148; library, 109, 118, 126, 148

Caldwell, Bowyer, 147
Call, Daniel, 117–18, 210, 211–12, 215
Campbell, 1st Baron (John Campbell), 142
Carey, Mathew, 188, 202
Carr, Dabney, 120
Carr, Peter, 130, 142
Carte, Thomas, 46
Carter, Landon, 107
Carter, Robert, 31, 34, 107, 122, 123, 125, 127, 142
Carter, Robert "King," 29, 120
Carter, Samuel, 105
Cervantes, Miguel de, 125
Chandler, Richard, 45
Charles I, 61
Charles II, 61, 63
Chew, Benjamin, 153
Chilton, Edward, 49, 75
Christian, Edward, 206
Church of England, 167, 186, 206
Churchill, Charles, 102
Churchill, Henry, 118
Clarendon, 1st Earl of (Edward Hyde), 50, 123

Clay, Henry, 127
Clayton, John, 100, 170
Coalter, John, 131
Coke, Edward, 189; *Book of Entries of Declarations,* 43; *Coke upon Littleton (First Part of the Institutes of the Laws of England),* 16, 18–19, 21, 33, 109, 130, 140–42; *Institutes of the Laws of England,* 33, 106, 119; *Reports,* 16, 18, 31, 46, 151
Colden, Cadwallader, 109
College of William and Mary, 40; legal education, 130, 141, 200–201, 211
Collett, John, 43
Colston, William, 78
common law, 4, 41
Commonwealth v. Myers (1811), 211
Conedon, James, 147
Constitution, U.S., 49, 187, 201, 204–5, 207, 208–9; Constitutional Convention of 1787, 117
Constitution, Virginia (1776), 201, 204–5, 214
Corbin, Richard, 44
Council of State library, 39, 40, 50–53, 107; bookplate, *38,* 44; compilation, 39–42, 44–47; loss of books, 42–43, 47, 50–51, 51–52; marks of ownership, 44
county courts, 21, 32, 41–42; libraries, 2, 4, 42, 77–79; navigation and staple acts, 65–68. *See also* justices of the peace; *names of counties*
Cowell, John, 17–18, 33, 162
Croke, George, 18, 31, 106, 151
Crompton, Richard, 189
Culpeper of Thoresway, 2d Baron (Thomas Culpeper), 74
Cunningham, Timothy, 31, 151
Custis, John, 67

Dalton, Michael: *Countrey Justice, 4, 12,* 20, 26n45, 32, 42, 106, 162, 163, 189; *Officium Vicecomitum, The Office and Authoritie of Sheriffs,* 4, 20, 26n46, 32, 42, 119, 162, 189

INDEX

D'Anvers, Knightley, 121, 142
Darwin, Erasmus, 125
Davis, Augustine, 188
Dean, Barbara C., 116
Declaration of Independence, 5, 117
Derickson, Tunis, 62
Dewey, Stephen, 116–17
Dibbell, Jeremy, 116
Dill, Alonzo T., 126
Dinwiddie, Robert, 103, 171
District Court, U.S., 197, 199
Dixon, John, 172, 173, 190
Dobson, Matthew, 125
Domat, Jean, 34
Dryden, John, 125
Dulany, Daniel, 107
Duncombe, Giles, 33, 105, 144–45
Dunlop, William, 123
DuVal, William, 116
Dyer, James, 18

Effingham, 5th Baron Howard of (Francis Howard), 67
Emerson, William, 125
Emlyn, Sollom, 47, 50
Eppes, John Wayles, 131
Erasmus, Desiderius, 122
Essex County Court, 78

Fauquier, Francis, 147
Federalist, 208, 214
Félice, Fortuné Barthélemy de, 118
Ferriere, Claude Joseph de, 47, 50
Filmer, Robert, 122
Finch, Henry, 18, 19
Fitzgibbon, John, 120
Fitzherbert, Anthony, 17, 26n45, 33, 46, 165
Fitzhugh, William, 18, 73
Fleming, William, 123, 125
Fontaine, Patrick Henry, 150
Fortescue, John, 18, 19
Forward, Jonathan, 105
Foster, Michael, 119
Francis, Richard, 105
Franklin, Benjamin, 117, 143, 144

Franklin, William, 142
Frederick County Court, 171
Fulbeck, William, 18

Gale, Thomas, 128
Gamble, Robert, 187
Gardiner, Robert, 106, 107
Garnet, Richard, 43
Garnett, Muscoe, 109
George II, 51
Gerard, John, 41
Gesner, Solomon, 51
Gibson v. Blande (1691), 69
Gilbert, George, 34
Glanville (Glanvill), Ranulf de, 33–34, 119
Godolphin, John, 26n46, 34, 145
Goldsmith, Oliver, 125
Goldsworthy, Jeffrey, 60
Gooch, William, 160, 161; *Dialogue*, 161–62
Goodwin, Mary R. M., 116
Green, William, 212
Grey, Anchitel, 44, 45
Griffin, Leroy, 72–74
Griffin and Burwell v. Wormeley (*Burnham Will Case*) (1683), 72–74
Grimston, Harbottle, 151
Grotius, Hugo, 34, 119, 124, 149
Guthrie, William, 45, 50, 123, 124
Guy, Pierre Augustin, 128

Hale, Matthew, 33, 46, 47, 50, 60, 119, 166, 189
Halifax, 2d Earl of (George Montagu Dunk), 172
Hamilton, Alexander, 197, 214
Hanover County Court, 148–49
Harper, Lawrence, 67
Harrington, James, 46, 122
Harrison, Joseph, 105
Hartwell, Henry, 49, 75
Hawkins, William, 33, 144
Hayberd v. Hawksford (1701), 74
Haynes, Samuel, 44–45
Hederich, Benjamin, 128
Hedgman, Peter, 106

Heineccius, Johann, 105
Helsham, Richard, 125
Hemphill, W. Edwin, 127
Hengham, Ralph de, 43, 128
Hening, Agatha Banks, 182
Hening, George, 181
Hening, Robert, 181
Hening, Samuel, 181
Hening, William Waller, 7, 68, 181–82; court reports, 183, 210, 211, 215; deputy adjutant general, 183; legal publications, 183–84; *New Virginia Justice,* 173, *180,* 181, 184–88, 190–91; *Statutes at Large,* 48, 107, 183, 200
Henry, John, 149
Henry, Patrick, 7, 53, 139, 143, 151; bar examination, 145–47; law library, 138, 145, 147–48, 149, 151–52, 152–53; legal education, 139–46; *Parson's Cause* (1763), 148–49
Henry, Sarah Shelton, 139
Henry, William Wirt, 147
Herbert, John, 123
Herne, John, 105
Hetley, Thomas, 120
Hickman, Richard, 29, 31
Hobart, Henry, 31
Hoffman, J. Henry, 52
Hoffman, Richard J., 129
Holden, Charles, 67
Holloway, John, 160, 161
Holmes, Hugh, 211
Holt, John, 98
Home, Henry, Lord Kames, 46
Hook, John, 187
Hopkins, William, 209
Houghton, John, 108–9
Hughes, Griffith, 102
Hume, David, 44–45, 46, 122, 123
Hunter, William, 102, 103, 141, 171
Hutcheson, Francis, 50

indentured servants, 75
Innes, James, 50
In re Derickson (1660), 62

Jackson, Andrew, 143
Jacob, Giles, 33, 105, 121, 148
James I, 59–60, 61
James, Ralph, 50
Jay, John, 120, 153
Jefferson, Thomas, 53, 82n22, 92n159, 197, 205, 214; Patrick Henry, 149, 150; William Waller Hening, 182, 187, 188; legal education, 116, 117, 130, 141–42, 143; library, 30, 103, 109, 120, 126, 153; manuscript laws of Virginia, 107, 200; reports of cases, 209–10; George Wythe's library, 115, 116, 128
Jekyll, Joseph, 76
John Bailey's Case (1798), 211
John Norton and Sons, 116, 117, 118
Johnson, Herbert A., 120–21
Johnston, George, 31
Jones, Gabriel, 104–5, 109
Jones, Hugh, 49, 92n158
Jones, William, 74
Joynes, William T., 212
judicial review, 213–15
jury trials, 152
justices of the peace, 4, 14, 187, 189, 190; manuals, 19–21, 26n45, 32–33, 42, 48–49, 162–63, 165, 181. *See also* county courts; Dalton, Michael; Hening, William Waller; Starke, Richard; Webb, George

Kames, Lord (Henry Home), 122
Kamper v. Hawkins (1793), 213–15
Keble, Joseph, 26n45, 32, 78, 79, 93n178
Keith, George, 124
Kennett, White, 46
Kippax, John, 109
Kitchin, John, 16

Lambarde, William, 19–20, 26n46, 32, 164, 189
Lancaster County Court, 77–78
Latch, John, 120
law books, 2–5; admiralty, 49; borrowing and lending, 30, 35, 39, 50, 105, 106, 116,

INDEX

131, 150; buying and selling, 4, 39–40, 77–79, 102–7, 117–19; civil law, 34, 47; commerce, 34; dictionaries, 17, 25n27, 33, 121; ecclesiastical law, 34, 49–50; English colonies, 43, 45, 46–47; equity, 33, 121, 148; law of nations, 34, 118–19, 149–51; manuals, 19–21, 26nn45–46, 32–33, 34–35, 48–49; maritime, 121; parliamentary records, 45, 51, 117, 118–19; property, 20, 33, 34; reports of cases, 16–17, 18, 31, 46, 47, 48, 119–20, 210–12, 215; Roman law, 47, 129; treatises, 18–19, 32, 119; witchcraft, 53. *See also* statutes of England; statutes of Virginia

law libraries, 4, 44. *See also* Byrd, William (1674–1744); Council of State; county courts; Henry, Patrick; Jefferson, Thomas; Mercer, John; Tucker, St. George; Wythe, George

Lee, Charles, 211, 212

Lee, Francis Lightfoot, 53

Lee, Philip Ludwell, 45

Lee, Richard, 18, 123, 127

Lee, Richard Henry, 53

legal education, 4, 99, 130–32, 141–42, 162–63, 191, 200–201, 211; commonplace books, 144; Inns of Court, 13, 15, 40, 41, 99, 174n13

Leigh, Edward, 25n27

Leigh, Benjamin Watkins, 185

Leland, Thomas, 46

Le Roy, David, 128

Library of Virginia, 50, 51, 52

Lightfoot, John, 124

Lilly, John, 105–6

Littleton, Thomas, 18–19, 21, 33, 106, 119, 141. *See also* Coke, Edward: *Coke upon Littleton*

Locke, John, 50, 122, 200

Logan, James, 126

Lower Norfolk County Court, 20

Lowth, Robert, 128

Ludwell, Philip, 118

Lyons, Peter, 148

Macaulay, Catherine, 46

MacLaurin, Colin, 125

Madison, James (bishop), 117

Madison, James (president), 187, 199

Magna Carta, 60, 77, 80–81n11

Mallory, John, 103

Malynes, Gerard de, 34

Manley, Thomas, 33

Mansfield, Lord (William Murray), 120, 197

Marana, Giovanni, 109

Marbury v. Madison (1803), 215

March, John, 105

Marshall, John, 124, 187, 199, 212; judicial review, 215; student of George Wythe, 116, 121, 130, 144

Marvin, John G., 120

Mason, George (1725–1792), 6, 98, 108–9

Mason, George (d. 1735), 98, 107

Mason, Thomson, 98

Maury, John, 148–49

Mazzei, Filippo, 124

McCall v. Turner (1795), 213

McCall v. Turner (1797), 213

McCarty, Daniel, 123, 125

Mercer, Ann Roy, 98

Mercer, George, 98–99, 103

Mercer, Grace Fenton, 97

Mercer, Hugh, 109

Mercer, James, 98, 105, 107–8

Mercer, John, 6, 97–98, 99–100; *Abridgment*, 48, 96, 100–102, 108, 109, 141; bookplate, *96*, 107; borrowing and lending, 106, 107–8; buying and selling, 102–7; *Complete Collection of the Laws of Maryland*, 100, 109; *Dinwiddianae*, 103; legal education, 99; library, 29, 31, 34, 105–9, 119, 120, 121, 171; subscribes to books, 102–3

Mercer, John (father), 97

Mercer, Katherine Mason, 98

Mercer, William Randolph, 105, 108

Meriton, George, 33

Middlesex County Court, 72–74, 78–79

Middleton, Conyers, 46

Milton, John, 50, 124–25
Minor, Benjamin B., 115
Molloy, Charles, 34, 106
Monroe, James, 212
Montaigne, Michel de, 122
Montesquieu, Baron de La Brède et de (Charles-Louis de Secondat), 50, 122, 200
Montgomerie, Hugh, 67
Moore, Edward, 109
Morgan v. Bally (1698), 71–72
Moryson, Francis, 48, 62
Mosely, William, 31
Munford, William, 131, 185, 210, 211, 215
Mutual Assurance Society of Virginia, 182

Nelson, Robert, 117
Nelson, William, 47, 52, 106, 142
Netherlands, 61, 64; Second Anglo-Dutch War, 64–65
New Kent County Court, 160
Newton, Isaac, 125, 128
Nicholas, Robert Carter, 146
Nicholson, Francis, 78
Nicholson, Thomas, 188, 190
Northampton County Court, 62, 69, 71
Northumberland County Court, 66
Noye, William, 16, 26n46

Ohio Company, 98, 103
Orange County Court, 171

Page, John, 107, 202
Paine, Robert Treat, 153
Paine, Thomas, 122
Parker, James, 32, 105
Parks, William, 48, 70, 100, 102, 103, 139, 141, 159, 169–70
Parsons, Theophilus, 143, 153
Parson's Cause (1763), 148–49
Pelloutier, Simon, 124
Pendleton, Edmund, 47, 50, 199
Perkins, John, 33
Petyt, George, 45
Petyt, William, 45
Pinkerton, John, 124

Plowden, Edmund, 18, 120
Pollexfen, Henry, 31
Pope, Alexander, 125, 148
Postlethwayt, Malachy, 125
Potter, John, 128
Prince William County Court, 99–100, 107
printing and print culture, 3, 6, 7, 16, 100–103, 161–62, 169–70, 172, 183–86, 188–89. *See also* Parks, William
Pufendorf, Samuel von, 34, 118–19, 124, 149, 150, 153
Pulton, Ferdinando, 77, 93n170
Purdie, Alexander, 172, 173
Purvis, John, 48, 106

Quincy, Josiah, Jr., 39

Rabelais, François, 125
Randolph, Edmund, 98, 139–40, 210, 212
Randolph, John, 43, 146–47, 210
Randolph, John, 100, 209, 210
Randolph, Peyton, 31, 43, 107, 118, 142, 146
Rapin-Thoyras, Paul de, 50
Rastell, John, 17, 33, 105, 107, 162
Rastell, William, 17, 43
Raymond, Thomas, 46
Read, Clement, 118
Reinhold, Meyer, 126–27
religion, 167, 186. *See also* Church of England
reports of cases, 3, 16–17, 18, 31, 46, 47, 48, 119–20, 210–12, 215; unpublished, 209–11
Rex ex rel. Ballard v. Ship Dolphin (1670), 65
Rex ex rel. Bland v. Ship Hope (1670), 65
Rex ex rel. Cole v. the Sloop Katherine of New York (1686), 86n83
Rex ex rel. Crofts v. the Ship Crown of London (1686), 86n83
Rex ex rel. Custis v. the Barque Fortune of Boston, Lincolnshire (1687), 86n83
Rex ex rel. Custis v. the Ship Katherine (1687), 67
Rex ex rel. Spencer v. Lynes (1685), 86n83

INDEX

Rex ex rel. Spencer v. the Ship Constant Matthew (1678), 66
Rex ex rel. Stringer v. the Ship Katherine of London (1685), 66–67
Rex v. Tom Cary (1693), 69
Rex. v. Lewis (1689), 72
Richardson, William H., 47–48, 50
Richmond County Court, 74, 78
Richmond Female Academy, 183
Roane, Spencer, 199, 216
Robertson, William, 44–45, 46, 47, 52
Robins, Obedience, 23n9
Robinson, John, 161
Rolle, Henry, 47, 52, 142
Rollin, Charles, 127
Roy, Mungo, 98
Royle, Joseph, 103
rule of law, 73–74
Rushworth, John, 50, 53, 109

Saint Germain, Christopher, 34
Salkeld, William, 31, 46, 47, 106, 151
Salmon, Thomas, 46
Sandys, George, 124
Sayer, Joseph, 31
Scarburgh, Charles, 67
Scarburgh, Edmund, 65, 71
Scarburgh v. Bradford (1663), 71
Selden, John, 34
Shakespeare, William, 102, 124
Sheffield, John, 109
Shelton, Eleanor Parks, 139, 141
Shelton, John, 139, 141
Sheppard, William, 26n45, 33
Shippen, Thomas Lee, 117
Shower, Bartholomew, 52, 120
Simpson, Thomas, 125
Simpson, William, 32
Skelton, Reuben, 142
Slater, John, 200
slavery, 20, 21, 22, 201, 205–6, 207, 208, 212–13
Small, Abraham, 205, 207
Smart, George K., 122–23
Smith, Adam, 200
Smith, John, 49

Spence, Joseph, 129–30
Spencer, Nicholas, 66
Spicer, Arthur, 18
Spotswood, Alexander, 75
Sprat, Thomas, 50
Stackhouse, Thomas, 124
Stafford County Court, 69, 99–100
Starke, Richard, *Office and Authority of a Justice of Peace,* 49, 172–73, 184, 185–86, 189
statutes of England, 4, 59–60, 68–70, 75–77, 167–68; abridgments, 16–17, 77; artificers (1563 and 1604), 68, 69; bigamy (1604), 68; Coercive (1774), 53; Customs Fraud Act (1662), 63, 67; drunkenness (1606), 68; engrossing (1552, 1563, and 1571), 68; forcible entry (1429), 71; frauds (1677), 72–74, 76; infanticide (1624), 72, 75; limitations (1540), 70; navigation (1660), 18, 61–63, 65, 77, 79; perjury (1563), 70–71; plantation and trade (1696), 67, 78; poor law (1601), 71–72; printed editions, 31–32, 42, 44, 45, 48, *58;* quarantine (1604), 71; recovery (1624), 69; riot (1411), 71; Stamp Act (1765), 98–99, 153; Staple Act (1663), 63–64, 65, 66–67, 79; tanners (1604), 71; testimony by Quakers (1696), 68; toleration (1689), 68, 186; Tonnage and Poundage (1660), 34
statutes of Virginia, 68–70, 100–102, 206; artificers (1632), 68; bigamy (1658), 68; code, 69–70, 171–72, 184, 185, 190, 206; drunkenness (1632), 68; engrossing (1632), 68; frauds (1748), 74–75; infanticide (1710), 75; law books (1666), 2, 20, 42, 77–78; lawyers (1732), 165; limitations (1710), 69–70; manuscript, 106–7; printed editions, 32, 44, 48, 70, 106, 117, 141, 160, 162, 206; slavery (1662), 22; testimony by Quakers (1705), 68; tobacco inspection (1730), 161–62, 168–69; toleration (1699), 68; trials of slaves (1692), 69; Two-Penny Act (1758), 148; vagrancy (1672), 71–72
Staunford, William, 40–41, 200

Sterne, Laurence, 124
Stith, William, 49, 124
Stotham, Mathew, 105
Strange, John, 46
Stuart, James, 128
Surry County Court, 71
Sweeney, George Wythe, 131
Swift, Jonathan, 125
Swinburne, Henry, 4, 20, 22, 26n46, *28,* 34, 42, 106, 145, 162, 163
Syme, John, 150

Taylor, Creed, 182–83
Tazewell, Henry, 215
Tazewell, Littleton Waller, 130–31, 182
Theolall, Simon, 43
Thomas Sorrell's Case (1786), 211
Thorpe, George, 40, 163
Thurloe, John, 50
Tillotson, John, 124
tobacco, 62, 161–62, 168–69
Toland, John, 46
Torbuc, John, 45
treasurer's office, 161
Tucker, Beverley, 131–32
Tucker, Frances Bland Randolph, 198
Tucker, Henry St. George, 211
Tucker, John Randolph, 212
Tucker, Lelia Skipwith Carter, 199
Tucker, Nathaniel Beverley, 211
Tucker, St. George, 7, 76–77, 143, 184; judicial review, 213–15; law library, 199–200; law notebooks, 209, 210–16; law professor, 200–201; legal education, 197; library, 50, 109, 120, 212; student of George Wythe, 117, 197; *Tucker's Blackstone, 180,* 196, 202–9
Turnbull, George, 105
Tyler, John, 76–77, 140, 141

U.S. Constitution. *See* Constitution, U.S.
U.S. District Court, 197, 199
Uztariz, Geronimo de, 109

Vattel, Emmerich de, 119, 150
Ventris, Peyton, 31, 106, 120
Vesey, Francis, Sr., 31
Viner, Charles, 105, 121
Vinnius, Arnoldus, 118
Virginia Company (London Company), 13, 40, 59–60, 62, 167–68
Virginia Constitution (1776), 201, 204–5, 214
Virginia Convention (1788), 117, 152
Virginia Court of Admiralty (1776–89), 49
Virginia Court of Oyer and Terminer, 41
Virginia Court of Vice-Admiralty (1698–1776), 49, 67, 185
Virginia Gazette, 39, 103, 105, 150
Virginia General Assembly, 14, 31, 41, 70, 148, 160–61, 167. *See also* statutes of Virginia
Virginia General Court (colonial), 41, 44, 72–73, 75; bar, 98, 151, 198; ecclesiastical jurisdiction, 49–50; navigation acts, 65. *See also* Council of State library
Virginia General Court (post-revolutionary), 197, 198–99, 212–15
Virginia Supreme Court of Appeals, 51–52, 199, 214, 215–16
Virginia High Court of Chancery, 121, 130, 182–83

Waller, Benjamin, 43, 49, 182
Waller, John, 123
Walthoe, John, Jr., 43
Walthoe, Nathaniel, 43
Warburton, William, 102
Washington, Bushrod, 210, 212
Washington, George, 150
Washington, Joseph, 105
Webb, Conrade, 159
Webb, George, 76; legal education, 162–63, 174n13; *Office and Authority of a Justice of Peace,* 7, 32, 48, 101, 121, 141, *158,* 159, 162–66, 164–69, 169–70, 171, 184, 185, 189
Webb, Lucy Foster Jones, 159
Webster, John, 53
Welwood, James, 46
Wentworth, Thomas, 34
West, Richard, 76

INDEX

West, William, 20–21, 26n46, 33, 41, 162
Westmoreland County Court, 18
Wilkinson, John, 32
Williams, William Peere, 47, 52, 151
Williamsburg, 30, 39–40
Wilson, George, 31, 46
Wingate, Edmund, 17, 33, 77, 101, 106, 107
Winston, Edmund, 140
Wirt, William, 127, 146, 149
Wood, Gordon, 79
Wood, Thomas, 33, 106, 151, 189
Wormeley, Ralph (d. 1703), 18, 72–74
Wormeley, Ralph, of Rosegill, 107, 123, 125

Wythe, George, 5, 146, 184, 187; bookplate, *114;* borrowing and lending, 116, 131; judge, 128–29; law books, 117–19, 131, 151; law professor, 117, 141, 143, 144, 200; legal education, 116–17; library, 115–16, 122–26, 126–31

Yeates, Jasper, 153
York County Court, 77, 78
Yorke, Philip, 76
Young, Wa., 26n45

Zaller, Robert, 60

EARLY AMERICAN HISTORIES

✦✦✦

Douglas Bradburn and John C. Coombs, editors
Early Modern Virginia: Reconsidering the Old Dominion

Denver Brunsman
*The Evil Necessity: British Naval Impressment in the
Eighteenth-Century Atlantic World*

Jack P. Greene
Creating the British Atlantic: Essays on Transplantation, Adaptation, and Continuity

James Corbett David
*Dunmore's New World: The Extraordinary Life of a Royal Governor in
Revolutionary America—with Jacobites, Counterfeiters, Land Schemes, Shipwrecks,
Scalping, Indian Politics, Runaway Slaves, and Two Illegal Royal Weddings*

Turk McCleskey
*The Road to Black Ned's Forge: A Story of Race, Sex, and
Trade on the Colonial American Frontier*

Antoinette Sutto
*Loyal Protestants and Dangerous Papists: Maryland and the
Politics of Religion in the English Atlantic, 1630–1690*

Jack P. Greene
Settler Jamaica in the 1750s: A Social Portrait

Warren M. Billings and Brent Tarter, editors
"Esteemed Bookes of Lawe" and the Legal Culture of Early Virginia